THE FIFTIES
A Women's Oral History

THE FIFTIES

A Women's Oral History

Brett Harvey

ASJA Press

San Jose New York Lincoln Shanghai

The Fifties
A Women's Oral History

ASJA Press
an imprint of iUniverse, Inc.

For information address:
iUniverse, Inc.
5220 S. 16th St., Suite 200
Lincoln, NE 68512
www.iuniverse.com

Originally published by HarperCollins

ISBN: 0-595-22959-X

Printed in the United States of America

For Ronnie

Contents

Acknowledgments

My first and deepest debt of gratitude is to the ninety-two women who allowed me into their kitchens and offices, who sat with me on their patios and porches, and told me about their lives in the fifties. Although I can't name them, I thank them for their generosity, their humor, and their eloquence.

More than any other genre, oral history relies on an ever-widening network of people who recommend people who recommend people. Kathy Braun, Beverly Brown, Faith Childs, Ellie Fuchs, Ann Grahn, Amber Hollibaugh, Diane and Jerry Kranz, Carol Levin, Laura Lewis, Marion Samuels, Janet Spar, and Lou Vuolo all generously provided names and connections. Jake Dengel, Ellie and John Trotter, and Eileen Jagoda did that and more: they also put me up, fed me, transported me, and were superb company on the road.

Mirra Komarovsky, Joan Nestle, Ann Snitow, and Alix Shulman gave me the benefit of their wisdom—personal as well as scholarly—in interviews. Maureen Rodgers's wonderful gift of a carton of *Life* magazines from the fifties was an endlessly rich source of material.

My thanks also to the helpful archivists at Barnard, Bryn Mawr, Mt. Holyoke, Radcliffe, Smith, Vassar, and Wellesley colleges, to the Schlesinger Library on the History of Women at Radcliffe College, and to the alumnae office of The Baldwin School.

Jonathan Tasini, Shelagh Doyle, Sonya Jaffe Robbins, and the members of the Feminist Ex-Press also provided constant support and encouragement throughout the writing of the book. I'm also grateful to my colleagues in the National Writers Union—particularly Russell Miller—for taking up the slack while I was working on the project.

The Virginia Center for the Creative Arts, that paradise, allowed me a month of concentrated work at a difficult moment.

Ellen Willis and Judith Podell read chapters and offered helpful criticism and suggestions. Sara Friedman was an invaluable reader, sounding board, and friend. I'm indebted to my agent, Charlotte Sheedy, and my editor at HarperCollins, Craig Nelson, for their enthusiasm for this project, and to Craig for his expert guidance throughout it.

I'm grateful to Bonnie Bellow, Marnie Mueller, and Nanette Rainone for their steadfast and precious friendship. And to Richard Fulmer, who helped me navigate the depths and shoals of writing this book with skill and sensitivity.

My gratitude to Judith Levine knows no bounds. Her love, encouragement, and respect kept my spirits up. Her intellectual honesty and sharp-eyed criticism kept me (I hope) on track. Her humor kept me laughing, hence sane.

Finally, I thank my children, Robert and Katie Vuolo: their support and affection sustain me.

Introduction

D id you ever think about the fact that all the fabrics we wore in the fifties were *stiff?*" my friend Ronnie once asked me. I hadn't, but the minute she said it I thought: faille, shantung, felt, taffeta, pique. Nothing clung, or fell, or draped—everything was crisp.

Forties clothes were truly sexy—those swingy little dresses in soft, flowered rayon prints with shoulder pads had a jaunty, competent femininity. Fifties clothes were like armor. Our clothes expressed all the contradictions of our roles. Our ridiculously starched skirts and hobbling sheaths were a caricature of femininity. Our cinched waists and aggressively pointed breasts advertised our availability at the same time they warned of our impregnability.

In the daytime we wore tight, revealing sweaters, but they were topped by mincing little Peter Pan collars and perky scarves that seemed to say, "Who, *me?* Why, I'm just a little girl!" At night our shoulders were naked, our breasts half-bare, the lower half of our bodies hidden in layers of tulle. Underneath it all, our flesh, like our volatile sexuality, was "contained" by boned girdles and Merry Widows, in an era when "containment" was a political as well as a social obsession.

Americans have a kind of fondness for the fifties. We think of it as a jokey, cartoonish decade, full of too-bright colors, goofy space-age designs, outlandish people and events, extreme ideas. We collect streamlined appliances, big-finned cars, poodle skirts and Hula Hoops as artifacts from an exotic and slightly ridiculous era. We pore over *Life* magazines of the period, enthralled by the crisp black-and-white photos of couples in bomb shelters, the ads in which smiling, wholesome teenagers toss back Cokes, and families speed down country roads in gigantic Chryslers with Dad at the wheel. Behind our bemused fascination lies a yearning for a past as black-and-white as those old *Life* photographs. Under our nervous, condescending laughter at the old "Father Knows Best" episodes lies a longing for a time when women were women, men were men, and the rules were clear.

What some of us tend to forget—and what many of us are too young to remember—is that the engine that drove the rules was fear.

There was much to be afraid of in the postwar era, or so we thought. An American girl who was fifteen years old on VJ Day in 1946 had experienced two profoundly disturbing events. Her childhood had almost certainly been touched, if not severely disrupted, by the Depression. Her father might have lost his job, her mother gone back to work. Her family might have been split up and she and her siblings separated, farmed out to relatives.

World War II created new kinds of instability. Fathers, uncles, friends, and fiancés vanished, some never to come back. In spite of more jobs, higher wartime earnings, and an easing of certain kinds of hardships, a sense of deprivation and scarcity persisted. Rubber and gasoline shortages meant you couldn't travel far from home. Public transportation was congested, housing was scarce, schools were overcrowded. Meat, butter, sugar, and many other things were rationed. Blackouts, air raids, warning sirens in the night, first aid courses in how to bandage the wounded, and, more than anything else, newsreels showing ruined cities, exploding buildings, endless lines of haunted-looking people trudging down muddy roads with their suitcases on their backs—these things created fear, uneasiness, a sense of vulnerability.

And though America had emerged from the war a major power, the world itself appeared more dangerous than ever. We had an enemy, Russia, who not only had an A-bomb, but powerful missiles aimed straight at us. The "Red tide" of Euro-Communism was headed our way as well, our leaders warned us, an evil force whose goal was nothing less than the destruction of "our American way of life." This fear of the enemy outside was easily manipulated by demagogues like Senator Joe McCarthy into a suspicion of subversion within, which rapidly spread into a queasy fear of difference itself.

This is an oral history of American women who came of age in the 1950s. It's about how these women, products of a great depression and a great war, made decisions—about school and work, marriage and motherhood.

"What decisions?" most women retorted when I called to ask if I could interview them. "Who made decisions? I just drifted." This is not, of course, strictly true. People are making choices even if they appear to be, even perceive themselves to be, drifting. But in the fifties as in no other decade, the current of the mainstream was so strong that you only had to step off the bank and float downstream into marriage and motherhood. "Before I knew it, I was married." "Before I knew it, I was pregnant." The phrase came up again and again in my conversations with women. The "it" we didn't know can be construed many ways: Before we knew who we were. Before we knew what we wanted. Before we knew what was happening to us. And before we knew what feminism was to teach us: that we had a right to control our own destinies.

For women, the postwar era represented a dramatic retreat

from the trends of previous decades. From the twenties through World War II, women had been steadily expanding their sphere by going to college and going to work in growing numbers. The war years brought huge numbers of women into the work force doing jobs that had been previously open only to men. It was a turbulent time when everyone's life seemed to change practically overnight. Thousands of people left home, migrating to urban areas. Not only were women making money, but many were living alone or with other women, many experiencing independence and self-sufficiency for the first time. The rigid sexual codes of previous times rapidly gave way to a more free-and-easy sexuality. Even the movies of the thirties and early forties glamorized the image of the plucky, resourceful career gal, epitomized by Rosalind Russell in *His Girl Friday* (1940).

When the war was over, all these changes raised worrisome questions among government leaders and social scientists. What if women had come to enjoy their independence and didn't want to give up their jobs to returning veterans? What if women's sexuality couldn't be curbed? What if not enough of them were willing to return home and start creating the nuclear families that would in turn create the demand for goods that the nation's prosperity depended on?

The response of government, aided by the social scientists and the media, was a massive effort to channel all these disturbing energies into one safe harbor: the family. In *Homeward Bound: American Families in the Cold War Era*, Elaine Tyler May explains that the home was the perfect vehicle for domestic containment: "Within its walls potentially dangerous social forces of the new age might be tamed, where they could contribute to the secure and fulfilling life to which postwar women and men aspired. . . . More than merely a metaphor for the cold war on the homefront, containment aptly describes the way in which public policy, personal behavior, and even political values were focused on the home."

A young woman approaching adulthood after the war was surrounded by powerful inducements to early marriage. The whole country seemed full of young men eager to date, to marry, to get on with their lives. They were glamorous, these returning soldiers. They'd been through something; they'd seen the world; they were sexually experienced; they were practically irresistible.

Magazines and newsreels were full of beaming couples buying homes, appliances, and shiny new cars. By 1956 Americans were buying 20,000 television sets a day and two out of every three families owned at least one set. Night after night, situation comedies like "Father Knows Best" and "Ozzie and Harriet," television dramas and commercials, drove home their powerful messages about male and female identity, their blueprint for family life.

As women, we were constantly warned about dangers, many of them hidden. The advertising industry taught us about the germs, odors, and wetness, insidious and often invisible, that could sabotage our confidence and make us unlovable. We learned we needed to be "extra-careful" about "personal hygiene," and that vaginal odor was "a grave womanly offense." We knew bad breath could make the difference between "laughter and love and marriage almost before you know it" and "boredom and loneliness."

"Insecurity" and "self-doubt" were our buzzwords. We worried about not being clean enough, or womanly enough, about not finding husbands, about not being good enough mothers. We were afraid of "getting a reputation," of "being a cock-tease," and we were terrified of getting pregnant. We made our life decisions on the basis of safety and security. We chose solid, reliable mates and valued maturity above all other personal qualities.

Increasingly, marriage and family were expected to be a woman's whole world. Her intelligence, energy, creativity, and sexuality all were funneled into the constricted sphere of family life. This narrowing of women's sphere was reinforced by the lack of desirable options outside of marriage. The professions, except for nursing and teaching, were virtually closed to women, and most of the jobs available to them were dead-end and poorly paid. Sexual experience was difficult to come by and risky unless you were married. Sexual activity could result in the loss of reputation—an essential commodity if marriage was to be your sole identity. More important, in the absence of legal abortion, an extramarital pregnancy could be—and almost always was—disastrous.

When I began working on this book, I saw fifties women as the hapless, passive victims of a culture that forced them into their biological slots. I had an image in my mind of the prevailing culture as a giant thumb pressing women back and down into the mold of wife and mother. But the real women I interviewed refused to fit neatly into my theories. They lurched, struggled, wavered, veered, regrouped, and floundered. They did things that made me angry and uncomfortable, like turning down interesting job offers, turning their backs on men they were attracted to, and marrying men who were boring but responsible, ignoring the encouragement of fathers and teachers. Many of them turned their backs on their own talents and desires, refused to take risks, retreated from situations that would have tested their mettle, chose smaller, safer, more comfortable spheres. I wanted these women, in Walt Whitman's words, to "give up toys and fictions and launch forth as men do amid real, independent stormy life."

As time went on and the stories accumulated, my understanding of the predicament of fifties women deepened. Women made their choices out of complex knots of motives that included their own emotional needs and family dynamics as well as cultural and social pressures. A woman's decision to set aside her own interests and devote herself to her husband's career, for example, might come out of a subtle interplay between her conflicting desires and fears—for work, for a family, for security, the wish to accommodate others, a fear of testing herself, rebellion against a parent's ambition for her. And reinforcing all the above, the messages her culture gave her about her role as a woman.

My own story contains some of these contradictions. Born in 1936, I'm a little younger than most of the women I interviewed, more a fifties girl than a fifties woman. I spent most of the decade learning "how to be a woman" from *Seventeen* magazine. On the other hand, I had a mother who hoped I'd "do something," and I went to girls' schools, where I was encouraged to do well and there were no boys around to distract and compete with me.

At twenty-two, after three years at Northwestern University studying theater and Beginning Bohemianism, I came to New York to make my fortune as an actress. I worked hard at it, and a year later I had a highly successful season in summer stock under my belt, as well as a coveted Actors' Equity card, and a letter of introduction from a famous actor to a very big agent. On the eve of my first audition for my first Broadway play, I got pregnant. (Did I forget to mention that I'd fallen in love with a fellow actor during my summer in stock?)

Crisis. Should I get an abortion? (My mother would have engineered it somehow.) Should we get married? (We would have married eventually anyway . . . wouldn't we?)

We decided to get married. I felt relieved. Off the hook. I wasn't sure I wanted the life of a professional actress, I reminded myself. As much as I loved acting, there was an element of self-exposure about it that repelled me. Then there was this baby inside me that I seemed to want more than I could have imagined. I felt my existence to be vindicated with this baby, although I wasn't sure why. I gave up acting and became a full-time mother. My husband didn't ask me to give up acting;

he didn't have to. There was a tacit agreement between us that *he* would have the career.

When I revisited this decision years later, viewing it through the lens of newly acquired (and insufficiently digested) feminism, I saw it as an outright retreat. I blamed myself for what I saw as my failure of nerve, the culture for brainwashing me into thinking I was no good unless I was a mother, and my ex-husband for depriving me of my career.

Writing this book has forced me to look at that moment again, this time with more respect for its complexities (and for myself). The decision, I see now, came out of a desire, submerged but powerful, for connection, for family. I believed that if I succeeded as an actress, I risked losing the man: the pregnancy would necessarily call a halt to a career that threatened him. I couldn't, in 1959, imagine having both accomplishment in the world *and* love.

Many of the women I talked with felt this way. What constrained them was not always the blatant sexism of barred doors and low expectations. It was their own profound belief, internalized from a lifetime of messages, that achievement and autonomy were simply incompatible with love and family. The equation was inescapable: independence equalled loneliness.

Most of the ninety-two women I interviewed for this book are now between fifty-eight and sixty-eight years old. I focused on women in this age range because they would have been in their late teens to midtwenties during the fifties—a time of intense and critical decision-making about college, marriage, children, and work. I tried to get women to home in on those moments of decision, to remember what they were thinking, feeling, what their friends were doing, what messages they were getting from their parents and teachers.

The book moves more or less chronologically through the phases of a woman's life. The first six chapters are about the progression from college to marriage to motherhood. They also include the wild cards that could interrupt that orderly progression: sex and pregnancy.

Chapters 7 through 10 are about women who deviated from the norm in one way or another, either by entering male-dominated professions, or loving their own sex, or going against the political grain of the time.

These rebellious spirits didn't come out of nowhere. Under the glassy surface of the fifties, sea changes in women's behavior and attitudes were taking place, changes that had been under way since the 1920s. The fifties only slowed them down for a while. The liberalization of ideas about women's sexuality continued despite efforts to contain that sexuality within the institution of marriage. The baby boom turned out to be only a blip in the century-long decline in the birthrate. And despite the domestic revival, the numbers of women entering the work force climbed steadily during the decade, although the patterns were different from those of the war years. By 1960, twice as many women were working as had been in 1940, and the proportion of working wives doubled during the same period. In fact, the increase in employment was greatest among older, middle-class wives whose children were in school. However, the jobs they got were in low-paying, sex-segregated fields. Rosie the Riveter didn't necessarily leave the work force; she just moved—or was moved—over into clerical and sales jobs, or the "helping professions" of teaching, nursing, or social work. While the growing numbers of women working outside the home did not alter the balance of power within the family, or directly challenge assumptions about women's roles, it meant that the realities of women's lives were being transformed.

The civil rights movement was also gathering steam during the fifties. The 1954 *Brown* v. *Board of Education of Topeka* decision striking down "separate but equal" education was followed by the Montgomery bus boycott in 1955, spearheaded by two middle-class black women, Rosa Parks and Jo Ann

Robinson. The civil rights movement, so unassailably *right*, with its roots in the black churches of the South, made working for social justice respectable again. It served to dissolve the Cold War consensus that equated advocating social change with subversion, opening the way for the liberation movements of the sixties and seventies.

Other crosscurrents were roiling under the becalmed waters of the fifties. In spite of the harsh repression of homosexuals, gays and lesbians who had tasted a degree of freedom during the war, created their first organizations, the Mattachine Society and Daughters of Bilitis. Beat writers like Jack Kerouac and Allen Ginsberg were challenging the status quo, and if their critique didn't extend to the status of women, their rebellion eventually helped shake loose the heterosexual hegemony of the fifties. Rock 'n' roll and rhythm and blues were rumbling like an earthquake beneath a pop music scene dominated by the blandness and inanity of Mitch Miller and Patti Page.

Many of the women I interviewed for this book had a hard time sticking to the subject of the fifties. They kept hurtling forward to the sixties and seventies because that's when they changed their lives. Nearly everyone I talked to had made substantial changes in the two decades after the fifties, though not every woman viewed these changes as rebellions. Some who finished college and went to work simply saw it as a new stage in their lives. Others deliberately kicked over the traces: they divorced their husbands, remarried, or came out as lesbians and created radically different lives with women lovers. Some took up interests or explored talents they'd left behind when they married or, finding it was too late to regain lost ground, turned in new directions.

Women sometimes resisted my efforts to pull them back to the fifties. They seemed to feel almost ashamed that they'd been so docile, so quick to submerge their identities into their husbands'. They needed to be reminded that they were hardly alone; that millions of American women were doing just what they were doing.

Their stories demonstrate the complex range of strategies that women of the fifties employed to accommodate themselves to their narrow spheres. Many emerged as triumphant survivors. But their survival should not distract us from a hard-eyed look at the costs of a decade that asked women to use only a fraction of themselves, to be satisfied to live through their husbands and children, and to forego the pleasure and power of free sexual expression.

THE FIFTIES
A Women's Oral History

Chapter I

Going All the Way

We found no basic differences in the anatomy which
is involved in the sexual responses of females and
males, and we found no differences in the physio-
logic phenomena which are involved when females
and males respond sexually.
—*Kinsey Report on Sexual Behavior
in the Human Female*, 1953

Remember that the average man will go as far as you
let him go. A man is only as bad as the woman he is
with.
—Kiowa Costonie,
How to Win and Hold a Husband, 1945

A young unmarried couple is making out in a parked Buick
in a secluded spot on a winter evening in 1953. The windows are steamed up and Jo Stafford is crooning "Teach
Me Tonight" on the car radio. His right arm cradles her head
and his tongue is deep in her mouth. His left hand has insinu-
ated itself under her coat, under her sweater, and rests firmly on
the stitched cotton point of her right bra-cup. Her right hand
rests, ever-so-lightly, on his crotch, ready at a moment's notice
to fly up and block his left hand should it venture under her bra,

or attempt a descent to the waistband of her skirt. In the game of sex as we played it in the fifties, he is "on second base." If he "gets lucky," she will "go all the way" and he will have "scored."

He's thinking: How far will she let me go? Does she really want me to stop or is it an act? She's thinking: Will he stop or is it really up to me to stop him? Do I *want* to stop him? Will he ever call me again if I don't let him do it? Will he think I'm a tease? Will he ever call me again if I *do* let him do it? What if I got pregnant? Does he really love me? Would he really marry me?

What makes this a uniquely fifties encounter is the fact that it takes place in an automobile. Young people had been necking and petting since the 1920s when Victorian sexual standards began to erode. But it wasn't until the fifties, when nearly every American family had a car, that they acquired that treasured commodity, privacy. The backseat of a Buick might have been uncomfortable, but it was infinitely preferable to the front porch or living room of your parents' home.

On Thursday, August 27, 1953, two bombshells exploded in the American press: news that the USSR had detonated an H-bomb, and Dr. Alfred Kinsey's report on female sexuality. It may seem ludicrous to equate the news of the Russian bomb with the news that 95 percent of American women had petted before marriage. But in fact the two events were given nearly equal weight by the press, and generated almost equal amounts of anxiety among the public.

Kinsey and his staff interviewed 5,940 American women and his findings were electrifying. He reported that up to 95 percent of them had petted before the age of eighteen; that 50 percent of married women born after 1900 had had sex before marriage (albeit with their intended husbands); and that 69 percent of women who'd had premarital sex were unrepentant.

More than anything else, the *Kinsey Report* revealed the gaping difference between our ideals of sexual conduct and the behavior of real men and women. But while a segment of the population recoiled—a letter to *Look* magazine protested that the *Kinsey Report* "cannot represent the mental, moral, or spiritual integrity of American womanhood"—the *Kinsey Report* also represented a milestone in the acceptance of women as sexual beings. The very fact that women's sexual behavior and attitudes could be the subject of a scientific study was remarkable in itself.

But for the young women struggling in parked Buicks across the country, this sea change in attitudes meant little. They had their hands full—literally—keeping their valuable reputations intact, their boyfriends attentive, and their own desires in check.

Alix Berns, who grew up in Brooklyn, New York, talks about how she and her girlfriends handled their curiosity about sex. A stocky, energetic social worker, at fifty-eight she still vibrates with sexual energy.

"I was in a gang of kids who'd all been through elementary school together. We were all high-achieving Jewish kids and the girls didn't date the boys in this crowd—they were almost like brothers, not interesting as dates. We were interested in the 'bummy' Italian or Greek boys, the street corner hoods that we'd meet in the movies from time to time. We tried to dress like the girls we thought would attract them—flats, flashy blouses. This was like another identity we tried on to learn about social things because the boys in our group were such good pals—and so uninteresting.

"With these bummy guys we didn't really have conversations. We talked about food and where we lived and stuff, just a few words at a time. We pretended we weren't that good in school. We didn't ever actually date them—that would have been too scary—we flirted with them. Even at the time I knew it was a learning thing. I was learning how to act sexual with boys and also how to deal with them, how to keep them at a distance. It was a way to get validation for our sexuality because we thought the guys we hung around with didn't notice those things."

When Alix was a little older, she found a "safe" way to explore her interest in sex without jeopardizing her future.

"I started going steady with this guy, Sal, who lived in New Jersey. This suited me perfectly—someone who lived somewhere else and wanted to be with me and came to see me and who was my boyfriend. So I had the security, the Saturday night date, but I could spend most of my time with my girlfriends, who were very important to me.

"Sal and I did 'everything but' sex, and through this relationship I was learning about sexual feelings. Everyone was scared I was going to marry him, but I always knew in my heart of hearts he wasn't 'the one.' He was very handsome and sophisticated, 'smooth,' as we used to say, but he wasn't intellectual enough or funny enough. Also, I'm a great romantic and I had the movie of my deflowering in my head. I wanted it to be perfect. Anyway, there wasn't any really reliable birth control around."

As conservative as we may find it today, going steady was actually a form of teenage rebellion in the fifties. Parents, educators, and teen advice-givers inveighed against the practice, suspecting—correctly—that it provided sanctions for necking and petting. But in fact, going steady was a peculiarly fifties response to the vicissitudes of dating: it guaranteed security. Wearing his ID bracelet, his class ring, his pin, or his letter sweater, you were sure of a date every Saturday night, an escort to every social occasion. His pin was a badge, a public token of your popularity. These were mini-marriages, in which young people could explore their sexuality in relative safety. But adult critics failed to notice that most young people, even as they were necking and petting up a storm, had thoroughly internalized the basic rules:

that sex outside of marriage was wrong, and that nice girls didn't do it.

In the Midwest, the rituals were different, but the rules were basically the same. Sheila McCarthy's description of her dating life in an Indianapolis suburb could have been lifted straight out of "A Date with Judy," the classic teen radio program of the late forties.

"By Thursday night, if you weren't invited out for a Saturday night, you were despondent. It was good if you also had a date for Friday night, but not with the same boy if you could avoid it. Friday was a lesser night. Saturday was the glittering night. Thursday night you washed your hair and did your nails. Preparations. Shopping, planning, ironing, curling. Anticipation. Waiting for the phone to ring.

"What you did on the date was go out to a roadhouse where there was *nothing!* Not even any music. The boys drank beer, the girls drank cokes, and on the way home you'd get stopped for drinking. That was the excitement. I got a steady boyfriend as soon as I could, picked him out from the non-Catholic school with the speed of light. He had auburn curls and danced well and would take me to the movies. Non-Catholic was the important thing. We kissed continuously. I was tremendously interested in sex. Over the course of two years, we progressed down from the lips. I remember the moment his hand touched my pale blue cashmere-covered breast because I was immediately stricken with the first migraine headache of my life. There was no question of consummation. It would never have occurred to me. There was never even a struggle. But there was tremendous tension and fondling and heavy breathing. I was quite shocked to find years later that a girl in my class who was so popular was putting out."

As a young woman in the fifties, the responsibility for controlling sexual situations was squarely on you. In other words, you were supposed to tell the boy when to stop. You were caught in a triple-bind. If you went too far, you could be stigmatized as fast; if you didn't go far enough, you risked being labeled cold, a prude; and if you behaved normally under the circumstances—allowing your own passion to flare, then pulling back in terror or guilt—you were in danger of being called a cock-tease. The tension and anxiety surrounding sexual encounters was heightened by ignorance about male and female sexuality. Were you a nymphomaniac if you got turned on in a necking session? Were you causing irreparable damage to the boy's health (as he claimed) if you didn't relieve his sexual frustration, or blue balls?

Claire Lassiter remembers her painful struggles with her first boyfriend in high school. Claire was raised on an isolated Vermont farm and felt herself to be plain, socially backward, and—one of the worst things you could be in those days—too tall.

"All the boys in school were shorter than I was. I knew not to slouch, I'd read my teen magazines, so the way I handled this was, I tried to bend at the knees so that I would look shorter.

"In my junior year, this boy, Terry, took a shine to me. He used to drive out to the farm to take me out and we would have these long struggles in the car. I wasn't even that attracted to him—I was just so grateful to have somebody interested in me. So in these struggles I wasn't at war with my own impulses so much as just busy keeping him at arm's length for all I was worth. Once he asked my permission to get out from behind the steering wheel and, of course, I said no. Then one day he showed up for a date with another couple, and when I looked out my bedroom window and saw that the other boy was driving, I realized immediately why. I sent my parents downstairs to tell him that I couldn't go because I was so terrified of having to deal with him in the backseat without him hampered by actually having to drive. I never heard from him again."

Gwen Barnes and her boyfriend were engaged in a more

complicated dance in which the conflict was heightened by Gwen's own desire. Gwen, a robust fifty-five-year-old bookstore owner, came from a big, actively Presbyterian family in western New York.

"In high school I dated a boy who was very good-looking, which was unusual for me. Usually it was my sister who dated the cute boys. But what happened was, on our first date we had a car accident. I always thought he stayed my boyfriend for four years because of that. We were at cross purposes. I used to tell him, Charlie, I love making out with you, but I would never want you to be the father of my children. And he used to say, Gwen, I wish I could go out with someone who would go all the way, but you're the kind of girl I want to marry.

"The first time he French-kissed me, I thought, what is this? This must be wrong. I'd never even *heard* of it! I couldn't ask my sister about it because I didn't want to show my ignorance and I also didn't want to let her know I was doing this thing. I remember going home at night and praying and crying, because I thought what I was doing was so bad and I was enjoying it so much. I'd pray, please, God, help me stop doing this. We had terrible fights in the car, Charlie and I. The thing was, though, even though we acted out this struggle—he'd push, push, push, I'd say stop, stop, stop—we both knew the rules. I knew he would never push me beyond what I wanted. Once I asked him if he'd ever gone all the way and he said he had, with this divorced woman that he worked with. I was absolutely floored."

Kay D'Amico, a dance therapist who grew up in the Chicago suburbs, remembers the unspoken bargain between her and her boyfriend Vince, and how it ultimately broke down.

"Vince was a real catch in high school, what we called a BMOC (Big Man On Campus). He played basketball and he had his own Ford convertible. He was different from me, working-class Italian, so we were exotic to each other. We used to spend hours and hours on Saturday nights necking in his car. It would always go the same way. We'd get to a point where we were both incredibly turned on—oh God, I remember feeling as if the whole lower half of my body, from the waist down, had turned to liquid. We'd be inches away from doing it and Vince would be moaning, 'Oh baby, baby, baby!' and I'd be moaning, 'No, no, no . . . ' and I would be having this terrific struggle inside myself. Part of me just wanted to let everything go and *just do it!*

"In a way, I almost wanted Vince to forge ahead because then I wouldn't have to take responsibility. I knew he expected me to stop him—especially since I was this 'nice' girl from the 'right' part of town. So I knew what my role to play was. But I was pretty sure if push came to shove, Vince would pull back. Well, one night it got way out of hand and I just let myself go and all of a sudden I realized he wasn't going to stop and at the same moment he was *in*. Well, he pulled out right away, I mean we kind of wrenched away from each other. Then we proceeded to have this terrible fight. I was furious at him for betraying me—I remember I was crying and saying, 'I can't believe it— you were going to *do it!*' And he was slamming his hand against the steering wheel and saying, 'You *let* me! Why didn't you stop me?' Of course, when I think back on it now, we were both in a state of total frustration and we were each probably furious at each other for *stopping*.

"After a while we made up, but the relationship was never the same after that. And a year or so after we broke up I heard that he'd made a remark about me, that I was not quite what I was cracked up to be or something. He was implying that I wasn't a virgin, or that I wanted it. I was devastated because, of course, he was right, I did want it and I felt guilty about that. Oh, it was complicated."

Underlying this narrow path of sexual behavior was a marketplace view of sexuality in which, in its crudest form, sex was a commodity purchased by marriage. In this system, a woman's "value" was based on her virtue. Fifties advice books and teen magazine columns were full of warnings to girls about the dangers of "free" kisses, "cheap" behavior, "selling yourself short," and ending up as "secondhand goods." This economic model of dating and sexuality was reinforced by the reality that after World War II, for the first time in American history, women outnumbered men. Inevitably, this system resulted in the "sexual brinkmanship" familiar to everyone who came of age in the fifties, in which a couple went as far as they could possibly go, short of actual intercourse. As long as a penis had not actually entered your vagina, you were a "technical virgin."

At close to six feet by the time she was fifteen, Tyler Barrett felt she had compelling reasons to cling to her virginity.

"Because of my height and my general feeling of unattractiveness, I felt my marketability was not so high. I thought I needed my virginity as a kind of extra asset. It wasn't until I got to college that I got a real boyfriend—someone who was tall enough for me, in other words. Ned and I would sleep in the same bed naked. I never masturbated him but I do remember his ejaculating once and thinking, 'Wonder what *this* is?' I didn't even understand why *I* was having a discharge while we were doing all this petting. I thought something was wrong with me. I finally asked my dermatologist in Minneapolis about it. He explained that I was lubricating and it was perfectly normal. Then he made a pass at me."

The real enforcer of the rules was the fear of pregnancy. The likelihood of becoming pregnant as a result of a sexual encounter was very great. Contraception was rarely used by unmarried couples. A young woman, unless she lived in a big city and had access to something like the Margaret Sanger Clinic, would probably not have owned a diaphragm. In many areas of the country doctors simply refused to prescribe contraceptives to unmarried women. Even if a young man had condoms, he was unlikely to admit it to his "nice" girlfriend because she'd think he was expecting sex. Millie Caine, who grew up in northern New Hampshire, recalls her lonely struggles between her sexual instincts and her terror of pregnancy.

"I dated a little, but it was a painful time which I wouldn't want to repeat. I was the oldest girl in a big family and I was tired of keeping kids. Even with my help, I saw what it did to my mother. I had an aunt who had been a nurse in the war and because of her I knew I wanted to work for a living. A job was a way out, a way to be independent. Marriage was not necessarily part of my dream. I wanted to cut loose and see what the rest of the world was like. I was very interested in sex, but I was so aware that messing around with boys would lead to pregnancy and that would be the end of achievement. I saw this trap of pregnancy all around me. Sexual experimentation was out of the question. There was no abortion, as far as I knew about. Girls who were desperate used coat hangers—literally! One of my girlfriends died using a coat hanger.

"But I was worried about my own interest in sex. I started to go to this church group as a way to find a better group of friends to relate to socially. But I found out that they were just as horny in church as they were outside of it! It was everywhere! And there were the same strictures about not going to bed with somebody but it was worse in this church group because not only would you be possibly knocked up and pregnant, but you were disgraced. A sinner. So I just withdrew, pretty much, until I could get out of there, and got a reputation as antisocial, I guess. It took me a few years before I could loosen up around men."

Still, despite the risks and the social opprobrium involved in any kind of premarital sexual experimentation, some young women did manage to have active sex lives before settling down to marriage. Peggy Fox came from a big, sophisticated Irish Catholic family outside Chicago. The youngest of five daughters, Peggy went to Catholic schools from kindergarten straight through college.

"When I was about sixteen, my sister Nancy came home the day after her wedding in tears. It was the sex—she wanted no part of it. I thought, oh my Lord! Even then I knew *that* wouldn't be my problem, I knew I was interested. The first time I did it was with Pat Conlon, when I was seventeen. We did it right in my own bedroom in the daytime. It wouldn't have mattered to me what time it was. I decided I must be a nymphomaniac because I *loved* it. I thought, this is *the best!*"

After college, Peggy got a job in a Catholic bookstore in Chicago and moved back and forth between home and various apartments in the city.

"I had kind of a schizy social life in those days. I was dating these fast-and-loose guys, but I would always have an acceptable romance going at the same time. In other words, I'd be going out with these nice Catholic boys—and being chaste, I might add! But many's the night I spent on a cot in the stockroom in back of the bookstore with one of these other wild guys. The nice boys all wanted to get married, but I was having too much fun.

"I was forever bombing down to Holy Name Cathedral because they heard confessions all day long. So obviously I felt guilty, but it didn't seem to stop me. Because, in my heart I couldn't believe that something that felt this good could be a sin. See, I always, always had orgasms, from the first time I had sex. That was why I loved it so much. I kept thinking, Grievous offense . . . sufficient reflection . . . full consent of the will, and I'd ponder over it. Did I really consent? Surely it wasn't as bad as killing somebody. Better just go down and confess. Because all this time I was still going to Mass and Communion, would you believe.

"It never entered my mind to use birth control. It never really occurred to me that I could get pregnant. I knew birth control existed, but I didn't know anything about it. To go out and actually get it would mean that I *planned* to do these things, to have sex. Since I knew it was wrong, I kept thinking I wasn't doing it, or I wasn't going to do it again. Each time was the last time. Birth control would have been cold-blooded."

Miriam Wells was a straight-A student in her Cleveland high school, and already thought of herself as an intellectual when she went off to Radcliffe in 1954.

"I was a serious student and I was going to major in philosophy. I hadn't counted on being so distracted by sex. I couldn't think about whether things really existed or not, whether it really was a chair, you know. I was wondering if I should be sleeping with this or that man."

Miriam's first boyfriend was a vet, at Harvard on the GI bill.

"I didn't mean to sleep with him. I wanted to stay a virgin. But my sexual desire for him was very strong and I didn't have a strong enough will to oppose him. No one I knew was sleeping with anybody then. After I slept with him, some of his friends sent their girlfriends over to talk to me in hopes that I would talk them into sleeping with them. But I wouldn't recommend it. It was a very mixed experience for me.

"I didn't know anything about orgasms. The first time it happened, we were in his room in his dorm. It was fast—he came in and he came out. It was a sharp, poignant pleasure that had no resolution. It stayed like that, it never got any better. He would come in and then pull out and come into a handkerchief. I was always left hanging. I used to come back to my dorm and lie down on the floor and howl and pound the floor. But I didn't really know why I was so frustrated. It felt so lonely.

"I was terribly frightened about getting pregnant, but I never did anything about getting birth control. I'm not really sure why. Maybe I kept telling myself we weren't going to do it again. And I think I saw him as a kind of father, and that he would take care of such things. Later on, when I ran into him and we were talking about our romance, he said to me reproachfully, 'You should have told me to go to the bathroom and masturbate!' What he was really saying was that I should have taken responsibility, that I shouldn't have let it happen. But I was thinking about a pure love, a spiritual union. I never thought about masturbating."

Miriam's real sexual awakening came after her boyfriend had graduated and left.

"I was relieved, in a way. By then I had met this artist in Cambridge. He was forty or so, and he had a gold earring, like a little pirate. I went to bed with him once and had my first orgasm, this enormous orgasm. After I had the orgasm I sat on the edge of his bed and wept so hard for all the times before that I hadn't had this pleasure. Afterward, it was as if the whole world had changed—I felt it for days afterward. I never saw him again—we both knew it was just a one-shot thing and that we had no intention of taking up with each other."

In Bohemian enclaves of American cities young women had a little more freedom to explore their sexuality. Miranda Clark grew up in Greenwich Village, the daughter of artists and socialists. Her parents were divorced when Miranda was sixteen. We talk in her tiny Greenwich Village apartment, amid the clutter of her two crafts, weaving and jewelry-making. With her waist-length, iron-gray braid and Peruvian skirt, she remains every inch the Bohemian. Although Miranda's sexual initiation happened early, her story has some elements in common with her sisters in less sophisticated milieus.

"When I was fourteen a boy named Ira Skolnick kissed me on the lips during a game of Spin-the-Bottle. Later he gave me a piece of chewing gum and said, 'Here, this will help you calm down.' I was mortified that he would think I was so excited. My girlfriend Selene was considered fast. She wanted to sing opera. We used to spend hours after school talking about what sex would actually feel like and reading Krafft-Ebing aloud to each other. Selene got it together and slept with her boyfriend when she was fifteen, which in those days was extremely early to be doing this stuff. She was our frontier person, but she wouldn't tell us what it was like for two days. When she did tell us, it didn't sound like much to me.

"I finally did it a couple of years later when I was seventeen. The war was just over, and the boy was a returned soldier. He was twenty-four, which seemed very old. He was a friend of a guy I was going out with who was pressuring me to sleep with him but I wouldn't. But I took one look at this friend, Allen, and I knew *he* was going to get it. But I wasn't going to give it to him right away. He tried to convince me a few times and then, smart guy, he said, 'I'm not going to ask you again. When you're ready, you tell me.' It took me about three weeks. I don't know why I held out as long as I did.

"I don't know where I got the idea that I *shouldn't* do it, that it wasn't nice to do it. It wasn't from my parents. We were Bohemians! I knew I was an outlaw and part of me didn't want to be. Part of me wanted to be like everyone else. I didn't dress Bohemian, I wore plaid skirts and sweaters with Peter Pan blouses under them.

"As time went on, I got more and more lustful for Allen. One night we were sitting in Nick's down on Seventh Avenue and I said, 'Okay, tonight's the night.' We walked down to Whelan's, the all-night drugstore on Eighth Street, and bought condoms. We went to my house—my room was in the back of the house, pretty far from where my parents slept. We got in my bed and did it. All the time we were doing it, I kept thinking over and over, This is it, this is it, this is what it is! Afterward, he said, 'Did you come?' I knew what he meant because my mother had said to me when I was about eleven, 'Never let a man make you come because then he'll have power over you.' Great, huh? At the time, I didn't know quite what she meant by 'come' but I had an idea. And of course, I hadn't come.

"When my mother caught on that I was sleeping with Allen, she sent me right up to the Margaret Sanger Clinic on Sixteenth

Street for a diaphragm. I went with Selene and they had us fill out these questionnaires. I remember they asked us how many times a week we had sex and we didn't want to look like amateurs so we said twelve times a week. I said my husband was in the navy. They didn't care. While we were there, a woman in the waiting room said to another woman, 'My husband doesn't like the taste of the jelly.' Well, Selene and I were convulsed at the stupidity of this man *eating* the jelly!

"After Allen and I did it, I started dressing in black and acting more like a Bohemian. But you know, for all this socialism and Bohemianism, I still had this idea that I'd get married and some man would support me and that I ought to get a teaching degree so that I'd have 'something to fall back on.'"

Even the most conventional and pliant young women could be blindsided by sexual desire. Julia Harmon appears to be the quintessence of Southern womanhood: tall and statuesque, with a queenly carriage and a voice like butter-and-honey, she radiates warmth and charm. She was raised in Charlotte, North Carolina, the daughter of a prominent and well-loved Presbyterian minister. Julia was not only an obedient daughter, she took pleasure in it.

"I very much wanted to please my parents—it was my joy to please them. I not only expected to get married, I consciously looked forward to marriage as a form of identity. You see, I was identified as Carleton Harmon's daughter, Carleton and Ella's delightful daughter, who had a great future. My agenda was college, graduation, marriage, perhaps travel, perhaps a job or two, but the right, the best marriage, and then, home and family. The direction behind my entire education, I believe, was to make us better, fuller people so that we would be better wives. I was following the pattern my mother followed. My highest ambition was to build the same kind of home that I had come from."

Julia progressed smoothly through high school, where she had a suitable number of "beaux."

"There was an in crowd, and I was in it, I'm afraid—all of us had grown up together, had gone through kindergarten, grade school, choir school. A number of the boys went off to prep school and you juggled the hometown boys with the prep school boys, and that was fun. The social thing was very much a part of my upbringing. I went steady, everyone did, but we were very circumspect, sexually. Passionate good-night kisses, a little neck-ing on the porch before you went in, that sort of thing."

It wasn't until after her graduation from college that the orderly progression of Julia's life was disturbed.

"After graduation, I went home and took a job as assistant to the director of the local art institute, and before I knew it I was madly in love with the director. He was older, he was mar-ried. He was the first man I'd met who was creative, artistic. Yes, I really did jump the traces. For a while there, I had a kind of dual life. I was living at home, but I was also staying out a lot in the evenings, very late. My parents went away at one point and I moved in with this man for a week. Can you imagine?"

Nearly forty years later, Julia blushes and becomes slightly breathless. "I shock myself. Of course, in many ways I was still extremely circumscribed. I remained a virgin—a technical vir-gin, we used to say. But this was the first time I had ever really dared to do anything that I knew was wrong. I was compelled, I was excited. I couldn't help myself. But in a way I was glad I did it because it was *me* doing it! I wasn't doing it to please anyone, for the first time in my life. I was answering a call that I guess I had not heard before. His wife and children, of course, were safely back in Atlanta. Oh, my parents must have been heartsick. It lasted three or four months. His brother was a priest and he would come down and take me out to dinner and caution me, did I know what I was up to. He was worried about me. It didn't have much effect on me. In fact, I thought it was very exotic, exciting. I'd never known a Catholic priest before, and here was one without his collar taking me out to dinner in a fine restaurant, with wine.

"After a few months I went to Europe with a couple of friends. I think this was a plan that had been set in motion before I embarked on my love affair. I seem to remember weeping bitterly when it was time to go, but I did go, and no one was forcing me. I may have been a little relieved. We were in Europe·for three months, and by the time I came back, this romance was over. You can imagine how relieved my parents were."

Julia went on to marry a suitable man, have a family, and to become a dutiful corporate wife. She is still married to Chuck, and speaks with quiet satisfaction about her career as helpmeet, mother, and homemaker.

For the majority of American women, their sexual initiation took place within the framework of marriage. In fact, as the women in chapter 2 make clear, marriage was often the only way for a woman to have sex. On the other hand, the notion of the erotic marriage came into its own in the fifties. The belief that non-procreative sexual activity was wholesome and desirable in a marriage was propounded by nearly all marriage guides of the time. Among other things, social scientists understood that an early and eroticized marriage was the best way to contain what they saw as potentially explosive sexuality.

Claire Lassiter recalls her wedding night and honeymoon: "Don was really the first man in my life that I was dying to go to bed with. Although I was a virgin when I got married, we'd done everything you can possibly think of during our courtship. Lots of passionate evenings. You know, the odd thing is that with all the repression I've had in every area of my life, I've always loved sex. In spite of all my mother's lessons about patting them on the heads and shutting the door in their faces, and about how men would kill you, I never had any trouble engaging in sexual activity and finding it pleasurable. There was a place inside me that my mother didn't reach for whatever reason. I don't think she was ever a sexual person, and it may be that this was a way of being separate from her.

"We had our wedding night at the Plaza and it was a complete bust. I was mortified at the idea that people in the lobby, or bellboys, would know I'd be having sex that night. We were both thoroughly exhausted by the wedding and suddenly it was awkward to have to do this. I felt cold, uninvolved sexually and emotionally. We went ahead anyway, but without any real passion. The next day we got on a plane and went to Nantucket where we had this wonderful cottage. For four days it poured rain and was cold, and we spent the entire time in bed. That was really fun, really everything I could have hoped for, except that I ended up with a horrendous urinary tract infection and we didn't know what it was."

Gwen Barnes describes how she and her husband looked for ways to improve their sex life: "Sex was lousy at first. Well, we were both virgins, what do you expect? Neither of us knew a thing about what to do. I didn't have my first orgasm until we'd been married for several years. It was an accident—we sort of stumbled on my clitoris. Then once while Buddy was away on a business trip, he found some old book along the lines of *The Joy of Sex*, and underlined all these things and sent it up to me. That really helped us more than anything. That book, I remember, said, hey, spend some time. And there was enough closeness between us that it was okay to try some things. I remember one time, we'd been out and he'd gone to take the baby-sitter home, I took my clothes off and put on his overcoat and when he came in the door I flashed open the coat and yelled, 'Voilà!' So we were trying."

Dorothy Glenn actually left her husband because there wasn't enough sex in her marriage. Now divorced and a successful book designer, Dorothy spent much of the fifties as a housewife in a Los Angeles suburb. After twelve years of marriage and two children, Dorothy's restless unhappiness crystallized.

"I was thirty-two or -three and I guess I was at the height of my sexuality. The problem was, we just weren't having sex very much. We could go for a *year* without having sex! And it was not something that my husband was willing to discuss. There was something removed about him. I thought there must be something lacking in me that I could not get this intimacy that I wanted. I thought I was sexually deficient.

"I didn't have anyone to talk to about these things. My mother was back east and she was kind of shaky with her drinking anyway. I did try to talk about it with one friend who was older, and she said, 'What's so important about sex?' I remember having dreams of isolation, of being on a boat with a bunch of children—mine and everybody else's—just being adrift on this boat, having all the responsibility and no power. I couldn't steer the boat. It was such a powerful dream I still remember it. I did try to get help. I went to a psychiatrist. In fact, my husband even went for a while, but this psychiatrist's idea of a solution was that my husband should bring me flowers. I was involved with the Episcopal church at the time and I went to talk to the priest. He agreed that there had to be sex in a marriage. But he didn't say much more than that.

"I came to feel I had to break out, I had to leave. It was around 1958. I don't know how I did it. To this day, I don't know how I had the courage. My friends were pretty shocked. Well, I remember now: I had an affair—mainly to check out the idea that it wasn't my fault. This wasn't even with somebody I was crazy about. It was somebody I felt safe with, somebody in our circle of friends.

"And it worked, more or less—that is, even with this man I didn't have much of a relationship with, I really enjoyed the sex and I was orgasmic. I didn't leave my husband to be with anybody else—although I assumed I would marry again eventually.

Once I decided what I was going to do I moved pretty fast. I got a lawyer, we put the house up for sale—God, when I think of it now! I haven't often in my life been driven to do something. But I was driven to leave that marriage."

Dorothy Glenn's story illustrates the slow but steady liberalization of our ideas about women's sexuality. Twenty years earlier, the idea of a woman feeling entitled to sexual satisfaction in her marriage would have seemed fantastic.

The sexual revolution has been getting a lot of bad press lately. A *New York Times Magazine* "Hers" columnist recently lamented the disappearance of virginity as "a source of feminine strength." But if we construe the sexual revolution as the whole package that includes changed attitudes about sexuality, the availability of the birth control pill, and the legalization of abortion, its impact on women's lives has been enormous. Thanks to the sexual revolution and feminism, women have greatly expanded their ability to have sex on their own terms, to have it free of the paralyzing fear of pregnancy, and to have it with other women. And though traces of the sexual double standard still linger, a woman's identity and self-worth are no longer tied to her "virtue." If it accomplished nothing else, the sexual revolution made it possible for a woman to explore and express her sexuality without having to get married to do it.

Getting Caught

You had to ask around. You asked friends and they asked friends, and the ripples of asking people widened until some person whose face you might never see gave over the secret information that could save you.

—JOYCE JOHNSON, *MINOR CHARACTERS*

Being forced to have a baby and give it away to someone else now seems preposterous to me—as grotesque and absurd as being asked to throw myself on my husband's funeral pyre. To make young women feel this kind of shame and disgrace, all because of some whimsical social decision—it's unforgivable and inhuman.

—PAT SULLIVAN

It's no accident we called it "getting caught." The phrase has a mean, smirking ring that captured the way we felt about sex outside marriage: that it was a sneaky, illicit game, and that you took your chances when you played it. "Getting caught" applied only to girls, and it implied that they deserved to get caught. Pregnancy was the punishment for sex outside of marriage. Of course, not only unmarried girls got pregnant and needed abortions, as the *Kinsey Report* made clear. I've focused primarily on young, unmarried women because their vulnerability and inexperience, and the shame and guilt associated with their pregnancies, made their plight more desperate.

It may be difficult for young women today to imagine a time when the fear of pregnancy was an unavoidable part of every sexual encounter. That meant that you were not able to have sex with a man—*ever*—without a part of your brain being occupied by this terror. To be unmarried and pregnant in the 1950s was to be in the deepest kind of trouble. First of all, there was the shame; a kind of shame that's unfamiliar to girls now: a profound and overwhelming feeling that you were bad and dirty in the deepest part of you; that you'd done something irredeemable.

Then there was the terrible quandary of what to do. If you even *knew* about abortion—and many young women didn't—you knew it was a dark, dirty, and exceedingly dangerous business. You probably had no idea how to go about getting one, and the fear of being found out made it hard to ask.

If you were anywhere near a large urban area, and you were resourceful, or had good help, you might be able to find your way to a Florence Crittenten Home, or one of the other places where unmarried girls could go to have their babies and give them up for adoption.

Single motherhood was not a viable choice if you were white and middle-class: the stigma was simply too crippling to live with. If you were black, your family and community might treat you with more compassion, but your life was irrevocably changed. The only option left, the one most white women took if they could, was marriage. But even marriage didn't shield you from censure if your baby was born at thirty-five weeks.

At the beginning of the nineteenth century, there were no laws regulating abortion in America; it was performed in the home by nonprofessionals—midwives, folk doctors, women themselves. Legislation against abortion coincided with the emergence of physicians in the 1800s as a class of medical professionals. Physicians seized on abortion as part of their project to enhance the status of their profession by claiming a moral high ground as well as superior scientific skills. As historian Kristin Luker says in *Abortion and the Politics of Motherhood*, "Given the primitive nature of medical practice, persuading the public that embryos were human lives and then persuading legislatures to protect these lives by outlawing abortion may have been one of the few life-saving projects actually available to physicians."

Their efforts were successful: by 1900, legal abortion had passed into the hands of the medical profession. Every state in the United States had passed laws against abortion, usually including exceptions to save the life of the mother.

Still, historians seem to agree that until the 1950s abortion remained relatively—and I stress *relatively*—accessible through informal female networks, from physicians driven by competition for patients, and from a thriving criminal underground. There was a tacit acceptance of illegal abortion by both the public law and enforcement officials. Between 1946 and 1953, for example, the New York County District Attorney prosecuted only 136 abortion cases, this in a city that had 411,413 live births during the same period.

In addition, until the fifties, the interpretation of "to save the mother's life" was vague enough to allow doctors broad latitude in their decisions to provide so-called therapeutic abortions. According to Kristin Luker, ". . . the doctrine of medical judgment permitted physicians to use an almost unimaginably wide range of criteria for deciding upon an abortion *and neither the public nor individual physicians appear to have been very troubled by the discrepancies.*"

In any event, therapeutic abortions were generally available only to married women. Single women were at the mercy of the illegal abortion network. This network encompassed a huge range of practitioners. At one end were the skilled and compassionate physicians like the famous Dr. Robert Douglas Spencer in rural Pennsylvania, who provided safe and thorough abortions for thousands of women who were fortunate enough to find their way to him. Dr. Spencer charged only ten dollars for nearly thirty years, raising his fees only when forced to, and often performed abortions at no charge for women who couldn't pay. Although he insisted he never paid off the police, Dr. Spencer maintained close and friendly ties with local law enforcement and town officials. Most of the principled doctors who performed abortions during the fifties were "protected" by local police or by organized crime in return for payoffs.

At the other end of the spectrum was the dark, fearful, and dangerous underworld of criminal abortion. If you didn't have good luck, good information, or access to money, you were at the mercy of back-alley butchers or well-meaning but incompetent quacks. You were very likely to find yourself in a dim, dirty room that smelled of disinfectant, in the hands of a so-called doctor whose breath stank of bourbon, and who might cop a feel before going to work. He usually warned you not to scream or he'd walk out and leave you in the middle of nowhere. You were given no anesthesia and you kept your shoes on because he needed you to be able to jump up and get out in a hurry if the police came to the door.

Often all these abortionists did was to pack your uterus and send you away to abort at home, alone. If you were very, very lucky, you didn't get infected by dirty hands or catheters, your uterus wasn't perforated, and you safely expelled all the fetal tissue. But thousands of women ended up in emergency rooms hemorrhaging from incomplete abortions, or raging with fevers from septic infections. By 1962, black market abortions were killing an estimated five to ten thousand women a year.

Despite these horrors, thousands of women resorted to abortion. The *Kinsey Report* estimated that 20 percent of the sexually active single women in this survey had had abortions. In 1957, Planned Parenthood calculated that between 200,000 and 1.2 million abortions took place annually in the United States.

Poor women had less access to safe abortion than their middle- or upper-class sisters—just as they had less access to good medical care generally. Young women with money could sometimes fly to Puerto Rico, or get their abortions from discreet Park Avenue physicians. But such women were in a minority. When abortion is illegal the problem of getting one has always cut across class lines. Young women from small towns and rural areas usually had no information about or access to abortion of any kind. Girls who were financially dependent on their male relatives were also effectively prevented from getting abortions.

Barbara Tuttle was the kind of girl for whom getting an abortion should not have been a problem. The only daughter of a powerful Midwestern politician, she met every fifties standard of beauty. She was tall (but not *too* tall), with a sleek chestnut pageboy and a perfect figure. She was also smart enough to get into Stanford, no mean feat in 1951. A talented singer and musician, Barbara had dreams of being a musical comedy actress, an ambition fiercely opposed by her powerful, conventional father.

"Almost the moment I got to Stanford I fell in love and got engaged. My fiancé was premed and an Olympic diver—a very smart, gorgeous, straitlaced guy. He was joining the navy and the plan was that we'd get married in June of my sophomore year and I'd quit school and go be a navy wife in Pensacola. However, they changed his orders and he was sent to sea instead, so we had to postpone the wedding.

"During my junior year, while I was trying very hard to be a loyal fiancée, I got involved in writing music and lyrics and starring in this big Stanford show, which was directed by W., who, you know, went on to become a very big man in Hollywood.

Well, this was all pretty intense. We were working together
night and day on this huge production which finally took place
in an auditorium that held thousands, with a full orchestra. Ter-
rifically exciting. All this time I was getting these letters from
my guy on this destroyer, the S.S. Something-or-other in Korea,
and they seemed so distant from my real life. But I dutifully
answered every letter, feeling guiltier and guiltier."

After the cast party, the night the show opened, Barbara
slept with W. and became pregnant.

"Ken was coming in on his ship from Korea and this gigantic, elaborate wedding was being planned. By this time I barely
remembered why I was marrying him, but so much machinery
had been set in motion and I was in a kind of daze. So here I
turn up pregnant and the world comes crashing down. My
father could have afforded to send me anywhere in the world
for an abortion, but I simply couldn't tell him. I truly believed
he would have killed me.

"I went to my uncle, who was a physician, hoping he could
find me a regular doctor who could give me an abortion. He
asked around and no one would touch me. So my mother and I
went down to the Mexican section of L.A., to this dirty little
house where I literally had to lie down on a kitchen table! This
guy—I don't even know if he was a doctor—packed my cervix
with something and told me I'd have to wait a few days and
then I'd get cramps and all the packing plus the fetus would
come out. So my mother and I went to this seedy motel room
and waited for three days while I had horrible cramps and
bleeding. Finally I expelled this fair-sized thing down the toilet.
I was lucky because my uncle had given me loads of antibiotics
so I didn't get an infection.

"No sooner had I recovered from the abortion than Ken
arrives—fresh-faced, clean-shaven, all ready for his wedding, in
his dress uniform, with all his mates—to meet me, this fallen
woman. Mr. Clean meets Miss Dirty. I felt absolutely like a

filthy, soiled creature. You know when something is illegal and you have to go through all this subterfuge to get it, you really *feel* like a criminal. I had to tell him I couldn't go through with the wedding, but I couldn't tell him why.

"Everyone was furious at me—Ken, his family, my father, all our friends—because they all thought I'd treated him so badly to call off the wedding. When I got back to college, I told a few of my close friends the real reason and they turned against me. Well, they were friends of Ken's too and I guess they couldn't forgive me. I felt really isolated.

"You see, this just wasn't done. In college, if you were actually sleeping with someone you kept it totally secret because we all lived this pretense that 'nice girls don't do it.' If you did get pregnant, you simply got married—or you left school. You disappeared. What you *didn't* do was to go have an abortion and then come back and expect everyone to treat you the same."

Despite the wealth in their family, neither Barbara nor her mother evidently had direct access to enough money to procure a safe abortion. Nor did her wealth protect her from the hostility and disapproval of her friends.

Isolation and despair made women do terrible things to themselves in order to end unwanted pregnancies. Paula Miller was twenty-four years old and the mother of two small children when her husband died suddenly of a cerebral hemorrhage. They had just moved from the Midwest to southern California and Paula knew almost no one in the community. A few months after her husband's death, Paula had a brief affair with a man who was passing through her town.

"He was different from me—he had almost no formal education and he was also an ex-con. But he was very sweet and he loved the kids—and he was a good lover. I was terribly lonely at that time."

When she found she was pregnant, Paula was terrified. "I was really desperate not to have this baby. I was alone, a widow—I couldn't take on responsibility for another child. I went to a doctor I'd heard had performed an abortion on another woman, but he refused to give me one—I think he thought I was a spy. Then I pulled another doctor's name out of the phone book because it was a Jewish name and I thought, well, at least this guy isn't going to be a Catholic. He turned out to be this darling doctor, who was in sympathy. He said he couldn't do it himself, but to come to him afterward so that he could be sure that everything was allright.

"Time was getting on and I couldn't find anyone to do it, so I tried to do it myself. I didn't have much information about what to do—this was something you didn't talk about. And anyway, I didn't yet have any close friends out there. I did it in the bathroom, at night after the kids were asleep. I used a knitting needle, and I probed and poked and tried to guide it into the right spot, but nothing seemed to happen that night, so I thought I'd failed. When I woke up the next morning there was blood all over the bed. So then I went to the hospital and this Jewish doctor took care of me, gave me a D & C. You know, I've told almost no one about this because I felt it was such an idiotic thing to have done. After all, I could have died, and I was solely responsible for these two small children."

Even women fortunate enough to find a more or less reliable, clean, and compassionate doctor, did not necessarily have an easy time of it. Diana Sperry was a young actress who had come to New York from Iowa City in 1953. She was living at a residential hotel for women when she got pregnant.

"All while I was growing up I was so sure I'd be a virgin when I got married. But after I'd been in New York for a couple of months I fell in love with this really bad guy. He was an actor, very handsome, very smooth, a real operator. He used to wear tweed jackets and smoke a pipe. By the time I caught on that he was a phony, I was pregnant. I was too scared and ashamed to tell anyone and, of course, I couldn't go home to my parents with this. I had overheard some of the girls at the hotel talking about a girl who'd gone to a good doctor in Philadelphia. So I invented a phone call from a girlfriend—there was a phone in the hall and people could hear you—and then I came bursting into the room where these girls were and told them I'd just had this call from a friend who was hysterical because she was pregnant. That was some acting job! They gave me the information and I don't think they ever knew it was me."

Diana borrowed a car and drove alone to Philadelphia. "This doctor had a regular office in a brownstone. After he interviewed me, he said to come back in a week with $350. I burst into tears. I had the money, but I felt I just couldn't go away and come back. I was afraid everyone would find out and I wouldn't be able to borrow the car again. I don't know, it seemed like the end of the world. Well, he took pity on me and went ahead and did it. He didn't do a D & C, he dilated my cervix and packed it with something. Then I had to drive back to New York. In the car I started to get these terrible cramps, but I was terrified to take the painkillers the doctor had given me because I thought they'd make me sleepy. Oh, I remember gripping the wheel and just screaming with the windows shut. That trip seemed to take about fifty hours. I don't remember what I did with the car, but I do remember how desperate I was to get back inside my room, and staying there for about two days with these cramps until the fetus aborted. I was so scared this mess would turn up in the plumbing somewhere—you know, clog it up and have to be pulled out and everyone would know what I'd done."

Rich or poor, your chances of finding an abortion were unquestionably better in an urban area. Every neighborhood in the cities had its informal abortion networks. Anita Vance, a jazz singer, had her first abortion in Detroit when she was seventeen. Raised by her Scots-Irish grandparents in the grinding poverty of a Pennsylvania coal-mining town, she moved to

Detroit to live with her mother and stepfather when she was fourteen. Her love of jazz was her only escape from an abusive and alcoholic family and drew her to the black community, where she found acceptance. At seventeen, she fell in love with a jazz drummer and became pregnant.

"A friend of mine told me about a black doctor who would do it. So I got the money together—maybe fifty dollars or a hundred dollars and went to his office after office hours. This was in a black neighborhood. He was very nice, but it was painful—and scary. I was scared of getting caught, of bleeding to death. You heard all these stories. I don't remember if anyone went with me—a girlfriend maybe. I just remember lying on that table and this terrible stabbing pain. Afterward, he told me how to take care of myself, and I remember he said to call him if I had any trouble. I was so relieved when it was over. I never had any regrets."

In 1952, Anita, who was singing regularly, though not yet professionally by now, went to New York with D.J., a jazz pianist who was playing with Charlie Parker. She and D.J. were married and in 1953 she had an ectopic pregnancy and found herself in a situation that was very common in those days.

"After my period I suddenly started having very bad cramps, and then it seemed like my period came back. I got scared because I seemed to be bleeding so much, and I went to Roosevelt Hospital. They accused me of trying to abort myself. That made me so mad because I was crazy to have a child at that time. This doctor fixed me up, and said, 'Well, you're OK now but don't try that again.' I came back home and started hemorrhaging again, but I couldn't go back to Roosevelt because I knew they wouldn't believe me, so I thought I'd just wait till it went away. I was singing in a club at the time and the woman who ran the club didn't like the way I looked and she made me go see her gynecologist. He was the one who figured out I was having an ectopic pregnancy, and he sent me to Beth Israel and

I had to have an operation—they took out one of my tubes."

Anita did have a daughter, Lisa, with D.J., who left her when the child was a year old. Anita moved in with another musician and became pregnant again.

"I was using a diaphragm, but I don't know, I guess it didn't work or I forgot it. I knew this guy was a loser. He didn't want the baby, and he wasn't giving me very much money anyway. I was working days as a secretary and singing whenever, wherever I could. I never gave up that day job because I wasn't going to have that poverty again, and I knew I couldn't rely on any man. I couldn't have supported another child—I would have had to go on welfare. And I kept thinking about this little girl I had, what's she gonna do? This time I had an illegal abortion in New York and that was awful. It was this Cuban doctor and I think he'd turned his apartment into an office just for abortions. He gave me some kind of gas or something. I went under and when I came out of it, he said, 'Usually the girls are so grateful they do something for me.' He wanted me to have oral sex with him. I just said, 'Oh, well, I can't do that for you—I'm too sick.' He was okay about it—he was afraid I'd puke all over his thing."

It's estimated that between 150,000 and 200,000 women a year gave up babies for adoption during the fifties and sixties. (After 1973, adoptions leveled off at about 50,000 a year, reflecting the legalization of abortion, as well as a change in public attitudes toward single motherhood.)

Pat Sullivan, an English professor at an upstate New York university, still feels haunted by the daughter she gave up for adoption thirty years ago. An upper-middle-class Cleveland girl with a convent education, Pat got pregnant during her senior year at Radcliffe.

"When I got to Radcliffe, suddenly there were people to talk to, people liked me, I didn't have to be sarcastic and hostile. I even felt pretty. I wore black knee-socks, a black turtleneck sweater, black jumper. I slept with the first boyfriend I had there and I liked it very much. I loved it. I developed an attitude that sex verified a relationship, so what was the point of going out with someone if you weren't sleeping with him?

"The summer before my senior year, I was working in New York. There was this man I'd known at school, somewhat older, a veteran. He was married—it was well-known that he had knocked someone up—and they had a child. He was a captive of the Hemingway myth and he was the center of a certain group of mavericks around Cambridge. He was the first man I'd ever heard use the word 'fuck' in conversation, and since he used this word a lot I was under the illusion that he'd be good at it.

"I became quite infatuated with him. That summer he turned up in New York and took me out to dinner. I was very excited, very turned on. After dinner we went back to his room at the Statler Hotel and went to bed. I remember being so surprised that it wasn't more interesting. He used a condom. There was no question of anything else: I would have had to tell a doctor! It was illegal to give out contraceptives or even information about them in Massachusetts then. And I didn't even know Margaret Sanger existed in New York. How would I know? There wasn't anyone to tell me anything. We never talked about it. Of my group of close friends, I'm pretty sure I was the only one who wasn't a virgin.

"Anyway, at the moment of entry, he pulled off the condom, saying something like, 'I hate these things.' I knew I was pregnant immediately."

As soon as she was sure she was pregnant, Pat flew home to Cleveland, intending to ask an old boyfriend who was now a medical student to give her an abortion. He was horrified and refused.

She then tracked down a housemother she'd had in her freshman year who had told her students to call her if they ever got into trouble. The housemother gave her Dr. Spencer's name, but as ill luck would have it, Pat called during one of the two brief periods when he'd been thrown in jail.

"Then I started remembering all these mysterious things about my friends . . . a friend who had made a mysterious weekend trip to Cuba, for example. I called her. It turned out they were having a revolution and you couldn't go. By now I was back at college. The friend who had gone to Cuba had an older brother who said he could help me. I had to come up with six hundred dollars, which was about the equivalent of a thousand dollars now. I did call the father and asked him for some money and he said, essentially, you're on your own, kid. I never contacted him again. I borrowed the money and went alone to New York, to an address on the east side, the kind of impersonal, modern, white brick building that airline stewardesses lived in. I waited for ages in a kind of waiting room until a short Hispanic man with a pencil moustache came in. I remember he was carrying his instruments in a knitting-needle bag.

"If I'd ever had a real abortion before I would have known immediately that this wasn't one. I felt nothing. But what did I know? He just poked around a little, gave me some pills, took my six hundred dollars and sent me away. I went back to my friend's apartment and waited for something to happen and nothing ever did. I never bled. When I realized that I was still pregnant, I became terrified that all he had done was crippled or blinded the baby."

Pat finally found her way to a kind doctor who, ironically, told her that he would have given her an abortion if she'd come to him sooner. He found her a temporary home with an older lady who needed companionship. He also set in motion the adoption of her baby when she had it. Meanwhile Pat had to tell her parents in order to get their permission to live off campus.

"When I told my mother she was completely silent for about five minutes. Then she went to bed for a few weeks. She never mentioned it again."

Pat continued to attend classes at Radcliffe wearing a loose-fitting raincoat, and took her final exams a few days before she delivered. Nobody noticed that she was in an advanced stage of pregnancy. When she went into labor in the middle of the night, the woman she was living with drove her to the hospital.

"I was scared. I felt I'd been taken over by an alien creature. I knew nothing about childbirth and I didn't want to know anything. I didn't want to be present. I wanted it to be over with and get out of there. It was like going in and being torn limb from limb. Completely terrifying. Afterwards, my three close friends who had been coconspirators, came to the hospital to see me and they went in to see the baby and they said, in awe, 'It's a *baby!*' We'd never thought of it in terms of an actual baby.

"They didn't want you to see your baby, but I certainly wasn't going to go through all that and not see it. I'd never had the slightest interest in babies, but when they handed me that baby, it was like lightning striking me. I thought, Oh. This is what love is. Then the nurse asked me what the baby's name was. I was undone—it had never occurred to me that I would have to name it. I gave it my own name—it was a girl and I couldn't think of anything else. Then she told me I could go home and took the baby away. That was all. I felt bad, very very bad. There's nothing worse than love mixed with shame."

Linda Marino got pregnant when she was nineteen. She was living at home in Teaneck, New Jersey, working at the phone company. The man who got her pregnant was married and refused to help her because he was afraid his wife would find out.

"Back then, it was the Dark Ages, you didn't just have a child and keep it the way you would today. I told my mother— my parents were divorced and she'd just gotten remarried to a man with two young children of his own. She was not unsympathetic, but there was just no way that we could afford to take care of them *and* me, and keep another baby. See, my mother herself had been pregnant with me when she got married—

she'd been very young at the time, too. She didn't want me to relive her life. Teaneck was a pretty small town then, everybody knew everybody, and they looked down their noses at you. I did think about having an abortion, but the only abortions available at that time were back-alley, and I was afraid they'd do something to me that would hurt me and I'd never be able to have children. So the more I thought about it, I decided I just couldn't have an abortion."

Linda's aunt made some inquiries and found out about a home in Paterson, not too far away, but "not a place that the people I knew would frequent. We told everyone I was visiting an aunt in Michigan. This home wasn't in the best section of town—it was a big old barn of a house called the Florence Christian Home. There were about thirteen or fourteen girls there with me, and we were all due around the same time. It was a nondenominational home, but it was Christian, and you had Bible study every morning for an hour or so, with a service on Sunday. I didn't mind that because at that point in my life I felt I needed some kind of guidance.

"We all had little jobs assigned to us, everyone had to work. My first job was cleaning the room that we used for a chapel, but after a while when the girl who was cooking had her baby, they moved me in there because they knew I loved to cook. This was one of the better places because the woman in charge, Mrs. Henderson, was basically compassionate, and she was really the only one you saw. We had some social workers that came in and talked to you, but most of the time it was just her.

"I heard about places where you weren't allowed to get friendly with the other girls, and you couldn't even tell them your last name. We didn't have that, and in the afternoons when we had a little free time, four or five of us would go out together, take a walk for an hour or so. When we walked out of the home, people would look at us strangely—anyone who lived in the area knew what this home was for—and at the stores the people behind the counter would give you looks. You felt like the scum of the earth all the time giving up your baby when the time came.

"There was not too much talk about anybody trying to keep their baby. The home itself made all the adoption arrangements. You didn't have to pay to stay there—they were paid by the adoption agencies.

"The day I was released from the hospital, Mrs. Henderson picked me and the baby up and took us to the Edna B. Conklin Home in Hackensack and took me inside and we turned the baby over. This was unusual. Most birth mothers do not get to see their children. But the day after I delivered, I was weeping in my bed and this young doctor came along and tried to calm me down. He promised that he would do something for me. Later that night he came by and took me to the nursery and sat me in this rocker at the back of the nursery and put my daughter in my arms. He said, 'If you breathe one word of this . . . ' and then he left us alone for about fifteen minutes. I stared at her and talked to her, just poured my heart out to her about how I couldn't keep her but how I would come and find her some day."

Linda stayed at the home for six weeks after she had her baby, until any evidence that she'd had a child disappeared. At the time I interviewed her, she was still searching for her daughter. She told me bitterly, "You know, all these wonderful do-good social workers say, go on with your life, you'll forget. Well, I have news for you, you don't forget. You don't have a baby and then forget. Today I would sooner have an abortion than give a child up for adoption. Not knowing where your child is, whether it's dead or alive, maybe ending up like Lisa Steinberg, that's something no human being should have to go through."

As barbaric as it seems to force a woman to give away her child, it may be even crueler to force her to keep a child that results from rape. Doris Cutter's story is a graphic example of the dilemma of an uneducated girl with no resources, dependent on a domineering and abusive parent.

Doris was born in Tulsa, Oklahoma, the oldest of six children. Her father was a pumper for an oil company—a man with the deadly combination of religious fanaticism and alcoholism. Marriage was going to be Doris's escape route.

"I knew exactly what was going to happen to me after high school. I would get married to a good man and have a nice little home and three or four kids and I would never leave Oklahoma. That was my picture."

In her senior year, Doris started dating Jack and they made plans to get married right after graduation. When Doris's father, who disliked Jack, found out about their marriage plans, he forbade her to see him, setting in motion a fierce battle of wills between father and daughter.

"I went down and tried to join the air force because I thought that would get me out of the house and we could take it from there. I wanted to let my parents know how serious I was about getting away from home—that if they wouldn't let me marry Jack, I was going to do this. I took all the tests and did very well in them. They sent a recruiting officer out to talk to my father and get his signature. I didn't tell my daddy he was coming—you didn't do anything until the last minute because his temper was so bad.

"Now my father had all these ideas about women in the services, that they were whores. That they joined the service so that they could be around the men. My daddy threw this man out of the house. He said, and I quote, 'No daughter of mine is ever going to join the service and become a whore.'"

Jack had joined the navy meanwhile, and gone to California for basic training. Doris's mother, trying to get her away from both her father and Jack, used her savings to enroll Doris in an airline school in Kansas City, but the school turned out to be a scam, and its promises of stewardess jobs fraudulent.

When Doris came home to Tulsa, she was just eighteen, and went to work as a cocktail waitress.

"My father didn't like it at all, but I was eighteen and he couldn't stop me. I guess I did it—went to work there, I mean—to drive him crazy, but I also did it because the money was a lot better than working in the dime store, which was where I'd worked all through high school. And it was more fun. It gave me a chance to be around people my own age.

"I had this friend that I worked with that my daddy didn't like—she was, I guess if I'm honest, she was a tramp, but she was a very nice person and I didn't feel that what she did was anybody's business. She had a car and every time she'd come to pick me up my daddy would yell that I was going out with that slut again, you're going to be just like her. Stuff like that.

"One night after I got back, I went out with my girlfriend to this nightclub where there was dancing, and there was a guy there that I knew, the brother of a girl I worked with. He was married, I knew that, and was living apart from his wife. And he knew I was engaged. We were dancing and, you know, flirting, and having a good time. Well, my girlfriend had to leave because she had to get up early the next morning, and this guy said, 'Don't worry, I'll drive you home.'

"So he's driving me home, but instead of turning where we're supposed to turn, he starts going down this dirt road on the edge of town. I said, 'Where are we going?' and he said, 'Oh, I just want to talk a little.' I guess I was naive, but I really believed him. All evening he'd been real polite and nice, a real gentleman. So we pull over where it was pretty desolate and immediately this man turns into a total stranger, like an animal, he's all over me tearing at my clothes and everything. I remember I was wearing this cute little outfit, it was pedal pushers with a side zipper with little plaid cuffs that matched the top. He kept saying, 'You've teased me long enough,' but I didn't even know what he was talking about. I couldn't believe he was really going to do anything to me, but when he broke the zipper on my pants I got really scared and I started crying and saying, 'Don't do this to me, I'm a virgin.'

"When he saw I was going to fight him, he pulled a gun out and said, 'If you don't do it I'll shoot you.' He'd had a lot to drink and I was afraid he'd do it. But I was also thinking maybe he'd had so much to drink he wouldn't be able to do anything to me. No such luck. After he did it to me, he said, 'You're no fun, I don't know why I wasted my time.' He dropped me off at my girlfriend's house.

"Next day I was black-and-blue with bruises, my face, my arms, I couldn't go back home like that, so I called my parents and told them I was going to stay at my friend's house for a few days. My friend wanted me to tell someone that I'd been raped. But this man had told me that if I told anyone he'd kill me or someone in my family. But I really don't think that was why I didn't tell anyone. I just couldn't tell anyone. I was ashamed. For sure I couldn't tell my daddy—he'd either beat me because I was a slut or he'd go out and find this guy and kill him. Which wouldn't have been such a bad thing, but it scared me, I was scared my father would go to prison."

When Doris missed her next period, she decided to go back to Kansas City.

"It was a place I knew from being in airline school there and it was a big city. I was already afraid I might be pregnant and my instinct told me to get where nobody knew me. I went to get a job at AT&T and they gave me a physical and that involved a blood test. I got the job, but I was terrified that I was pregnant. About a hundred times a day I would run to the bathroom to look and see if I got my period yet. About two weeks into the job they called me in and told me they had to let me go because I had lied about being pregnant. I don't think they could fire me for *being* pregnant, but they said, if I lied about that I might lie about other things and so I wouldn't be a reliable employee.

"I just didn't have any idea what to do. I kept thinking, how could God do this to me? I was such a good girl with Jack, I would never do it because I wanted to be a virgin when I got married.

"As far as I knew, there was no such thing as abortion. I never heard of anyone who ever had one. Oh, well, you heard about these butchers who would put knitting needles up inside you. You know, even Tulsa was a small town compared to New York or Chicago. I did try doing things to get rid of this baby. I tried falling down the stairs, and drinking castor oil, douches, everything I'd ever heard anyone talk about. I tried eating and drinking things that would make you sick because I had an idea that if you got sick enough, just the throwing up and all would make you get rid of the baby. I was very ignorant about where this baby was and how it would come out. I even thought about sticking something up me, but I was just too scared to do it. Nothing I tried worked."

Out of money and with no job prospects, Doris heard of a home that took in women and children who came to Kansas City with no place to stay.

"You either paid a little money if you could, or you earned your keep by sweeping the floors or making beds or baby-sitting. So I went there, and one day I was reading the paper and I came across this ad for a couple that wanted to adopt a baby and they'd pay the hospital bill, so that seemed to be the answer to my prayers."

Doris met the couple and they arranged for her prenatal care. However, against her better judgment, Doris had called her mother to confide in her about her pregnancy. Her mother told her father, who called her, enraged.

"See, I don't think my mother believed me when I said I'd been raped, and I'm *sure* my daddy didn't believe it. He said, 'If you don't bring this baby home, you can forget about ever coming inside this house again.' Now that may sound nice to you—like he was saying, any child of yours belongs to our family. But that wasn't what he meant at all. He meant that this baby was my punishment and I had to take it and be saddled with it, and if I didn't, he never wanted to see me again. I had every intention of giving up this baby. I thought, for the rest of my life every time I look at this child—especially when he becomes a man—I'm going to see the man who did this to me. I knew that wasn't a good way to feel about your child. But as much as I wanted to get away from my daddy, I was scared of him, too. And when he said I could never come home again, I figured he meant it. That scared me. I just felt like I had to keep that baby and go home with my daddy and that's what I did."

Doris's father and brother came to Kansas City and brought her and her baby home.

"We told the neighbors that I'd gone to California to marry Jack and it was better for me to come home with the baby because he was at sea so much. I had such mixed up feelings about that baby. It wasn't that I hated him and couldn't go near him—it was like he was a toy—remember, I was just nineteen at the time. I was ambivalent, I guess you would say."

Doris's troubles were by no means over. A year later she left home for good and moved to Wichita, where she fell in love with a man who abandoned her when she became pregnant. Unable to care for this second child, which, ironically, she had wanted, Doris reluctantly gave him up for adoption. Now, thirty years later, she is trying to find and make contact with this son.

In some communities, the shame of unwed motherhood was so great that a pregnant daughter was literally hidden away. Kitty Delson grew up in Newark, New Jersey, the eldest of six children of Irish immigrants.

"We were very poor, and both my parents were alcoholics. My mother especially was a scary, violent woman. My father was working at the shipyard and he used to bring these English sailors home with him and there'd be a lot of drinking. My sister and I were just young girls—she was sixteen, I was seventeen. I already had ideas about myself as an actress and these sailors were beneath me. But my sister went out with one of them and got pregnant. My mother was enraged, but there could be no abortion, of course, so Colleen was hidden away in the back room like an animal. The rest of us weren't supposed to talk to her. She had the baby there. She wrote to the guy and he sent for her and she went to England after the baby was born.

"I kept thinking of my sister in that back room and us bringing her plates of food and whispering to her as if she was a prisoner. The shame of it was terrible, I can hardly describe it. That was what happened when you got pregnant and it gave me a terror and a determination that it would never, never happen to me."

As the fifties flowed into the sixties, the separation of sexuality from reproduction, a process that had been under way since the beginning of the century, became complete with the introduction of the birth control pill. As women themselves developed a sense of their own bodily integrity and independence, they began to insist on the right to control their own reproductive lives. Inevitably, this led to the demand for liberalized abortion laws, and an organized political movement to achieve that demand. The Supreme Court's 1973 decision in *Roe* v. *Wade* declared most laws against abortion unconstitutional, and essentially granted women the right to first- and second-trimester abortions. The decision gave women of the seventies what the women of the fifties were deprived of: rational, humane choices about their own pregnancies.

The overwhelming feeling you get from listening to these stories is the sense of women being trapped—trapped by their bodies, trapped by their pregnancies, with no alternatives, nowhere to turn. It's hard to believe that, twenty years after *Roe v. Wade*, women are being forced back into that trap. Young women's access to abortion has been sharply curtailed by parental consent laws. Rural women and poor women who live far from urban centers are once again effectively deprived of safe, timely, affordable abortions. And adoption is again being promoted as a desirable solution to unwanted pregnancies.

Chapter III

Post-Doc or Paella?

At Sarah Lawrence for the first time I learned to think for myself. Those were the most wonderful years I can remember. The classes were like seminars with only eight or so people, and you did a lot of independent study. I took writing, literature, poetry, psychology and art. For the first time, I was actually using my mind.
—PAM DILLON, 60, TALKING ABOUT HER FRESHMAN YEAR AT SARAH LAWRENCE IN 1951

When I tried to talk to my father about what kind of work I might do after college, he said, "You know, Charlotte, I've been giving a lot of thought to that, and it seems to me that the world really needs good, competent secretaries. Your English degree will help you." He said this with perfect seriousness. I was an A student at Bryn Mawr, for God's sake!
—CHARLOTTE PALMER, 58

In 1955, the graduating class of Smith College heard an eloquent commencement address by the great liberal intellectual Adlai E. Stevenson. He exhorted them to eschew "tribal conformity," and added that in order to defeat totalitarian ideas the country needed "more idiosyncratic, unpredictable character . . .

people who take open eyes and open minds out with them into the society which they will share and help transform." In case any of his young listeners thought they themselves might play an active role in the battle against conformism and mediocrity, Stevenson benignly set them straight; most of *them*, he explained, were destined for "the humble role of housewife" whether they liked it or not, and that "when the time comes, you'll love it."

"The assignment for you," he went on, "as wives and mothers, has great advantages. It is homework, you can do it in the living room with a baby in your lap, or in the kitchen with a can-opener in your hands. If you're really clever, maybe you can even practice your saving arts on that unsuspecting husband while he's watching television."

Stevenson's address perfectly captures the ambiguities surrounding women's education in the fifties. Early in the decade, American educators had begun to notice a glaring incongruity between the kind of college education American women were getting, and the lives they would lead after graduation. What Pam Dillon experienced at Sarah Lawrence was the classic ideal of a college education: opening of the mind, exposure to new, challenging ideas, the development of the ego and identity necessary to function in the world. But of what use was all this to someone who would then spend most of her time tending small children, cleaning her house, and entertaining her husband's boss?

Claire Lassiter, who felt cursed by her height, was also gifted with a brilliant, probing mind. She won a scholarship to Smith College, where she experienced an intellectual awakening similar to that described above by Pam Dillon. She says of herself at the time:

"I had no sense of reality at all as far as squaring the idea of this wonderful education I was getting with the notion that I would marry and have children. I only looked at the present, never did any long-range planning about my life at all. If someone had asked me what I was going to do after college . . . well, I might have said, vaguely, that I wanted to do something for 'the world.'

"I was interested in the World Court, the League of Nations, and had an idea I'd like to work in that sort of endeavor, moving nations closer to each other. At the same time, I had a general sense that I would get married. About the closest I ever came to having a fantasy about combining my interests with marriage was, wouldn't it be wonderful to marry a college professor. It never crossed my mind that I could *be* that college professor. But the way to have access to that atmosphere of ideas and intellectual stimulation would be to marry an academic. All these half-baked ideas were milling around in my head."

Claire's confusion was symptomatic of the malaise that infected the entire field of women's education in the fifties. Some educators, noting the irrelevance of the classic, "masculinized" liberal arts education to the demands of homemaking and maternity, called for a new, "distinctively feminine" curriculum. In his influential 1950 book, *Educating Our Daughters*, Lynn White, Jr., president of Mills College, proposed a new curriculum that would better prepare women to "foster the intellectual and emotional life of her family and community." White called for college courses in clothing and textiles, house-planning and interior decoration as well as "the theory and preparation of a Basque paella, a well-marinated shish-kebab [and] lamb kidneys sauteed in sherry."

Many colleges and universities did institute courses on marriage and family life. In *The Feminine Mystique*, Betty Friedan asserts that "education for femininity" spread "to the proudest bastions of the women's Ivy League, the colleges which pioneered higher education for women and were noted for their uncompromising intellectual standards." Friedan gives the impression that the so-called Seven Sisters colleges capitulated to the "functionalists" by altering their curricula. But in fact, only Barnard College appears to have added a cluster of courses to its curriculum that were clearly aimed at defusing their critics. These included a course on personal finance and family budget-making, and another on "Interpersonal Relationships in Family and Marriage."

But though the elite women's institutions generally resisted the pressure to water down their curricula, they were clearly placed on the defensive. In 1950, a triumvirate of respected women educators—Millicent McIntosh of Barnard, Sarah Gibson Blanding of Vassar, and Mildred Horton of Wellesley—felt impelled to certify in the *New York Times* their belief that a woman's first responsibility was to her children. Throughout the fifties, the male president of Radcliffe, W. K. Jordan, routinely greeted incoming freshman by telling them "that their education would prepare them to be splendid wives and mothers, and their reward might be to marry Harvard men."

However, professors who might have been urging their students on to higher academic achievement found themselves frustrated and discouraged by young women's lack of interest. A noted Vassar professor lamented to Betty Friedan that his students "just won't let themselves get interested. They feel it will get in their way when they marry." The women who were the subjects of this debate were dropping out of college to marry in alarming numbers, or marrying the day after graduation, or not bothering to go to college at all. Although the actual number of women going to college had shown a steady increase over the decades, that figure was deceptive. In fact, the *percentage* of women among college students declined, from 47 percent in 1920 to 35 percent in 1958. In the 1920s and 1930s, women who went to college tended to stay there until their educations were complete. A 1959 study showed that 37 percent of college women were dropping out before graduation. The percentage of women receiving doctorates had dropped even more precipitously from one in six in 1920 to one in ten—a mere 900—in 1956.

In this atmosphere of low expectations all around, many bright women who might have gone on to graduate school weren't encouraged or pushed by their professors. Despite her obvious interest in going on with her education, some time during her senior year, Claire Lassiter's focus of attention shifted to marriage. She still isn't sure how that happened.

"I did once mention graduate school to my mother but she said I shouldn't ask my father to pay for anything else. In fact, it's possible that the idea of marriage took hold because graduate school was not a possibility. It's also possible I intuited that what my mother really wanted was for me to get married, and *not* to go to grad school, though it was never verbalized."

There's no question that Claire could have gotten financial aid had she decided to go to graduate school, but the possibility of a scholarship was never mentioned by her advisers at Smith.

A few institutions did try to encourage their students to pursue graduate degrees, but there was still the problem of finding a desirable graduate program that would accept women. Wellesley graduate Helen Schumann recalls that "once you declared that you were going on for further education, Wellesley zeroed in on you and gave you a lot of extra attention. I guess they were so pleased to find someone who wanted to do something else beside getting married right after graduation. The trick was to find someplace that would accept you as a woman."

After the war, soldiers on the GI bill flooded back into the colleges and universities, straining the resources of the institutions. Many schools cut back sharply on female admissions. Cornell University, for example, where women had been in the majority during wartime, cut female admissions to 20 percent in 1946. Many medical and engineering schools, which had begun admitting women for the first time during the war, now turned away female applicants in favor of veterans.

Often the only route into graduate school was to enter a program especially tailored for women. Helen Schumann, who wanted a graduate degree in psychology, found she had to enroll in something called a "terminal master's program" at Purdue. "Most of the graduate schools went straight through to the doctorate. But at a few of them you could get a master's and then go back later for the doctorate—those were the terminal master's, and those were the ones that accepted women. They figured you were just going to get married and waste their money."

Many of these special programs for women were inferior, truncated versions of the standard degree programs, as Sally Ann Carter found out when she entered one of them at Harvard. Sally Ann was the kind of girl everyone envied in high school—blonde, blue-eyed, vivacious—the kind of girl who had a date every Saturday night. Because she was also smart, everyone in her small Texas town figured she'd go to college, but everyone, including Sally Ann, also expected her to get married either during or right after college.

Much to her surprise, she got turned on to economics at Smith. "There were only about seven women out of our class of 450 who majored in economics. Incidentally, now it's the largest major at Smith. But I had a wonderful teacher, a woman in her sixties, who made the theoretical aspects of it fascinating instead of dry."

Sally Ann graduated summa cum laude in 1956. By then she'd fallen in love with a man at Dartmouth, and wanted to stay in the East to be near him. At the same time, she wasn't yet ready to get married, so she enrolled in the Harvard-Radcliffe program in business administration for women.

"In those days, though Harvard Law and Medical were both

integrated, the Harvard Business School was the last holdout. We used the same textbooks, had the same professors and most of the same courses, but our classes were held on the other side of the river at Radcliffe. It was a twelve- instead of a sixteen-month program, and we got a certificate instead of an M.B.A. The sense of being shunted off to the side, treated like a second-class citizen pervaded the course. We had four- to six-week internships in which we went out to major companies to work and the jobs were always clerical." Disgusted with the program, Sally Ann switched to education. "I *thought* I'd found out that I didn't like the business world. I did like studying and learning, so teaching seemed the thing to do."

Sally Ann's interest in business was deflected by an inferior graduate program and a job market which offered few opportunities for women. Her decision to go into education, an acceptable "woman's" profession, was practical. But it was also based on her expectation that she would be married.

Sally Ann did in fact marry shortly thereafter, but not for long (for more on her marriage, see chapter 4). She never had children and soon returned to her early interest in business. She's now a prominent realtor in Dallas, where the business she has labored to build is solid enough to ride out a depressed real estate market. Swinging away from the big mahogany desk in her high-rise office, she shakes her head in amazement as she looks back:

"I now realize that in the back of my mind there was always the assumption, even when I was getting my graduate degree in education, that any work I did was temporary, something to do until I assumed my principal role in life which was to be the perfect wife and mother, supported by my husband. As it turned out, I never had children, and I've supported myself for thirty years. If I'd known I was going to have to do that I would have made some very different decisions. I would have approached work with more seriousness and purpose."

The educational establishment vacillated between blaming women for their lack of purpose and admitting that institutions were failing their women students. A report published in 1955 by the Commission on the Education of Women bogged down in contradictions. On the one hand, the Commission stated that "little has been done to [help women] to develop their capabilities, make their contributions, and achieve satisfaction in whatever they choose to undertake." But the report also cautioned that "any proposals for broader participation of women in gainful occupations outside the home must not detract from the importance of their roles as wives and mothers." Further on, the Commission observes—without seeming to notice the contradiction—that while "Almost without exception, women consider marriage, homemaking and child rearing as major goals and responsibilities . . . they are also motivated, as are men in our culture, to use all of their abilities and energies." In the next breath the report asks, reprovingly, "Do women hinder their own development and advancement through a lack of clear purpose?"

Many of the women I talked to also blamed themselves for their "vagueness" and their failure to plan for the long term. But even a woman who was motivated to continue her education after marriage encountered a discouraging array of obstacles. If she followed her husband to a new university, she found that her academic credits were not transferable. Course schedules were inflexible and inconvenient for women with children. Most graduate schools didn't accept part-time students. While blaming women for abandoning their educations, the institutions were unwilling to make the allowances necessary to help them continue.

Bridget Moran says she's had a passion for mathematics ever since she can remember. A squarish woman with a blunt, humorous face, Bridget grew up in Texas, the daughter of an engineer and a schoolteacher. Bridget graduated from high school in 1947 and went to the University of Texas where she majored in mathematics. After a year, she dropped out to get married. "Sex tripped us up," she says. "There was no way in that time and where I lived that you could have sex without fear of being pregnant. In essence, I got married in order to have a sex life. I thought that was why everyone got married."

Bridget tried to continue her education at Texas A & M, where her husband, Tom, was on the GI bill. "A & M was a boys' school at that time and the only courses available to me were the ones they gave vet wives. The way it worked, if you could get ten of these wives together for a class, a professor would teach you anything. But you had to have ten women. I couldn't take math because I couldn't find ten other vet wives to take it with me. So I took horticulture and a basic history course."

After three months, Bridget decided her marriage was a mistake and returned home to live with her parents.

"There had never been a divorce in our family and I didn't know anyone who was doing anything like this. I wanted some kind of counseling, but the closest place for that kind of thing was Galveston and that was far away and I didn't have a car. So Tom and I got back together again. I kind of felt, what the hell, I had no choice."

Bridget gave up the idea of pursuing math and tried to settle into a domestic routine. "I never worked, there was no question of that. Tom supported us both. He was convinced that if I could take care of myself financially, I would leave. I took care of the house, did fancy knitting and strange cooking—you know, puff pastry—I canned, made pickles, lots of bread. I was living my life vicariously through what he was doing." Bridget enrolled in some education courses in a local junior college, but found them uninteresting. Meanwhile, she was trying very hard to get pregnant, and finally had a baby in 1954.

When her daughter was four, Bridget and Tom moved to

Huntsville so that Tom could get his master's at Sam Houston College. At last, Bridget was able to take courses in advanced math and calculus.

"Now this was the first time I'd gone back to school and done mathematics in a serious way and I really loved it. My husband was very happy about my doing this, too—he was proud of me. Then I got pregnant. I was trying to. In fact, I'd been back to the doctor when my firstborn was four months old, with this tiny baby in my arms, and asked him, 'Can I get pregnant immediately?' But in fact it took me four years to get pregnant again."

When her second child was a year and a half, Bridget returned to school, trading daytime babysitting with a fellow student's wife so that they could go to basketball and football games at night.

"I had a marvelous time because I was taking a junior level math course from probably one of the best math teachers in the world. This man taught without a textbook. You did everything in your head. It was the most exciting thing I've ever done. I used to think it must be like composing music. I'd think about it all the time, proving theorems in my head while I was changing diapers and washing dishes. No one else I knew was doing anything like this, none of the women. But the male students all knew how exciting it was to be in this man's classes. This professor stopped my spouse in the hallway one day and said, 'Mr. Moran, I think your wife may be better at mathematics than you are.' Tom couldn't wait to come home and tell me that. I don't know what he ever thought I was going to *do* with it . . . "

In her second year, Bridget began falling asleep in her eleven o'clock class. "That's always how I knew I was pregnant. I didn't want that baby—I was using a diaphragm. But I never thought of abortion. So I dropped out again and had the third one. I didn't go back to school again until 1975."

When her marriage ended in 1974, Bridget, now a single

mother of three, went back to school to acquire a marketable skill. She became a computer programmer and now works as a consultant doing sophisticated data analysis for various companies.

Anne Carpenter's story is a good example of the way women's own ambivalence about what they wanted interacted with the expectations and restrictions of the educational institutions they dealt with. Anne came from a background that might have been expected to foster accomplishment. The eldest of two daughters born to comfortably middle-class parents on Chicago's North Shore, Anne and her sister spent a great deal of time hiking, fishing, and mountain-climbing with their father.

"I suspect that he gave us a lot of things that might have gone to a son. We didn't ever do little girl things and we weren't very feminine. Daddy was a stickler for academics. He sneaked us out of public school in the eighth grade and sent us to a private girls' school, and then we were to go on to college. And this wasn't a question of eking out a couple of years of college before marriage. We were expected to get through.

"My mother, on the other hand, was extremely anxious that I get married and, of course, I also expected to. But I didn't have any clear idea how marriage would fit in with this idea of higher education. What I was supposed to do with this high-powered education, I didn't really think about. My mother's concerns were that I marry a nice young man of the proper sort, meaning of the proper ethnic background, of the proper kind of family, the proper social standing. So I had very conflicting values and, though I like to think that my father's values were predominant, in fact, my mother's values had a profound influence on me."

Anne went to Mount Holyoke where she managed to please both parents by doing well academically and alternating between two boyfriends, one at Yale and one at MIT. "Most of my friends planned to get married right after college, but everyone was motivated to finish. Holyoke was the kind of college you finished. And in fact, most of my class married immediately after graduation."

Anne had spent her junior year in the Netherlands as part of the Experiment in International Living. When she returned, she applied for a Fulbright in her major, zoology. "I was going to study fruit flies at the University of Utrecht—genetics, basically. And I got the Fulbright. I think they were looking for people in all kinds of disciplines and I'm sure no one else had applied to go to study *persophela melanagaster* at the Genetics Institute of the University of Utrecht. You can imagine my father was thrilled.

"I had a wonderful time in Europe. I traveled a lot and I did some research, but it was fairly desultory. I was much more interested in the social relationships I was having and the traveling. And in truth, the purpose of the Fulbright was not just for you to do a serious piece of research; it was to foster good international relations."

Anne had applied to and been accepted by Harvard Graduate School in biology, but she had turned it down because the scholarship they offered was too small. While in Europe, she had applied and been accepted again. "So I came back from Europe—with a certain reluctance—and went off to Cambridge to start at Harvard. Within two weeks I knew I didn't want to do this anymore. I didn't know *what* I wanted to do. It was so rigorous, academically—I just didn't have my heart in it. Academic achievement never came easily to me and I didn't want to spend all my time studying. I was living in an apartment with some friends, women who were working and dating. It seemed like these women around me were having a lot of fun. I just wasn't in the right frame of mind then.

"So I dropped out. Harvard was extremely upset with me. They called me in and asked me to see the school psychiatrist. It was pretty hard to get in to Harvard if you were a woman—they just couldn't believe I'd turned them down *twice*.

"You know, I think if everyone around me had been going to grad school, I probably wouldn't have dropped out. And I do think this concept of getting married and having a respectable boyfriend that my mother would approve of was another problem for me. After all I was twenty-four now and almost everyone was either engaged or married by then."

Anne got a job she hated—cutting up rats at the Harvard School of Public Health for minimum wage—and was married within a few months. She became pregnant almost immediately and she and her husband moved to a Boston suburb where he'd been offered an academic job.

"It was an interesting community because many of the people worked at Harvard or MIT—the men, that is. The women were all having babies. But it was a highly intellectual group of people. The women were all smart, had gone to college. We were all liberal democrats, discussed politics and the state of the world. But after a few years I began to think . . . well, am I going to do this for the rest of my life? By this time I knew I wasn't a 'born mother.' We had a play group in which we all took turns taking the children so that we could take turns getting out. It worked very well—except that I dreaded when my day came to have all the children. By now I knew I probably should have stayed in grad school. I was worried that every month I delayed going back to school my science degree was getting more and more out of date."

Anne first attempted to go back to school when her son was three years old. Thinking that teaching could be meshed with her children's schedules, she enrolled in some education courses at Boston University. She found them tedious and poorly taught, and when she became pregnant with her second child, Anne dropped out.

Finally in 1960, before her daughter was a year old, Anne became part of an educational experiment at Harvard called Plan M. "The 'M' stood for mother. This was the brainchild of a female grad student in education at Harvard whose thesis was that mothers could go back to school on a part-time basis, get a degree, become teachers, and do just as well at Harvard as the full-time students who didn't have any children. In fact, she thought they might even do better—that was also part of her thesis. Harvard had refused to let anyone into their program on a part-time basis; she got them to open up the program to twelve women a year for a couple of years.

"The minute I heard about this program I went roaring in there. I had quite a job to convince them that, in spite of having dropped out of Harvard twice they should let me into this program. I was accepted.

"It was supposed to be a one-year program but it took me two winters and one summer to finish. It was a wonderful program. The courses were marvelous. I rediscovered studying, loved the academic life. I worked like a dog. I even took some more biology courses. My husband objected to all this very, very strenuously on the grounds that mothers do not go back to school when their children are less than a year old. But I had to do it then because it was available and I didn't know how long it would last. I graduated from the program with honors."

Although she doesn't mention it, Anne was undoubtedly aware that even with an advanced degree in biology, her chances of finding a good job in the field were virtually nonexistent. Teaching was one of the few professions deemed acceptable for women, and its flexible schedule made it desirable for mothers of small children. For Anne, as for so many women, teaching became an attractive option by default. In her 1959 study, *A Century of Higher Education for Women*, Mabel Newcomer reported that "While teaching is high on the list of occupations when seniors are asked what they plan to do after graduation, it is low on the list when freshmen are asked the same question. The seniors are facing reality."

For black women in the fifties the realities of the job market were even more inescapable. While white women were dropping out or staying out of college, black women, driven by economic necessity, were flocking to college in droves. In addition, more and more black women were going on for higher degrees. In fact, by the midfifties, more black women than black men had earned master's degrees, even though black men held more Ph.D.'s. When educator Jeanne L. Noble surveyed black college women in 1955 about why they went to college, fully 90 percent of them answered: to prepare themselves for work. By contrast, an AAUW report of white college women found that only four out of ten of them went to college to prepare themselves for an occupation.

But there were also cultural differences between black and white women's attitudes toward marriage. Though these may also have been related to economics, they served to insulate black women from the pressures to marry early.

Joyce Purvis is a fifty-nine-year-old black middle-school principal in the Newark, New Jersey, school system. We talk in her office at the end of a long school day. Joyce was born in East St. Louis, Illinois, a small town across the Mississippi from St. Louis, Missouri. Her father was a laborer, her mother a factory seamstress.

"My generation, my cousins and I, was the first to go to college. For a black girl coming along in those days, the primary thing was education. My grandma used to say, 'You can *always* get married.' First of all, there were not that many men who had much to offer in the way of support. The outlook in terms of employment for men was not good. Also, culturally, it was not that important that girls get married early. It was more important to us that you rise about your present level, educationally and economically."

Joyce went to the segregated schools in East St. Louis, and got a state scholarship to Southern Illinois University in Carbondale, intending to major in business.

"Blacks were only about 8 or 9 percent of the student body at SIU, and we lived off campus in private homes, because blacks were barred from the dorms. This changed by the time I was a senior, incidentally, but only for the boys. They had black athletes on the track and basketball teams so they had to open the dorms to them. Anyway, I worked hard and I thought I was pretty well-prepared but the work was difficult, and instead of the A's and B's I was used to getting, I was getting C's at SIU.

"So I studied even harder, but studying hard didn't seem to do it. As I went along, I began to see a pattern, that it was happening in certain departments, with certain professors. There were some areas where it clearly didn't make any difference how much I studied or how hard I worked, I wasn't going to get above a C.

"I had this friend, Johnny, a black guy who had come from a more privileged background than I had; we entered the freshman class at the same time and we were the only two blacks to declare business majors. In those days, you had to declare your major in your freshman year. We took the same courses so we studied together and I was doing what a lot of girls did in those days: two sets of homework—mine and his. That was typical of college boys in those days, get your homework done or at least typed by any girl you could. The thing is, he was getting A's and B's and I was getting C's and D's.

"At the end of freshman year, we were allowed to start taking our business-related courses and we had typing, shorthand, and introduction to business. I got a C in typing, he received an A; I got a D in intro to business and he received a B. The head of the department called me in—she was also the instructor—and she pointed out to me that if I got an F that I would be on probation. Then she suggested that I change my major. When I asked her why, she said, 'What would you do with a degree in business, anyway? There are no jobs.' She also said, 'You do not need a college degree to be a secretary.'

"It took me years to put the pieces of that together: she was saying, there is no place in business for blacks and as a black woman the best you can hope for is to be a secretary. I was only seventeen at the time. It didn't occur to me to say, '*You're* not a secretary!' I went out of there just like a little whipped kitten. I found out later that this was the reason there weren't many blacks in the business department—they knew she didn't want blacks in her department."

I asked Joyce why she didn't at that point switch to a black school as many women did who had her experience.

"For one thing, the money wasn't there. The black schools were expensive and scholarships were not available except to agricultural and technical colleges in the South, but I was not interested in those schools, and I was definitely not interested in going any further South. So I changed my major to education. I chose education because it was easy for me, I'd always been a kind of natural teacher, teaching kids stuff in my backyard as a kid. I knew I wouldn't be unhappy in teaching. I wouldn't have to reach, make sacrifices. And, of course, many of my mother's friends were teachers so I had a lot of models of women going into education.

"By my junior year I had learned the ropes and I knew to avoid professors who didn't grade fairly, and to take the courses of professors who did. Of course, we had been raised to believe that this would happen, and to expect and anticipate it. Most of your energies went into protecting yourself instead of fighting the system. Especially since the numbers of black people there were so small.

"You know, we didn't have words for things then, like racist or sexist. We accepted things. There was nobody to say to me: this is unacceptable, she can't do this, go back in there, protest, go to the dean. I took it into myself and felt inadequate and it took many years to repair that damage. The main thing that healed it was experience, seeing that hey, I can do this, I'm *doing* it!

Joyce graduated from SIU in 1953 and went on for her master's at the University of Illinois at Champaign/Urbana. "Suddenly I was getting straight A's. It was a much bigger school, with a larger black population, and that made a big difference in how I felt about myself as a student. You felt more comfortable and more in control of what happened to you. You knew that if you studied hard, you had a good chance of getting A's. In fact, the school was big enough that a lot of the professors didn't even know your name, much less if you were black. They really didn't care. There were enough black students so that you could even have friendships that were based on things other than race."

Joyce admits she was not entirely immune to social pressures to marry, but points out a significant difference.

"I do think I married because everyone else was getting married. All my friends were doing it, or so it seemed. I was the last single woman in my group. But I was out of school and working when I got married. The progression was, you went to college, you got a good job, you got married. The thing you *didn't* do was quit college or quit work. You were not going to raise a family on one black man's salary. And you were not going to easily find a black man who was in premed or pre-law."

Joyce Purvis was deflected from her goal of becoming a businesswoman by an overt act of combined sexism and racism. But many other women were more subtly diverted from unsuitable ambitions to more acceptable paths. Jane Hunter became interested in architecture when her parents hired a woman architect, Lilian Rice, to build their house. Rice encouraged Jane to pursue a degree in architecture, and even promised her a job when she graduated.

"On the first day of classes, the dean of architecture called us all into the auditorium. There were three women in a class of at least a hundred. He said, 'I see we have three women here. We're not going to have them much longer.' Well, that made me furious. It made me even more determined to go on. Then, in my junior year I got a terrible respiratory infection, and I went to the university health service. The doctor there said I was working too hard. I did feel I had to drive myself, to work harder than any of the men because of what that dean said. I had all these projects I was doing at night—in architecture you often have projects that you have to stay up all night to do—and I was exhausted.

"He told me I had to cut back on my hours at school. This doctor was an older man and I guess he was being protective. He did scare me. My best friend was also suffering from exhaustion at the time and her doctor also made her cut back. So I transferred out of architecture into fine art. I lost some credits and changed my major to interior design. Only one of the three women in our class actually graduated."

Jane married a naval officer shortly after graduation and began raising a family immediately. She and her husband now live in Arizona where they run an antique business. She says she never wanted to work, that she was satisfied being a housewife and mother, channeling her artistic talents into decorating her home. But when I ask her if there is anything she wishes she'd done differently, she says, "I sometimes wonder if that doctor would have given the same advice to a man. I've often been sorry that I didn't just defy him, and *demand* of my body that I get well and do it."

A fatherly doctor who advises you not to work so hard when you're exhausted, ill, and probably feeling discouraged is hard to resist. Perhaps because she herself was daunted by the work ahead, and in the absence of any kind of institutional support, Jane interpreted the doctor's advice as a caution to retreat altogether.

There was only one college in the country that never retreated an inch from its rigorous standards for women, and that was Bryn Mawr. Dedicated to producing scholars and proud of it, Bryn Mawr offered an intellectually formidable program that included Greek and Latin, and required a premed caliber chemistry course for graduation. M. Carey Thomas, Bryn Mawr's president from 1885 to 1922, was widely quoted as having said, "Only our failures marry." In fact, what she said was, "Our failures *only* marry." Either way, she was expressing an attitude toward women's education that remained uniquely uncompromising throughout the fifties. It was inevitable that Bryn Mawr students often found themselves in conflict between the expectations of their college and the realities they knew awaited them after they graduated.

Charlotte Palmer, who graduated magna cum laude from Bryn Mawr in 1956, was a southern girl whose mother desperately wanted her to go to Sweet Briar. Tall and thin, with a long face that strikingly resembles Virginia Woolf's, Charlotte tells her story in a twanging Virginia accent, punctuated with gusts of self-deprecatory laughter.

"Mother's line was always, 'Put that book down and go out and play or you'll end up like your aunt Annie Lee.' What Mother had against Annie Lee was that she refused to make her debut and stayed in her room all the time reading poetry. This made her a drip in Mother's book. To make matters worse, she went to Bryn Mawr and ended up marrying her Latin professor. As far as Mother as concerned, this was a disaster. You got educated so you could attract the right kind of man."

Charlotte came from an old southern family, which had been reduced to shabby gentility by the Depression. She would have liked to have gone to Radcliffe, but a relative had endowed a one-thousand-dollar scholarship at Bryn Mawr with the stipulation that Charlotte have it if she qualified for Bryn Mawr and wanted to go there. Since the entire tuition was only fifteen hundred dollars, Bryn Mawr was the obvious choice.

"Mother was afraid I was going to Bryn Mawr because I had to. She thought it was an awfully dreary place—all those foreign students, you know. She never could understand why I didn't want to go to Sweet Briar, which she thought was heaven. But I saw it as a place where I could never be as successful socially as my sister, who was a real belle. I thought I was a drip, and most of the evidence pointed that way. Actually, I was probably as good-looking as my sister, but I wasn't as extroverted and lively. She had social ease. Poise. I did not. I knew I had to go someplace where what I *did* have was valued. I think I intuited that Bryn Mawr was a place where you didn't have to have a date on Saturday night—which would have been social suicide at Sweet Briar."

Charlotte remembers the combination of exacting standards and support she got at Bryn Mawr:

"They had a chemistry course that you had to take and this wasn't just some pro forma thing that satisfied a science requirement. You had to take chemistry with the *medical* students. This was an absolutely rigorous course; people were crashing all over the place. It was a horror! I got just mired in it and had a mini-breakdown over chemistry at one point. I was taking long walks in the fog and people were saying, Charlotte, are you alright? So I took myself to the infirmary and told them I just wanted to rest a little because I was having such a hellish time with chemistry. The head nurse said, fine, you just stay here as long as you want. I stayed a few days and then went back to my chemistry and did pretty well.

"Another time I was writing an important paper on Virginia Woolf, something about the sea being the symbol of the subconscious. I'd finally gotten a beau over Christmas vacation. This paper was due on a Monday and I had just enough time to finish and type the thing over the weekend and get it in on time, but it was going to be tight. I'm sitting there deep in it on Friday night and suddenly there is Paul, who has driven all the way from Ithaca as a surprise. About the worst thing that could possibly have happened. There was no way to finish the paper, no way to get rid of him, and, of course, I *wanted* to spend the time with him. You couldn't have boys in your rooms at that time. Well, the dean of freshmen took pity on us and allowed me and a couple of other girls who were in similar straits and their dates to have her house all day on Sunday. So we played with the boys on Saturday and on Sunday we all repaired over there and finished our papers while the guys typed them for us. It was all very collegial."

Although Charlotte loved the challenge and the intellectual stimulation she found at Bryn Mawr, she remembers how uneasy she and her fellow students felt about how their high-powered education would fit into their futures.

"We had a keen awareness of ourselves as scholars at Bryn Mawr. We knew what lay ahead, and we thought this was a blissful luxury that we were permitted now. Everything in the place, the very walls were redolent of this idea of being the very best you can be, strive, don't settle for less than perfection. But we had this tugging, nagging feeling that we were gonna let 'em down. I guess we recognized that it was unlikely that we could go full throttle after college. As much as we admired these brilliant spinster professors, we didn't want to be like them. We knew we were gonna try and marry the smartest person we could find . . . in fact, one of our great fears was, would you be able to find anybody that would let you be yourself and that would keep you interested. We felt like we were betraying the college in a way, that we couldn't live up to what was expected of us. It was perfectly fine with Bryn Mawr if you got married, you see, but you weren't meant to quit, you were meant to push on with your studies."

After graduation, Charlotte, who had by then decided she wanted to be a writer, went to England on a Fulbright. "I knew I was a writer for sure when I found I was a thousand times more excited about winning the *Mademoiselle* fiction contest, which paid five hundred dollars, than the Fulbright, which gave you three thousand dollars." When the Fulbright Committee refused to extend her grant for another year to allow her to write a novel, Charlotte came home.

"I applied to the writing programs at Stanford and the University of Washington. Stanford cost money but it sounded like a wonderful program and you didn't have to teach. Washington accepted me but they wanted me to teach three freshman English courses and I couldn't bear the idea. I had also been offered a teaching job for a year at a girls' school. Looking back, I should have taken that job and socked away the four thousand dollars and then gone and been a full-time writer in one of these programs. Or I could have gotten a scholarship. Or borrowed the money. But this is the kind of thinking we didn't do. It was a kind of failure of nerve or imagination not to just take the chance."

Faced with conflicting imperatives, to earn a living and to write, what Charlotte did was get married—to "the most interesting man around," who made six thousand dollars a year and "didn't mind if I wrote a novel. Bill was about as supportive of women as a man in his generation could be until we had children. Then it got to be, 'What, you're going to pursue *your* career at the expense of *my children?'* But that's another story." She laughs.

The decline of women's education in the fifties took its toll. By the end of the decade, five women's colleges had closed down, twenty-one had become coed, two had been downgraded to junior colleges. But the real tragedy lay in the waste of human talent and resources. Bridget Moran, for example, had a gift for mathematics that, in a man, would have been nurtured and supported by parents, teachers, institutions, and, no doubt, a devoted wife. Instead, Bridget's dogged struggle was conducted alone, in a climate indifferent to her abilities and ambitions. Bridget Moran's example is extreme, but many less spectacularly talented women were also deprived of the chance to explore and fulfill their potential.

At the heart of the problem was an old idea: that education in women is antithetical to their roles as wives and mothers. People concerned with the education of women have always had to battle this argument. The founders of the first women's colleges defied their critics and, insisting that education for women and men be equal, designed curricula that emulated Harvard and Yale. For a few decades the critics were silenced, but in the 1920s a backlash occurred with renewed demands for an altered curriculum that would prepare women for domestic life. Feminists protested, but Vassar responded by creating a "School of Euthenics" to educate women "along the lines of their chief interests and responsibilities, motherhood and the home." Even the University of Chicago experimented with a graduate program in home economics.

But lurking under the attacks on equal education for women was a real fear: that education awakens desires and ambitions that make women dissatisfied with the narrow domestic sphere. For college women of the fifties, the conflict was particularly intense because they felt the pull to domestic life so strongly. Many curbed their interest and refused to become "serious" about their college work. As one Vassar student told Betty Friedan, explaining why she had dropped out of a history course that excited her, "Suddenly I was afraid of what would happen. I wanted to lead a rich, full life. I wanted to marry, have children, have a nice house. Suddenly I felt, what am I beating my brains out for?"

Chapter IV

Mrs. Someone

All these years you have been growing up as yourself.
You may have pondered long and dreamily about
yourself as that strange new entity, Mrs. Someone.
Now that the time has come to be Mrs. Someone,
you have a concrete, down-to-earth social responsibility on your hands. You are now a full partner in a
shared enterprise, a 50% stockholder in the new firm
of Mr. and Mrs. You and your husband are a new
social unit in the social fabric of your time.

—*THE BRIDE'S REFERENCE BOOK:*
A GUIDE FOR YOUNG MARRIEDS, PUBLISHED IN 1956
BY *BRIDE'S MAGAZINE*

I felt lucky because I'd found someone I wanted to
marry! A lot of people I knew were marrying people
just to get married.

—CHERYL WOLFE, 65

I just wanted to get married and start my life.

—CATHY LEE SHIPLEY, 60

In the April 1956 issue of *Life* magazine, there's an ad for
"The Bride's House," a model home designed and manufac-
tured by U.S. Steel. In the living room, before a huge picture
window masked by opaque drapes, the young wife is entertain-

ing her in-laws; the older people are formally dressed (she still has her hat on!), and awkwardly posed on furniture that's just a shade too low for them. The young husband is in his shirt-sleeves; his bride wears a dress, heels, and hose. The headline trumpets: "Now! See how U.S. Steel's BRIDE'S HOUSE can give you new freedom to live as you please." Below, the copy carols, "What a wonderful way to live! Privacy! Space! Comfort!"

The ad is bristling with messages about what the institution of marriage meant to young people in the fifties. The ad says your home is above all your private domain, the place where your parents can only visit—and then not even long enough to take off their hats and get comfortable. Here, hidden from your neighbors by the double drapes on your picture window, you are free to do whatever you please—which includes, of course, having all the sex you want. Here, you're surrounded by your own *things* at last—your furniture, your luxurious wall-to-wall carpeting, your appliances. The newlyweds radiate pride of possession; the in-laws beam with satisfied approval.

The institution of marriage had a power and inevitability in the fifties that it has never had since. You simply didn't ask yourself *if* you wanted marriage and children; the only relevant questions were when and how many? And the answers were, as soon as possible and as many as possible. "I got a little secretarial job after college, but I thought of it as a prelude," recalls Bonnie Carr. "Education, work, whatever you did before marriage, was only a prelude to your real life, which was marriage."

In the years following World War II, Americans married in record numbers. In 1940, 31 percent of the population was single; by 1950, that number had dropped to 23 percent, and by 1960, to 21 percent They also married younger than ever: During the 1950s, the median marriage age dropped from 24.3 to 22.6 for men, and from 21.5 to 20.4 for women. (By contrast, the median marriage ages for men and women in 1990 were, respectively, 26.1 and 23.9.) But even these statistics don't quite do justice to the strength of the trend. By 1959, a staggering 47 percent of all brides were married before the age of nineteen. Another 1959 study revealed that two out of three women who entered college dropped out—usually to get married.

Once married, Americans began their families almost immediately. Women who came of age in the fifties had an average of 3.2 children, and most couples had completed their families by their late twenties. And contrary to popular belief, educated women were in the forefront of the trend. The notion that, in the words of a 1946 *Newsweek* article, "For the American girl books and babies don't mix," persisted in spite of clear evidence that the steepest increase in the birthrate occurred among highly educated women.

What accounts for this headlong rush into domesticity? To some extent, especially at the beginning of the decade, it was the natural result of the war's long period of deprivation. Young people, weary of loneliness and shortages, were eager to get back to normal and begin participating in the new postwar prosperity. But this was more than young sex- and love-starved Americans scrambling into marriage. It was an all-out embrace of domesticity that over the course of the decade elevated family life into a kind of national obsession. Even the Beat poet Gregory Corso pondered, "Should I get married? Should I be good?" and allowed himself to fantasize a wife "aproned young and lovely, wanting my baby."

Historian Elaine Tyler May sees this phenomenon, not as "the last gasp of traditional family life with roots deep in the past," but as a new project which arose out of postwar America's "intense need to feel liberated from the past and secure in the future." For many young women, the past meant a family fragmented by the Depression, and a coming-of-age shadowed by the war. The future seemed, at one and the same time, full of promise and hedged about by Cold War fears of the atom bomb, an aggressive Russia, and the insidious peril of creeping Communism. What better bulwark against these dangers and uncertainties than the warm, enveloping security of the family? A 1959 *Life* magazine cover story showed a newlywed couple spending their honeymoon in their own bomb shelter, surrounded by canned goods, water supplies, and generators: a perfect metaphor for marriage as a self-contained world— secure, private, surrounded by consumer goods.

But marriage in the fifties was not simply a retreat into safety and privacy. More than in any other decade, the family in the fifties was seen as a vehicle that would, in Elaine Tyler May's words, "fulfill virtually all its members' personal needs through an energized and expressive personal life." Although this was true for men as well as women, men were assumed to have a life outside the family, an identity in the world of work. Women were expected to seek—and find—*everything* in marriage and family: love, identity, excitement, challenge, and fulfillment.

"Marriage was going to be the beginning of my real life," says Joy Wilner, echoing Bonnie Carr. "It was all I thought about in college. I was so focused on finding this mate I wouldn't allow myself to get carried away by any of my subjects. My feeling was, life was not concerned with work, but with men and dating. When Ted came along, I made him into the right person. He was going to be a doctor, someone who would help the world, and I would help him. He was an idealist and we were going to build a life together—*his* life, essentially, only that wasn't how I saw it at the time. In fact, as it turned out, we had no common interests except our mutual interest in his career."

The postwar efforts of government, media, and the social scientists to move women out of the labor force and back to the home have been well documented. Returning GIs needed the jobs, the nation needed stability, and the economy needed consumers: young families to buy the homes, cars, and appliances that would fuel the economy. The battle-weary veterans returning home to rebuild their lives were thought to be in need of both shoring up and calming down. In order for them to adapt to "normal life," the theory went, their masculinity must be domesticated and, at the same time, their battered egos bolstered and repaired. Everyone agreed this could best be accomplished within the clear-cut sex roles of the traditional family. The trouble was that while the men were away at war, women had been experiencing the relative freedom that comes with economic independence, better job and educational opportunities, and the self-reliance that comes from coping alone. Many social scientists feared women might be unwilling to give up this newfound autonomy to devote themselves to family life. There was also a great deal of concern about the potential for uncontrolled sexuality. Jittery public health officials predicted that "sexual chaos" would be one of the results of an atom bomb attack, and developed elaborate scenarios to prevent epidemics of venereal disease. A strong family unit based on clearly defined sex roles seemed to be the solution.

At the same time, an ideology was developing among social scientists that, as it sifted out into the popular media, would provide the underpinnings for the domestic revival. In essence, this body of theory said that not only could women find perfect fulfillment within the family, but those who looked outside the family for satisfaction were unwomanly.

Much of this thinking was based on the theories of psychoanalyst Marynia Farnham and her husband, Ferdinand Lundberg. In their influential book, *Modern Woman: The Lost Sex*, Lundberg and Farnham indicted the woman who "[seeks] a sense of personal value by objective exploit (e.g., a career in the world)," and predicted for such a woman a host of ills, from "orgastic failure" to the loss of her "emotional qualities." Even more dire, she will inevitably "seriously damage [her husband's] sexual capacity," ultimately bringing about "psychic catastrophe."

Although the great majority of American women probably never heard of Lundberg and Farnham, the couple's ideas found their way into most mass market magazines. The centerpiece of *Life* magazine's 1956 issue on "The American Woman" was an article by five male psychiatrists on "Changing Roles in Modern Marriage." Blaming feminism for the "fatal error" of demanding equal rights, these gentlemen harshly denounced the "emerging American woman [who] tends to be assertive and exploitative." Granting magnanimously that women "have fully equipped minds," the authors suggest they "use them in every feasible way, from potting geraniums to writing books or making political speeches—even, when the children are of school age, to having a part-time job—so long as their primary focus of interest and activity is the home."

Seventeen magazine started educating its readers about their roles even earlier. In an article titled "How to Be a Woman," the magazine warns darkly that "being a woman is your career and you can't escape it." The magazine goes on to explain to its young readers that "there is no office, lab, or stage that offers so many creative avenues or executive opportunities as that everyday place, the home. . . . What profession offers the daily joy of turning out a delicious dinner, of converting a few yards of fabric, a pot of paint, and imagination into a new room? Of seeing a tired and unsure man at the end of a working day become a rested lord of his manor?"

It's not necessary to posit a conspiracy in all this to understand how the ideology of the times and the realities of the job market reinforced each other to curb women's ambitions and energies and narrow their options. That said, to view fifties women merely as pieces of flotsam tossed about by cultural forces is to do them a disservice. You can only see them this way from a distance. The closer I got to individual women, the more respect I came to have for the kind of maneuvering they did to get what they thought would make them happy.

For Vicky Carroll, marriage appeared to offer the solution to all her problems. A lively redhead who exudes sexual energy, Vicky now lives with her second husband on a small ranch in Arizona. I arrived early for our interview, in time to watch her chair a contentious community meeting with impressive skill and tact. It was hard to reconcile this competent, energetic woman with the vague, helpless creature she says she was in 1953. The overprotected child of alcoholic parents, Vicky's first taste of life's possibilities came when she went away to college. "I'd never been so stimulated," she remembers.

"I loved the kinds of people I met there, the dorm life, which I'd never had before. I was flying high. We'd sit in the smoker and talk intensely about life and philosophy and everything. Coming home on holidays I felt as if a long arm was dragging me back where I didn't want to be." But her grades were average and after two years her father summoned her home to Philadelphia, saying, "Hell, if you're going to pull straight C's, you can come home and go to the University of Pennsylvania and save us a lot of money."

While Vicky's mother was obsessively anxious to see her "marry well," Vicky herself was interested in journalism, which had been her father's major. But the journalism department at Penn was poor. "My future was a blank. It had never occurred to me that I could take care of myself—either I stayed with my dad or I got married. At one point I had toyed with the idea of going to Europe or to New York, but it was out of the question."

She'd started dating Dan while she was at Goucher, and their relationship was getting sexually intense. Vicky was eager for sex and terrified of getting pregnant. "I think my parents could have accepted it better if I'd picked up a gun and shot someone dead. Dan was a very nice, gentle, clean person. He didn't get drunk, make scenes in restaurants, fall down, get belligerent." With the Korean War threatening, Dan joined the navy and married Vicky in the same week. "I left Penn and became a navy wife . . . whither thou goest . . . and this navy life seemed glamorous and exciting and a way to get out from under my father's dominion." Given her options, it's easy to see why Vicky seized the one she did. Marriage would provide escape, sex, and an opportunity for some excitement, perhaps even travel. More important, marriage to Dan also gave focus to her life. "Now I knew what my job was: to be Dan's wife."

The importance of sex as a motive for marriage can hardly be overestimated. Premarital sexual experimentation was out of the question for most young women. The potential consequences—from pregnancy to loss of reputation—were simply too devastating to risk.

Under the circumstances, it's not surprising that the desire for sex drove many young women into premature and ill-considered marriages. "We were at the mercy of our hormones," says Vicky Carroll. Like many engaged couples, she and Dan did "everything but" before marriage. "We were playing the kind of brinkmanship game everyone was playing. It was sort of mutual masturbation, but we never actually slept together."

A woman with an appetite for knowledge and accomplishment as well as sexual experience was almost sure to find herself in severe conflict. Sally Ann Carter, the Texas homecoming queen with the steel-trap mind, started thinking seriously about marriage after she became disillusioned with her Harvard-Radcliffe program in business administration. When she saw that the program was a dead end, Sally Ann made a classic change of direction, to education.

Looking back, Sally Ann is not surprised that it happened that way. "I was so young. If business school had been challenging and exciting, if the program had given me a sense of getting a hold on the world . . . who knows? But you see, I wasn't thinking about a future with work in it. Teaching was a short-term job, something I could do until I was married and maybe during the early years of a marriage, while I waited to have children."

Sally had fallen in love with a Dartmouth man with whom she'd been spending weekends filled with sexual tension. "We weren't sleeping together because I thought it would be wrong; I wanted to be a virgin when I got married. I remember he came down for this November weekend and said he thought it would be best if we didn't see each other for a while. Those were his exact words. I interpreted that to mean that he didn't want to see me anymore, ever. It later turned out that he wasn't breaking up with me at all, that he'd meant exactly what he said. He'd been so afraid that if we kept going the way we were I'd get pregnant, so he thought we ought to stay clear of each other until we were ready to get married. This was a complete communications breakdown. He had no idea I would go off and marry someone else. But, of course, that's exactly what I did."

Sally Ann began dating another man almost immediately, and was married within three months. "I didn't feel I was in love. I thought, everybody else is doing this and I need to get my life on some sort of course. Of my ten close friends who graduated from college with me, three had gotten married immediately upon graduation, one had married before graduation, and, with maybe one exception, all the others were in the process—engaged or whatever. My parents begged me to wait a year. But I felt fairly driven. After all, I was a twenty-one-year-old virgin and my hormones were driving me as well. He was bright and capable and I thought we had a lot in common.

"I should have known better, and as a matter of fact, my body did know better. I started having these convulsions of vomiting every month. I'd end up dehydrated and in the hospital on an I.V. This went on for seven or eight months." On the eve of exploratory surgery, Sally Ann's surgeon told her he was convinced her illness was psychosomatic. "After that conversa-

tion with him, about stress and how it could affect the body, I
went away and never had the symptoms again." Sally Ann's
marriage lasted two years.

Given that so many women felt propelled into marriage by
sexual desire, I was struck by how many of the women I talked
to rejected men they were powerfully attracted to in favor of
men they felt they could "rely on." They seemed to feel that
sexual passion was untrustworthy, and that a man who could
inspire it was probably not good husband material. They chose
"appropriate" men—solid, nice, often older guys with good
futures ahead of them, who were acceptable to their parents:
men who would be able to support them and their children.
This was the mature choice, and maturity was at a premium in
the fifties. In her book about the fifties, *Private Lives*, Benita
Eisler describes herself at sixteen as "a creditable knockoff of a
forty-year-old."

Gwen Barnes, the bookstore owner who struggled so might-
ily with her boyfriend, Charlie, laughs often and heartily as she
remembers herself during the fifties. "I came from a truly functional family, the kind you see in the movies. We did the dishes
together and then we'd go into the living room and my mother
would play the piano and we'd all stand around and sing.

"My future was going to be like my mother's. I wouldn't
have to earn a living. I would be married, with children, and
taken care of by my husband. But my father wanted me to go to
college, since no one in the family had ever gone. My sister,
who should have gone—the one who was two years older than
me—got pregnant and had to get married right after high
school. So when she blew it, I was the one—all their hopes for
education were on me."

Gwen went to a Presbyterian college in Maryville, Tennessee, where she lasted only one semester.

"I wasn't doing well in college; I'd never picked up the
knack of studying. I seemed to be running and never catching

up. I kept thinking that if I could just get married all these problems would be over. Everything seemed as if it would be *easier* if I was married. During the Christmas holidays I started dating this guy I'd known since I was eleven. Buddy was three and a half years older, and he was a really nice, nice guy. I had dated him a couple of times before, but it was like going out with your brother. He had kissed me once and I hated it. I was never attracted to him. But that Christmas, something was different, and I can't tell you what the difference was. I think by then I was tired of trying to find someone. I still wasn't attracted to him, but I wanted to be settled."

During that same holiday, she and Buddy went to a party where she ran into her old boyfriend, Charlie. "When he shook my hand, this tingle went right through me, from my hand all the way down, and I thought, wonder why that doesn't happen with Buddy . . . ?" She roars with laughter. "Boy, Charlie could really make me tingle . . ." Though for a while Gwen felt torn between Buddy and Charlie, Buddy carried the day. "I was really into who would be the father of my children. I wanted a certain kind of person and Buddy fit the bill perfectly. He seemed solid, he had a job. He was my answer."

"Answer" was a word women used again and again to describe a particular man, or marriage in general. The implied question, of course, was what am I going to do with my life? A woman who looked to the job market for an answer was confronted with few appealing options. Even with an undergraduate degree in social work, for example, she could look forward to long hours, low pay, and little hope of advancement in a field considered "suitable" for women.

Betty Miller's story graphically illustrates the kind of dead end many women faced in the fifties. Betty is a soft-spoken, sweet-faced woman of sixty-two who has spent her married life in a small town in southern Indiana. I interviewed her in the vestry of the local Methodist church where she was volunteering that day. Betty was born near Terre Haute and went to the University of Illinois where she majored in social work.

"I don't know how I arrived at my major exactly. I don't remember making the decision. I may have been influenced by my mother who was a do-gooder. I guess it was an acceptable area for a woman to go into."

After graduation, Betty got a job in the welfare department in Fort Wayne. "I was living with one of my college roommates in her parents' home and I wasn't happy in that situation. I didn't feel as if I really belonged. I'd always been asthmatic, and it got very bad at that time. As I look back on it now, I think my asthma was related to being on my own for the first time. I'd never had to support myself or take care of myself before. All of a sudden I had a car and car payments to make and this small salary, living with these people I wasn't very happy with. And I felt homesick—I really didn't like Fort Wayne."

When an opening came up in the welfare department in her home town of Terre Haute, Betty jumped at the chance. "I started out at $150 a month and by the time I left, two years later, I was only up to $200. The men were making about $300. In those days most of the women who worked at the welfare department were married and they were just underpaid."

Betty was also beginning to feel "uneasy" about not being married. "At this point most of my friends were married. My sister was married to a very successful man and was making a beautiful home, so that looked pretty appealing. She was always trying to fix me up with people to get me married off." When she ran into Carl, a man she'd dated years before, at a party, "I did something I'd never done in my life. I ditched my date and came home with him." Betty and Carl started dating, but after a year, the relationship didn't seem to be going anywhere. When a girlfriend suggested she and Betty go to Ohio State to get their master's degrees, Betty thought, why not?

"When I told Carl about my plan, that seemed to be the

shove he needed and he said, 'Well, I think we need to get married.' I guess he was afraid if I went to Ohio he was going to lose me." Betty pauses reflectively, then laughs. "I'm not at all sure I didn't say that to him to see if I could get him to commit himself. Tell you the truth, I really wasn't wild about the idea of going back to school. For one thing, to get a master's in social work at that time took two full years and lots of field work and I felt like I had worked in the field enough. And I knew that a master's degree wasn't going to improve my salary at my present job because they didn't care what kind of degree you had or even if you had a degree. So I was saved, as it were, by the bell. I was relieved."

Betty's way of getting Carl to propose was clearly manipulative. But her situation had all the elements that made women in the fifties feel marriage was their best, if not their only option: an ill-paid, futureless job, the knowledge that more education would be fruitless, and a gnawing sense of being outside the mainstream because she was single. And, of course, she *wanted* a husband and family. When she met Carl, she seemed to recognize instinctively that he offered her the best and, she feared, her last chance, for marriage.

Lucille Baker was also "saved" by marriage, but her alternative was very different. Lucille is black, sixty-one, and about to retire from a demanding job as community affairs director of a civil rights organization in a large midwestern city. We talk in her office where we're continually interrupted by a buzzing intercom, testifying to her indispensability to this organization.

"My mother was not married when I was born, she was a sixteen-year-old unwed mother who had never finished high school. My mother's mother ran a boarding house, so that accounted for the economics of the situation." When she was twelve, Lucille and her family moved from their small town to the city where, for the first time, she attended an all-black school. "I had always been a good student and my teachers made me feel very comfortable, so I did well in high school. The bunch of girls I hung out with, we were all smart, and it was just understood that you would work hard and do well. I always knew I would have to support myself, that I would have to make something of myself."

Lucille finished high school in three years, at seventeen. "I was hoping to go to this small college in Ohio, because that was where all my friends were going, but I didn't have the money. I remember it was only five hundred dollars that I needed because I had saved about four hundred dollars myself. I went to my mother, and she just flatly refused. She really had the money to pay all the tuition. I think there was always a resentment of me. She always accused me of thinking that I knew everything. My stepfather might have given me the money, but he was in the army at the time. My mother's father had some money—he lived in a little town in Missouri and I asked him and he refused also.

"It was such a disappointment. I had registered and was all ready to go. As I grew up I attributed this to ignorance, just not understanding. I think it would have been different if I'd been a boy. See, my mother always thought I was going to get pregnant like she did. That was always between us. Had she sent me the year I got out of high school, I probably wouldn't have married. She just was not interested in education at all. My education.

"I'd done very well in photography in high school and I'd had a teacher that I could go and talk to. He suggested that, since I couldn't go to college, I should go ahead to photography school in New York, because this would be cheaper. Thoughts of New York just terrified me, but I was going to do it, even though I didn't know any photographers, certainly no women photographers."

That summer Lucille worked as an elevator starter at a big hotel downtown, saving her money for the trip to New York.

"It was right at the end of the war, very busy and exciting. That summer I met my husband, who was the editor of a magazine, kind of similar to *Ebony*, and this really impressed me. He ran around with all the interesting people in town. He was ten years older than I was and he'd just come out of the army. I kept telling him that I was leaving for New York in September, I had my bags packed. He kind of fathered me and told me things. He didn't like the idea of me going to New York at all—don't forget, I was only seventeen—but he was supportive. Well, I didn't go. I married him on my eighteenth birthday. Anything to get away from my mother. Going to New York would have been getting away, too, of course. But I was frightened of it."

She had good reason to be fearful. As a seventeen-year-old black woman, Lucille would certainly not have had an easy time of it in New York. Even if she'd been accepted at a good photography school, the problems of finding a suitable place to live would have been nearly insurmountable. She had no family in New York and it's unlikely that residential hotels for women would have been open to blacks.

"Here was this nice man who seemed to be going places and was going to have an interesting life. The people he associated with were older than me and they were doing things. They kind of babied me. And he told me I could always go back to school and do what I wanted to. So I married him and I'm still married to him. Forty-three years later."

Lucille did not, in fact, ever graduate from college, although she thinks she's probably amassed enough credits over the years to do so. She and her husband have recently finished putting the last of their six children through college and, as she puts it, "I'm no longer interested in getting a degree; I'm interested in sitting down." She thinks a moment, then adds, "I think I would wait to get married if I had it to do over again. Still, I've been very happy. But I would not encourage my own daughter to marry at an early age—or my sons."

Both Lucille Baker and Vicky Carroll married men they thought could provide glamour and excitement: an interesting life. Neither was in a position to go off by herself and have her own adventures, through travel, for example—Lucille because she couldn't afford it, Vicky because her parents wouldn't allow it. Unlike their male counterparts, young women were not encouraged to spend the time between college and a first job exploring the world. They were more likely to go from the controlled environment of home or school directly into the confines of marriage. But even women who had the courage and resources to explore the world a little often found that travel didn't necessarily translate into freedom and expanded horizons.

Tyler Barrett, the woman whose six-foot frame made her feel unmarketable, was one of the fortunate ones who had the opportunity. Her family ran a lumber business in northern Minnesota which, after a slump during the Depression, prospered in the late forties and early fifties. "I was too tall to date, even though at home I was the 'baby sister' of two brothers who were *really* tall," she recalls wryly. Tyler tried to content herself with having lots of male friends, to whom she served as a confidante about their romances. She poured her considerable energies into being a straight A student and campus leader throughout high school and college: student body president, head of the debating team, valedictorian. She had wanted to go to an eastern women's college, but eventually opted for Northwestern University. "I was afraid I'd feel like a fish out of water on the East Coast." At Northwestern, she majored in speech.

"One of my professors tried to encourage me to go into the field of speech and hearing therapy, but I wasn't interested. If I'd been thinking at all about planning a real future, a future of work, I think I would have gone to law school because semantics, language, communication, that's what I'm good at and what I love. But no one ever suggested anything like that. It never occurred to me that as an adult I might be expected to be a professional, a woman of work. My father and I were very close and used to argue and debate continually—he'd call me 'the senator.' But we both knew politics was out of the question for me. He also suggested I take typing and shorthand in my senior year, so that I could support myself until I got married. There were no models around me of women who worked, except a few friends of my parents who were . . . shudder! . . . *divorced!*"

Armed with her typing and shorthand, Tyler got a secretarial job at the Institute of Design in Chicago after graduation. "I was a terrible secretary but I liked Chicago and wanted to stay there for a while." After a few months, Tyler lost her job because of her poor typing and decided to go to Europe with her parents. When her parents went home, Tyler stayed on for what she thought would be three months, but stretched out to two years. She attended the University of Lausanne for a while, then batted around Europe for a few months, and ended up in Paris working for the Marshall Plan and the U.S. Bureau of Labor Statistics. "I had a wonderful boss who realized that I was a crappy secretary but that I was reasonably bright. He set me to work doing some kind of urban anthropological studies, which was really fun."

In Europe, Tyler suddenly found herself popular with men. For the first time, men were appreciating her intelligence, and telling her she had the figure of a Greek goddess. She had a series of romances and received several offers of marriage from "interesting but highly unsuitable men."

"It's a miracle I didn't get pregnant during that period, because I used no birth control. Mother had told me: douche after intercourse. Great advice. I was very lucky."

All the while she'd been in Europe, Tyler had been receiving a stream of letters from her father urging her to come home. "He kept warning me about the Korean conflict which was building up at that time. But, of course, there was no hysteria in Paris about this war, and I was loving being there, even though I was often lonely. Plus now I knew I could earn my own living."

By 1952, with the Korean War in full swing, Tyler gave in to her father's pressure and to her own homesickness. "I'd had my two years in Europe and I wanted to be home. Home seemed a place of succor, of nurture at that moment." She'd been offered a chance to transfer to a good job with the Labor Department in Washington. Tyler came home, but never took the Washington job.

"There were too many women there, I thought. I had a horror of being part of an army of brittle career girls—that was a thirties and forties stereotype. I never recognized that I probably could have had a good career in Washington. I was twenty-four years old, unmarried, and not knowing what I wanted to do. My mother had been married when she was twenty-four. This just seemed like the next thing to do."

Back in Minnesota, Tyler went to work in her father's business, where she met Frank, her husband-to-be. The fact that he was working for the family business gave him the stamp of approval.

"Although I was a partner in the business, there was no place for me because I wasn't an engineer or a CPA. Marrying Frank kept me in with my brothers and gave me a home. In retrospect I see that I had an immense need for stability and roots. Frank was good-looking, he coached the church basketball team, I thought my brothers liked him. I kind of had to rope him into taking me out, whether it was because I was the owner's daughter, or because he was just kind of a loner, an isolate. He was a lot of laughs, a good date, and we just moved into marriage. I don't think I really thought I loved Frank—I'm not sure I even asked myself the question. And on the honeymoon I realized with bitterness and tears that this was a dumb thing to have done, that I had far more energy than this man."

Tyler's energy, intelligence, and appetite for experience could have taken her in a very different direction. Her return to

Minnesota was in some sense a retreat. But Tyler's emotional need to be accepted by her father and brothers intersected with cultural expectations about women's roles. It's intriguing to speculate about how her story would have been different if her father and brothers had encouraged her to be a "woman of work," as she puts it. As it was, even travel, work, and sexual validation weren't enough to counterbalance her fear of independence.

Tyler and Frank were married for seventeen years and raised two children. In 1970, Tyler and Frank were divorced. "It was time to move out. The marriage had become a dead horse we were carrying around. I was reading about women's liberation and there were things I wanted to do," she says simply. After the divorce, Tyler went back to school for her advanced degrees. She now teaches anthropology and English at a Minnesota college, and makes regular field trips to New Guinea.

The relationship of these women to the culture of their decade was not simple. Their choices came out of a complex interlacing of their individual emotional needs with societal pressures and restrictions. They all stopped short of pushing themselves into unknown territory. Joy Wilner curbed her own interest in college work for fear of being distracted from her search for a husband. Sally Ann Carter turned her back on her love for economics and married a man she had serious doubts about. Tyler Barrett retreated from a challenging job and opted for a safe marriage.

But the alternative was dismal. The image of single women as incomplete and deficient human beings was everywhere in the culture. The jaunty, self-possessed career gals of the films of the thirties and forties had given way in the fifties to unflattering portraits of single women as pitiable and slightly ridiculous. "If there's anything worse than a woman livin' alone, it's a woman sayin' she likes it," snaps Thelma Ritter to a prissily repressed Doris Day in *Pillow Talk*. And that was a benign characterization compared to the brittle, predatory, and unstable spinsters that appeared in movies like *The Blackboard Jungle* (Margaret Hayes) and *Picnic* (Rosalind Russell).

Most of the women I interviewed for this book would probably have married in any case. A few of them, in a different era, might have chosen not to marry. But in the 1950s there was nothing around to indicate that a single life could be anything other than lonely, empty, and joyless.

Chapter V

The Motherhood Drift

> As soon as I was visibly and clearly pregnant, I felt, for the first time in my adolescent and adult life, not-guilty. The atmosphere of approval in which I was bathed—even by strangers on the street, it seemed—was like an aura I carried with me, in which doubts, fears, misgivings, met with absolute denial. *This is what women have always done.*
>
> —ADRIENNE RICH, *OF WOMAN BORN*

There has never been a better description of how it felt to be a mother in the 1950s. Nothing you could do elicited such universal and unstinting approval. Motherhood has always been a socially sanctioned condition, but not since the late 1800s had motherhood been so glorified and enshrined. The "baby boom," which began as a national response to the end of hard times, a gesture of confidence in the future, turned into a decade-long celebration of maternity.

The soaring birthrate reflected the fact that women were marrying and having their first children younger than at any time since the beginning of the nineteenth century. And in spite of the dire warnings of the experts that college-educated women were "failing to keep up with the baby boom," it was precisely urban, college-educated women who were having three, four, and even five children. Citing what it called "the social prestige of motherhood," *Life* magazine celebrated "the reappearance of the old-fashioned three- to five-child family in an astonishing quarter, the upper- and upper-middle-class suburbs."

All this took place at a time when women had better access to improved contraceptive measures. By the end of the forties, the idea of birth control for married couples had achieved public acceptance, and the improved methods available—condoms and diaphragms—were more effective than the douching and rhythm methods of the past.

Given all this, I was surprised by how many of the women I interviewed seemed to "drift" into motherhood, rather than *deciding* to get pregnant. Women who were quite definite and clear about other aspects of their lives, other choices they'd made, talked about their pregnancies—especially their first ones—with a sort of vague helplessness. Dorothy Glenn's explanation was typical: "I was kind of shocked to be pregnant. I wasn't exactly ready. Although I had a diaphragm, I hadn't tried very hard *not* to get pregnant. But there was no reason not to have a baby . . ." And Marge Fraley is still bemused by the way she and her husband "backed into" their first child. "I remember how long it took us to decide what car we wanted to buy, in I think it was 1956. It was between an Oldsmobile and a Ford, and we spent hours discussing them, weighing how much we could afford, how long it would take us to pay it off. But having a baby didn't ever feel like a decision. We never talked much about it—we just sort of stopped using birth control."

In fact, motherhood couldn't really be described as a "choice" in the fifties. For one thing, the ideology that equated womanhood and motherhood was powerful and ubiquitous. Its architects, Ferdinand Lundberg and Marynia Farnham, in their widely popular book, *Modern Woman: The Lost Sex*, actually defined femininity as "receptiveness and passiveness, a willingness to accept dependence without fear or resentment, with a deep inwardness and readiness for the final goal of sexual life—impregnation." They went on to warn that for the sexual act itself to be pleasurable to a woman "she must, in the depths of her mind, desire, deeply and utterly, to be a mother."

Despite the authors' overwrought language and proscriptive tone, their ideas gained tremendous currency, and informed a wide range of popular media. A December 1956 issue of *Life* magazine devoted to "The American Woman" carried this introduction:

"Ask any thoughtful woman what the most satisfying moments of her life have been and she will never mention the day she got her first job or the day she outwitted her boss on his ground. But she will always speak of the night when, as a teenager, she wore her first formal, and twirled in the arms of a not-so-bad date to tingly music. Or the night the man she loved took her in his arms, bringing a special look to her face. Then there was the moment when she held her first baby in her arms. It was not just releasing, it was completely fulfilling."

Fan magazines like *Photoplay* and *Modern Screen* carried gushing paeans to motherhood by stars who scrambled over each other to proclaim that nothing was more important to them than their families (although relatively few of them actually retired from the screen to raise children). Magazines overflowed with photo spreads of the stars cuddling their newborns, cavorting around swimming pools with their toddlers, and hosting elaborate children's birthday parties—to which the press was always invited! In a 1950 *Photoplay* article typical of the genre, Esther Williams's sister, Maureen Williams Sellstrom, describes the star discharging a nurse and slipping out of her "gala evening dress" to "take charge in the nursery." In an unconscious echo of Lundberg and Farnham, Sellstrom characterizes Williams, who had four children, as "deeply acceptant of motherhood. . . . For Esther, motherhood had been synonymous with fulfillment from the time she had been a child herself."

In such a climate, childlessness in a woman was viewed with

pity only so long as people assumed she *couldn't* have children. The rare woman who appeared to *choose* not to have children was often viewed with suspicion. Childless couples were thought to be selfish and even vaguely un-American. When Ellen Rodgers and her husband moved to a small town in western Kansas, they raised eyebrows among their neighbors because they were childless and because Ellen worked as an engineer.

"Out there, the fact that Brian and I'd been married eight or nine years and didn't have any kids, everybody thought that was pretty strange. I got the impression they thought something was *wrong* with us. I was unprepared for the fact that people would come right up and ask you all kinds of questions. Just casual friends would feel free to say, well, you've been married this long and you don't have children, what about it? That used to astound me."

Rachel Gruen, a Long Island housewife at the time, remembers well the despair she felt when she was unable to get pregnant.

"I wasn't working, I stayed home, took care of the house. I was marking time until I got pregnant. As time went on, and it didn't happen, I got increasingly desperate. All my friends around me were busy having babies. There was a sense that this was my function, that nothing was more important than having a baby. It would also give me a reason for not doing anything else. I actually never had any wild desire to have a baby. This was just the way it was supposed to work. I took all these tests and nothing seemed to work. I felt totally inadequate. In fact, it turned out Frank had a very low sperm count, so that was the problem. But even after we learned that, I still felt somehow responsible that I wasn't getting pregnant. I felt there was something wrong with me as a woman."

The ideology that glorified motherhood was reinforced by the paucity of other options for women. Motherhood *can* be experienced as a powerful and creative act and in the fifties, powerful and creative acts were hard for women to come by. The project of rearing children was touted as the ultimate challenge to women's skill, resourcefulness, organizational, and even scientific talents. It was also her exclusive domain, the one area in over which she could exercise complete control. Compared to what awaited her in the job market, motherhood presented itself as an alluring career with pleasant working conditions, opportunities for creativity, and good job security.

Finally, the decision to become a mother can never be separated from the lack of contraceptive alternatives, especially legal abortion. To say that birth control was more available in the fifties than in previous decades is not to say that it was universally easy to get and use. Many of the women I interviewed described being discouraged or refused birth control by their doctors. Others said they'd never been sure how to use their diaphragms. And many simply didn't know where to obtain contraceptives, and were afraid to ask their family doctor.

The Comstock law of 1873, which prohibited the circulation of birth control information and devices through the U.S. mail, inspired most states to enact similar legislation. Although a federal appeals court narrowly overturned Comstock's anticontraception provisions in 1936, state legislation remained intact. Even as late as 1960, twenty-nine states had laws on the books strictly regulating the dissemination of birth control information even to married women.

Birth control failed, as it always has, and was misused: one out of every four women in a 1955 study reported at least one unintended pregnancy. By the early 1950s, "therapeutic" abortions, the usual recourse for married women, were becoming exceedingly difficult to obtain. Responding to growing differences of opinion among physicians themselves about the morality of abortion, and undoubtedly to the groundswell of pronatalism in the country as well, hospitals in every state established boards to rule on requests for therapeutic abortion. These boards usually consisted of obstetricians, internists, and psychiatrists, and their effect was an immediate and dramatic curtailment of the number of therapeutic abortions performed in the United States. At New York Hospital, for example, the number of therapeutic abortions per thousand live births dropped from 7.4 between 1941 and 1944 to 4.8 between 1951 and 1954.

At a 1955 Planned Parenthood conference on abortion in the United States, Dr. Alan Guttmacher described how the abortion board at Mount Sinai came about. Before Guttmacher arrived at the hospital, therapeutic abortions had been decided by consultation of two senior staff members. Concerned that Mount Sinai was getting a reputation as an "easy" place to procure an abortion, Dr. Guttmacher instituted a five-member board which included the chiefs of medicine, psychiatry, obstetrics, and gynecology, and representatives from pediatrics and surgery. This board met once a week, and letters from two consultants recommending an abortion had to be circulated forty-eight hours before the meeting. In addition, one of the consultants had to appear before the board to answer any additional questions. The decision of the board had to be unanimous in order for the abortion to be granted. As a result, Dr. Guttmacher reported with some satisfaction, "applications for interruptions of pregnancy have decreased tremendously because of the vigilance of the board and the fact that a case has to go through such a procedure."

With legal abortion so scarce and in the absence of any consistent criteria for making decisions, it was inevitable that a kind of quota system would emerge. Women who had the resources to manipulate this complex system—by securing a psychiatrist's support, for example—were more likely to be granted abortions. Poor women not only had a slimmer chance of getting abortions, but when they did get them, they were often subjected to involuntary sterilization as well. As therapeutic abortions became ever more difficult to get, women naturally turned to the illegal abortion underground. In fact, a 1958 study showed that most illegal abortions were performed on married women who already had at least one child.

But, as we saw in chapter 2, financial resources did not nec-essarily guarantee easy access to abortion. Pam Dillon, who married the day after she graduated from Sarah Lawrence, was eager to have a large family. "I loved being pregnant. It was such a huge high that I got pregnant again seven months after I had my first child. After a while, we moved out to the suburbs and I went into the house and started having babies and hardly ever came out—or so it seemed. In fact, I had three more chil-dren. I became an earth mother. I made my own yogurt, I made my own bread, I did my own upholstery, I practically made their shoes! In fact, I did make moccasins for them once. By the third child, I was beginning to feel somewhat overwhelmed. I had no help whatsoever. Cleaning ladies would come to the door and take one look past me and just turn around and walk away. They wouldn't even come in.

"When I got pregnant for the fifth time, I wanted an abor-tion. I went to my ob/gyn—I never shopped around for an obstetrician, I went to this guy because he was eminent and came highly recommended. He always treated me like a child, but I was used to that. But when I went to him to ask for an abortion, he said, 'Oh nonsense, you'll love having a fifth child. After all, you've *got* four, what's one more?' I was enraged. And desperate. Somebody told me about a doctor in New Jersey who was doing abortions. So I went out there, found this place all by myself, sat in the waiting room for about half an hour. When I told the doctor I wanted an abortion he just stared at me and said, 'I don't know what we're going to do about that.' Finally my husband's sister, who worked in a hospital, found me a doctor who gave me an abortion. There was just no way in hell I could have handled a fifth child."

Emily Gilman is the wife of a prominent obstetrician in Atlanta. She has the soft, self-effacing manner of a woman who has always adapted herself to the needs of others. "I wasn't absolutely sure I wanted children, but I knew Forrest wanted them. We were trying not to get pregnant until he finished medical school and his internship, but after that, I guess we thought, why not? My second child was not yet three when my third was born. Three children in less than three years was a little close. If . . . well, I don't regret having the third, but I might well have considered an abortion if I hadn't been so sure my husband would never have allowed it. I'm still not sure exactly how I got pregnant that third time—I was using a diaphragm.

"Later, when the pill looked fairly safe, my husband said it was all right for me to take it. I used to go to sleep with the children at nap time every afternoon, and then feel as if I could hardly get up to get supper. My husband said it was probably the pill, but it may have been depression, too. It did seem to get better when I switched to the IUD. But then the children were older, too."

Rose Kramer's story demonstrates how ambivalence about a pregnancy could be resolved by the lack of alternatives. At sixty-one, she's a New Age therapist practicing in a sunny office in Pittsburgh filled with plants and crystals. In 1952, she was working as a nurse in a Philadelphia hospital. Rose came from a poor family in a depressed Pennsylvania town. She had a beautiful singing voice and dreamed of going into opera, but had no idea how to go about making such a career a reality.

"One day my best friend called me up and said, out of the blue, I've decided to become a nurse—why don't you come along? I can't say I had any burning desire to be a nurse. I felt like I was floating then, and did whatever came my way. Here was a plan, and I tagged along. It was also a way to get away from home."

Rose met Robert while they were both singing in a local church choir. "Robert was a very formal young man with impeccable manners. He reminded me of a young Franchot Tone. We started dating and then we began to do what you didn't do in the fifties—we slept together, and I got pregnant. I was absolutely terrified. I picked a doctor out of the phone book, and bought a dime-store wedding ring. The doctor told me I should go home and go to bed because I might lose the baby, and he gave me a prescription for some medication.

"I remember coming out of the doctor's office and feeling this great sense of shame, feeling sure that they knew I wasn't married. I walked to the corner and tore the prescription up and threw it in the garbage and thought, well, if I lose this baby it's okay. Then I got on the bus and it was a very bumpy ride. I found that I was holding myself so carefully. I sat on the bus thinking, what am I going to do? What am I going to do? I liked Robert a lot, he was not like most of the men I'd dated, but I can't really say I told myself, this is okay because we're going to get married. I told Robert that I was pregnant, and I told him with the idea that he should do the 'right thing.' His reaction was immediately, we'll get married. Once he said he would marry me, I felt everything would work out."

I ask Rose if she ever considered abortion and her first reaction is, "There was no such thing as abortion in those days, or if there was, I didn't have any idea about it." When I point out that, as a nurse, she must have had *some* contact with abortion, she remembers that therapeutic abortions had, in fact, been done at her hospital: "Two doctors had to say it was in the woman's best interest—I think one of them had to be a psychiatrist. And they only did them on married women. It just never occurred to me that I could have one. None of my classmates, none of my friends ever had one. If abortion had been as available then as it is now, I might have had one. But that's a big 'if.' I didn't really ever consider it."

Pregnancy—motherhood—could present itself as the answer to questions about one's identity. Kay D'Amico was also unmarried when she became pregnant in 1958. At the time she was studying dance in New York and living with Tony, a fellow dancer—an arrangement she was keeping secret from her conservative family back home in Illinois. "At first I was horrified. I mean, I wasn't married and, in my heart of hearts, I don't think I ever intended to marry Tony. But then I found I was also kind of excited, and as the crisis developed, and Tony and I started having these conversations about what we were going to do about this pregnancy, my excitement grew. After a while it crystallized into the feeling that ah, *at last I knew who I was. I was a mother.*

"You see, as much as I wanted this career as a dancer, I was also terribly afraid of it—afraid of not making it, of the hard work involved. For the first time in my life I was absolutely sure of my reason for being alive. And as that certainty took hold, of course, the idea of an abortion, which we'd been talking about sort of tentatively, receded in my mind. I found myself thinking—and saying to Tony over and over again—'Well, of course we were going to get married *eventually*,' and the more I said it, the more I believed it. I'm not sure he did, but I think I sort of swept him along in my growing conviction that this was inevitable—this baby, this marriage."

Kay abandoned her career and settled down to care for her new daughter, Lisa. Two years later, she "found herself" pregnant again.

"I was using a diaphragm—don't ask me how it happened. Did I choose to get pregnant? No . . . and yes. Not consciously, of course. I don't remember exactly wanting another child . . . but I wanted something." Kay pauses thoughtfully, "You know, it was more like, if I didn't have another child, what would I do? I could already see Lisa moving away from me, even though she was only two. I could see that she was already needing me in a less elemental way. A hole was opening up out there ahead of me. The old tormenting questions about who am I, what do I want to be, were threatening to come back. The only time I'd been completely free of them was when I was pregnant and while Lisa was an infant. As awful as those new-baby weeks were—the exhaustion, the sleeplessness, the endless laundry, the tension and anxiety between Tony and me—I wanted it all back because it filled up my life, it gave this feeling of absolute sureness." She stops again and says, as if seeing it for the first time, "I was afraid *not* to have another child."

Carol Freeman had always expected that she'd marry and have kids, but her mother, a Russian Jewish immigrant with little education, was determined that Carol graduate from college. Carol's mother, who had been widowed, supported Carol and her sister by running a dry-cleaning business in San Diego. After two years of college, at the age of nineteen, Carol fell in love with a navy man. They married, over her mother's strenuous objections. "She loved Mark, but she told him if he didn't let me finish school she'd go after him with a meat cleaver."

Carol got pregnant on her wedding night. "It was frightful. Here I was, nineteen years old, I wanted to finish school, and I really didn't want a child. I had a diaphragm, but I guess I didn't use it or I didn't use it right. As it turned out, I had a miscarriage at two months, which was a real blessing. I was damn relieved because if I'd had a child then . . . well, I just can't imagine it. I think I would have been scared to death to have an abortion because I'd heard about the back rooms, the kitchen tables. I had a college friend who had an abortion down in Mexico and it was hair-raising. She wasn't married and she came here because she wanted to hide the abortion from her friends and family. She never told me the details, but I understood that it was a real sleaze operation, and that she never quite got over it."

Carol's second pregnancy came three years later at an interesting moment. She and Mark had moved to Washington, D.C., where he'd been offered a job in a law firm. "I was delighted to move there because I wanted to see the world. I was totally into political science at that point and I'd already finished one year of grad school. I was working on a thesis about the reorganization of Congress and I loved doing research at the Library of Congress. Then I got pregnant. I was surprised, but I just took it as a matter of course. It was time to have kids. Even though I was enjoying doing the research for my thesis, I was very worried about actually having to write this dissertation. I was afraid I couldn't do it. So when I got pregnant I felt sort of saved! We moved back to San Diego, to the suburbs, so that we could be near my mom when the baby was born."

When Claire Lassiter found herself pregnant a month after she was married, she felt she had gotten what she deserved.

"On our honeymoon in Nantucket I'd picked up this horrendous urinary tract infection. The weather was bad and we'd spent four days in bed and who knew you were supposed to keep taking the diaphragm out and cleaning it? When we got back to New York I went to this ancient, deaf doctor and he gave me some pills. Maybe he never understood what I had because in a week or so I developed this high fever and it turned out this infection had reached my kidneys. The doctor wanted to hospitalize me but I prevailed on him to let me go home instead. He made me promise we wouldn't have sex for six weeks. Well, of course, the one single time we ever did it without protection happened at the end of this period and I got pregnant.

"I always knew I wanted to have children, but I really, deeply, did not want to have that baby at that time. I just wasn't ready. I liked my life as it was. I liked being married, and working and living in New York. On Sundays we'd go over to Central Park and Dan would play football—Dan knew tons of people and we were always doing stuff with this big gang of people, young couples. We had a tiny apartment, with no room in it for a baby. But I guess I felt, you've made your mistake and now you have to pay for it. I did think about trying to get an abortion for a few days. We talked about it, but I just couldn't bring myself to do it. Partly, I couldn't bring myself to terminate this piece of life inside me. And partly, I thought I'd brought it on myself, that it was my own fault—after all, it's not as if I was raped or something. I'd been stupid and disobedient and was that a good reason for aborting? The answer was no."

Claire attended natural childbirth classes to prepare for the birth of her baby, but in her eighth month, Dan's father died and she and Dan moved to Florida to look after Dan's mother.

"Down there, they'd never heard of natural childbirth. My doctor down there gave me a private room and that was it—no support or encouragement. It turned out that I had a ten-pound, five-ounce baby with his face turned the wrong direction. They knocked me out cold and delivered the baby with forceps.

"I emerged from that labor physically wiped out. Couldn't sit in a chair for two weeks. I hadn't expected to feel this badly. Also, the baby made me very nervous, I didn't have any idea what to do with it. I didn't have any of those wonderful satisfied mother feelings at first. Suddenly I was responsible for this creature. I was trying to nurse the baby and I was terrified that I was inadequate and that it wasn't getting enough to eat. Of course, he was monstrously healthy already—after all, he was ten pounds at birth. We put him on cereal in a month, for God's sake!

"But I had none of this bonding you're supposed to have from nursing—I was just tormented with anxiety and guilt. When I went back for my postpartum checkup or whatever it was, I asked the doctor to put me on the pill. I still think that if I'd been on the pill I wouldn't have gotten pregnant. I hated the goop and the glop and the having to stop in the middle of things to do all this stuff. He refused to do it. This doctor actually referred to your genitals as 'down there.' He insisted that I continue to use the diaphragm—not because the pill was dangerous or anything. He didn't even bother to explain, just dismissed my request and sent me on my way."

For all the glory that it conferred on women, childbirth itself was often a thoroughly dehumanizing business, followed by a lonely struggle with feelings of inadequacy. The prevailing idea that ambivalence about any aspect of pregnancy or maternity was neurotic made women who didn't immediately experience waves of "maternal" feeling after childbirth feel terribly guilty.

Claire's experiences with a patronizing obstetrician and an alienated labor were by no means unusual in the fifties. Male obstetricians routinely treated their patients as if they were children. Female obstetricians were rare, and those who had survived the gauntlet of medical school often felt they had to emulate their male colleagues in order to maintain credibility.

Anne Carpenter, the woman who kept turning down Harvard scholarships and ended up in "Project M," chose a famous obstetrician to deliver her first child.

"I didn't like him, didn't feel he was a kind person, but he had this reputation. It was a long, long labor, a forceps delivery, and when I got home I really didn't feel well and I kept feeling worse and worse and pretty soon I started bleeding profusely. I kept calling the doctor and he kept saying it was normal. I *knew* it wasn't normal because I was losing tissue. I tried to tell the doctor about that, but I was a little uncertain about it and when he dismissed it, I really believed he knew best.

"By about five weeks after the baby was born the bleeding was so bad I went back into the hospital. He said he couldn't find anything so he packed my uterus and sent me home again. The next week I had a major hemorrhage. Emergency. I couldn't even get out of the car. They discovered there was a large hole in my uterus that had to be sewed up. I now believe the placenta had never been properly removed.

"This doctor never admitted being at fault. He just kept patting me on the head and saying, there there, don't be hysterical. Even afterward, when I reminded him that I'd called to tell him I thought I'd lost placental tissue, he simply denied it had happened and said, no, no, that couldn't be. I believe he nearly cost me my life. What it *did* cost me was that I lost one of my fallopian tubes and there was a question whether I should get pregnant again with this sewed up uterus. I wanted badly to have another child. You *had* to have two children."

Peggy Fox laughs out loud when she remembers the delivery of her first child. "I had one of these 'great man' doctors who thought he was God's gift to expectant mothers. When Billy came, he came very fast and I was such a good little convent girl that I didn't complain about the pain until it got really unbearable. At that point they had to rush me into the delivery room because the baby was presenting. My obstetrician was down in the cafeteria or something, and he arrived a moment after Billy was born. He came roaring into the room, enraged, screaming at everyone, 'Why wasn't I called?' and making this huge scene. Everyone in the room was in a state of panic, apologizing and explaining, it was pandemonium and they all completely forgot about me. I'm sitting up on the table blubbering, 'This is the happiest moment of my life,' and nobody even heard me. The great man never even spoke to me—all he said as he stormed out was, 'Don't bill this woman!'"

Elaine Moeller remembers how grateful she was to get some help from a visiting nurse:

"We were living in a Quonset hut near the University of Washington when I had my first child. My life changed literally overnight and I was totally unprepared for it. I went from working full time to being alone in the house with a new baby, a full-time mother. No adults to speak to during the day, totally isolated, nervous. It was awful. For a long time I felt like an inadequate mother. My nipples were retracted and I was tense and uncomfortable, so the nursing didn't go well. I read all the time about how to do this, and kept trying to do it according to the books. I tried calling my obstetrician and he wasn't any help. Finally my pediatrician sent me a visiting nurse, who asked me what made me feel happy and comfortable. Then she set me up on the sofa, a cigarette, a novel propped in front of me, and Beethoven on the record player, and when I was all settled and comfortable, she handed me my baby to nurse—and that did it. She was solid gold."

Montana-born Grace Crawford's wide-set eyes and high cheekbones hint of the Cherokee blood in her mother's family. Grace's family were homesteaders who lost farm after farm during the Depression. She married her childhood sweetheart, Kevin, when he returned from the war in 1945.

"After the war, we finished college together at Montana State University. Kevin was getting his engineering degree and I was studying art and art history. We were living in what I called 'Lower Slobovia,' a kind of student ghetto, with a coal stove which heated the hot water. We lived like two gay bachelors, sharing the work, and we had a wonderful time. Housekeeping was kept to a minimum—we cleaned only when we had to.

"In my senior year, I got pregnant. I was shocked. I had a diaphragm, but I didn't really know how to use it. There was no birth control information readily available. I was fairly ignorant, and didn't know how careful you have to be." Grace and Kevin went on to have twins, then another son. After their fourth child was born, Grace and Kevin went to a local doctor to get the birth control pill.

"We didn't realize this doctor was Catholic. He told us we were the kind of people who should be having children and refused to help us. Anyway, we found another doctor who put me on the pill and that ended that. I probably would have had ten children but for the pill because we had a very active sex life."

Joy Wilner was also looking forward to having her first child, and got pregnant, on schedule, during her husband's last year of medical school.

"I felt totally fulfilled, totally happy. We were the perfect couple—Ted was supportive of me and I was supportive of him and we never argued. Well, we didn't know how. We'd had no experience with conflict. Everything was fine. I had my next child sixteen months after the first. The second child was neither exactly planned nor unplanned. I didn't really intend to get pregnant again, but on the other hand, we weren't using birth control because, after all, we already had *one* . . .

"After the second baby, that was the first time I can remember conflict, feelings of being trapped, wondering what I was doing with my life. These weren't very distinct feelings, not like I wonder if this is the right man for me. Just uncomfortable feelings. At some point I expressed some of these feelings, in a very tentative way, to Ted and he said, 'Well, if you feel that way, maybe we should get a divorce.' I was terrified. The idea of divorce was inconceivable. I never mentioned the subject again.

"At the same time, I got such pleasure, real physiological pleasure from my children—from playing with them, feeding them, watching them develop. Then we moved and Ted went into general practice, and at about the same time I had another child. I became his secretary, his nurse, and I was also handling the children, keeping them out of his hair. And of course, we were also establishing our identity as the doctor and his wife, so there was a lot of socializing. It was a busy time. What amazes me now is that it never occurred to me *not* to do this. His career was just my life, the substance of my life. There came a time when I felt I didn't have the strength for all this and I started breaking down. I can remember going into the shower and screaming—in the shower so that no one could hear me. Even then I didn't have conscious thoughts of 'I hate this life'—I didn't think there was anything objectively wrong with the way I was living, just that I couldn't take it any more."

Nancy Karlsson suffered a kind of breakdown after the birth of her second child. She and her husband, a salesman, were living in Seattle, Washington, at the time. "My marriage was in trouble because of my husband's drinking, and I had been thinking about trying to get a divorce. Then I found myself pregnant and I felt I didn't see how I could leave. I didn't want to have a second child, but there wasn't anything to do about it. I was trapped.

"The night I came home from the hospital with the baby, I woke up in the middle of the night and I couldn't get out of bed. I had to crawl to the bathroom. I was in excruciating pain. A doctor came to the house and he said, 'What do you mean, you can't get up?' I said, 'If the house is on fire, I'll get up. Otherwise I'm not getting up.' He told me I probably had rheumatoid arthritis. It's an acute inflammation of the joints—you can only lift your arms so high, and walking can be very painful. Evidently it can be latent while you're pregnant, and there are a lot of explanations for it, psychological ones. It has to do with the kind of state of mind you're in. For about a month I could do very little—I had to have a nurse. My husband was scared and for a while he quit drinking and was very supportive—he was a really sweet person when he was sober. In a few months I got better. Then we bought a house and moved, and I kind of forgot about leaving for a while."

Never before had it been so important to produce *perfect* children—with unblemished bodies, high intelligence, and "normal" personalities. When Carol Freeman's second child, a son, was slow in developing, she was horrified:

"It was terrible, having a child who didn't talk at the right time, didn't walk when he was supposed to. All children were supposed to talk and be clever and verbal and fun and perfect. And here comes this kid who is miserably unhappy, can't communicate, and I can't communicate with him which was wildly frustrating. So I have this darling little girl child who is doing everything and this darling little boy child who is doing nothing. Something is very wrong. Of course, we—I—took him to a child psychiatrist.

"This doctor didn't make any judgments on me, he just said, be patient, maybe he'll just be slow. That was the worst thing he could have said. I had this horror of having a stupid child. It seemed almost morally bad, reprehensible to me. When it turned out that my son had a very severe hearing loss, I was so relieved. Something could be *done* about this. My husband was traveling all the time, so it was my job to take care of this problem. Well, you did what you had to do. I may have even felt a little like it was my fault that he had the problem. So I was very wrapped up with getting him diagnosed, finding a therapist, driving him around to all these different tests and doctors.

"The funny thing is, I was actually *advised* to send my son to nursery school because it would be good for him. But with my daughter, I would have been seen as pretty way-out if I'd sent her to nursery school. You were supposed to stay home with your kids. But my son was always a big job."

So pervasive was the idea that all a child's imperfections were the mother's fault that Carol felt responsible even though the psychiatrist didn't blame her. But most mental health professionals did not hesitate to indict mothers exclusively for childhood problems ranging from shyness to juvenile delinquency. Experts like John Bowlby, whose 1950 study, *Maternal Care and Mental Health,* was extremely influential, argued that anything short of full-time maternal devotion was disastrous to the child. "Maternal deprivation" became a buzzword and mental health experts beat the bushes for examples of its dire consequences. As Barbara Ehrenreich and Deirdre English describe in *For Her Own Good: 150 Years of the Experts' Advice to Women,* "Psychologists demonstrated the noxious effects of maternal deprivation on baby monkeys, baby rats, and baby ducks, including weight loss, enlarged adrenal glands, heightened susceptibility to infectious diseases and chemical poisons, and stunted growth. In the logic of the experts, it followed that the mother who failed to meet their exaggerated standards of mother-love might as well be watering her baby's milk."

The trouble was, there was another cadre of experts denouncing "overprotective" mothers. The leading theorist of this school was Dr. David Levy, author of *Maternal Overprotection*. Levy asserted that such mothers in fact harbored "unconscious hostilities" toward their children—especially their sons, whose masculinity could be hopelessly damaged by their mothers' cloaked aggression.

Another leading early childhood expert, Dr. David Goodman, asserted that the solution to maternal overprotection was simple: better marital sex. In a chapter in his parents manual, unambiguously titled *Live Your Gender!*, he asserted: "The truly feminine mother, fulfilled in her marriage to a truly masculine father, does not over-protect, dominate or over-fondle her children." (Not surprisingly, the foreword to Dr. Goodman's book was contributed by Marynia Farnham, whom Goodman thanked for the "inspirational stimulus of her remarkable book.")

Although seemingly contradictory, the two theories, of maternal deprivation and overprotection, had one thing in common: the notion that mothers had accumulated an almost unlimited power. Paradoxically, this idea gained currency at a time when women had virtually no real economic power, despite the advertising industry's attempts to set them up as purchasing decision-makers in the home.

A key figure in this orgy of mom-bashing was novelist and conservative social critic Philip Wylie. In his best-selling 1942 book, *Generation of Vipers*, Wylie coined the phrase "momism," to describe "the megaloid momworship" he believed was dominating American life. Wylie laid the blame with mothers themselves, describing them with remarkable vitriol as parasites—"an idle class, a spending class, a candy-craving class"—preying on their children, especially their sons.

But it was psychiatrist Edward Strecker, consultant to the Surgeons General of the Army and Navy who launched the most vicious attack on mothers. In his book, *Their Mothers' Sons*, Strecker claimed that military hospitals were overflowing with "psychoneurotic" men—weak, cowardly, and infantilized—all the products of immature "moms" who dominated their sons with excessive and suffocating attention. Strecker's typology of bad mothers included the "self-sacrificing" mom, the "ailing" mom, the "Pollyanna" mom, the "protective" mom, the "pretty addle-pate" mom, and the "pseudo-intellectual" mom.

The effect of all this on mothers was to make them scrutinize their every action for its potential to harm their children. Many mothers felt almost paralyzed with self-consciousness. Kay D'Amico remembers with a shudder her own dread of being a bad mother. "I had the idea that every little thing I did could have this terrific impact on this tender little psyche. The worst was when Nick, my second child, was born. I was so concerned that my two-year-old, Lisa, not be jealous, that if she came into the room and found me hugging or caressing the baby, I'd literally jump guiltily, and have an impulse to put the baby down fast, and act as if I didn't care about him. Now, of course, I'm just appalled by this. But I was reading so much then, and trying so hard to be a good mother, to do a better job than *my* mother had done."

Most of the women I talked with wanted children and would have had them in any case. But many might have waited to have them, or had fewer of them. And some would clearly have preferred not to have children at all.

I was also struck by how many women—like Kay D'Amico and Carol Freeman—saw pregnancy as a reprieve, a way to avoid taking the next step in a career, or testing themselves academically by writing a dissertation or going to graduate school. This is not surprising. In the fifties, motherhood offered validation and a measure of control over a limited sphere. Any other path promised only uncertainty, conflict, and the risk of failure.

Chapter VI

Living the Dream

No man who owns his own house and lot can be a communist. He has too much to do.
—WILLIAM LEVITT, BUILDER OF LEVITTOWN

To walk down a Levittown street in the spring of 1950 was to be struck with the newness of it all: freshly painted houses with western pine exteriors; the ruts that guided the '47 Chevys and Fords up to the carports; grass, growing braver each week; skinny saplings, three to a house, standing like embarrassed sentinels along the curving sidewalks. Noise, bikes, wagons and baby carriages. Knots of housewives sitting on lawns, next to busy playpens. Gangs of three- and four-year-olds shriek and giggle in and out of houses. . . . Above all there is the uncluttered bowl of the sky—a great, clean, blue presence coming down all over Levittown.
—WILLIAM DOBRINER, *CLASS IN SUBURBIA*

I always felt there was something wrong with me that I was so unhappy in the suburbs.
—CAROL FREEMAN

In the first years after the war, a wave of relief and euphoria swept the country. People had jobs, savings to spend, and, with the end of wartime shortages, plenty of things to buy. In 1946, *Life* magazine found the nation "on the threshold of marvels ranging from runless stockings and shineless serge suits to jet-propelled airplanes that will flash across the country in just a little less than the speed of sound." The catalyst between the public's desire and ability to spend and the nation's need to stimulate production was the advertising industry. "Tomorrow" and "the future" were magical words that appeared repeatedly in ads for everything from synthetic fabrics to automobiles. Americans were in love with the "new" easy-to-clean, wrinkle-free fabrics with names like Enkalure, Celanese, and Avcoset. Industry retooled its factories to produce automobiles bigger and shinier than ever and now advertised as "built with rocket technology!" For the first time, car ads were aimed at the woman of the family, extolling "interiors as tasteful and colorful as your own home." *Life* magazine carried pages of ads for gigantic refrigerators packed with Coca-Cola, Jell-O molds, cherry-topped puddings. "Holds 490 lbs. of food!" gasped the headline for a General Electric refrigerator ad. Air-conditioning, frozen foods, and contour sheets were among the profusion of labor-saving, life-enhancing products that came on the market in the postwar era.

In case they needed any urging, young couples were made to feel it was their patriotic duty to consume. A *Bride's Magazine* handbook for newlyweds urges them to look for brand names "when you start out to buy the dozens of things you never bought or even thought of before." It adds that by buying brand names "you are helping to build greater security for the industries of this country . . . what you buy and how you buy it is very vital in your new life—and to our whole American way of living."

The most urgent problem facing the nation after the war was

the acute housing shortage. Veterans and their families had to double-, triple-, or quadruple-up with parents and friends. People were living anywhere they could, crammed into barracks, Quonset huts, trailers, chicken coops, garages, trolley cars and grain bins. An Omaha newspaper advertised "Big Ice Box, 7 by 17 feet, could be fixed up to live in." Young people, buoyed by postwar optimism, tended to view their crowded conditions as temporary and treat them with good-humored grace. Connie Boyden remembers roughing it with her veteran husband in a place called Shanks Village, New York.

"This was a military embarkation camp in Orangeburg, New York, that Columbia bought to house students and faculty. It was all Quonset huts and there were five thousand of us living there, all the same ages, all connected with Columbia in some way or another. It was a great way to start a marriage. We were part of this wonderful community, all these young veterans, eager to start life, all poor and struggling, living in these barracks. There was only about one car to every five families, so the husbands were always carpooling into the city. The wives would get together and coffee klatch, but it wasn't stupid, we were actually doing community projects. We were political, we were reacting to McCarthy and the Korean War. It was an exciting time."

Julia Harmon, who went on to become a "corporate wife," also treasures her early years in Lexington, Virginia:

"Chuck had just been hired by a corporation that was based in Lexington, Virginia, so that's where we went right after we were married. We lived in these funny-looking prefabs that the government had built during the war for service personnel or students who were doing something for the war effort. They were dreadful when you think about it—the walls were so thin that things used to happen like a man calling out to his wife in one would be answered by his neighbor's wife next door. We were just as happy as can be, though, and when our son was born, we took two of these prefab things and put 'em together.

"We loved the life there, we had our new little baby and a wonderful circle of friends in the university and in town. I took courses at the university—wonderful courses. I think that may have been where we were the happiest."

The federal government responded to the housing crisis by providing billions of dollars of mortgage insurance for veterans, effectively underwriting a massive new housing construction program. Although it also called for construction of some low-cost public housing, the real thrust of the government's efforts was to encourage single dwellings outside city limits. Builders from Long Island to Los Angeles leapt into the breach. The rolling farmland surrounding major cities was flattened into huge tracts of mud, and row upon row of identical boxlike houses was thrown up with lightning speed.

Architects and architectural critics condemned the "uniform, unidentifiable houses lined up inflexibly at uniform distances on uniform roads." Social critics decried the homogeneity of race, class, and age the new suburbs fostered, and predicted the death of individuality and diversity. But to young Americans hungry for stability and normalcy, all this was beside the point. The new developments promised nothing less than the American Dream: an affordable home, a safe, green place to raise their children, and a community of other young families.

Levittown was among the first of the suburban communities and became synonymous with the idea of suburbia. It was built in 1947 by William Levitt on 6,000 acres of Long Island potato fields. By ignoring union restrictions, eliminating middlemen, and employing automobile assembly-line techniques, Levitt was able to build an astonishing thirty-six houses a day. Teams of workers went from house to house laying foundations, putting in floors, fitting windows. Two days before the first houses went on sale, hundreds of eager veterans and their families (Levittown houses were at first available only to veterans) began arriving to wait out the weekend camped on army cots, beach chairs, and sleeping bags. One vet remembered that he and his wife rushed out to Levittown, "followed the map we were given and bought the first house we saw without even going inside."

Cele Roberts was in that early wave of Levittowners. She still lives in the house she and her husband bought in 1949, although, like most of the Levittown houses, it's been remodeled and added to many times over the years.

"I was twenty-five and pregnant. We'd been living in a one-room apartment on the lower east side of Manhattan, and though I liked the city streets, the hurly-burly, I couldn't envision raising children there. I wanted that suburban dream life. We'd come out to visit our friends. They showed us several houses and told us that for a hundred dollars down we could move into a house that had venetian blinds, a washing machine, a refrigerator.

"Of course, the houses didn't have basements, they were built on concrete slabs—there was quite a lot of controversy about that. How could you have a house without a basement? Did it have a carport? Did it have a garage? Certainly not, but you were only paying $7,990 for this house, and the monthly payments were low, $58 a month, they promised us. That was just about what our budget could handle in those days. My husband was a substitute teacher at the time. Even though these were cheap houses, they weren't cheap when you were making $3,000 a year. But the VA took part of the mortgage—I think my FHA mortgage was about 4½ percent.

"The house was surrounded by a lake of mud. But I was thrilled—it was a very exciting thing to have a house of your own. And everything you dreamed about was there, everything was working, brand-new, no cockroaches. You got a beautiful stainless steel sink with two drains, cabinets, drawers, a three-burner General Electric stove with oven, a Bendix washing machine. The only thing I had to buy for the house when we moved in was a fluorescent tube over the kitchen sink—the fix-ture was even there!

"We had the ranch-house model, and every house was laid out the same, all on one level, of course. Eight hundred square feet, but the rooms looked roomy at the time. There was an unfinished attic. You had two bedrooms, a fireplace, and a living room with a picture window sixteen feet. The only thing I didn't like, all the floors were sort of a black tile, which you couldn't put wall-to-wall over because they had the radiant heat, which was from coils under the floors. Those black tiles were impossible to keep clean, especially during the first year because we were living in a construction site, so there was always this mud.

"When we looked out our picture window, it was a blessing because there were no houses behind us—nothing but a long, grassy hillock, because I had an end property. The yard was 67 by 120 feet, which was a few feet larger than most and Mr. Levitt didn't leave you with just a house—you got three fruit trees like sticks, plop, plop, plop, in the front yard, and even a weeping willow tree. These little sticks were carefully monitored by the landscape guys and if they didn't grow, they would come by and put in new ones. Of course, once they did grow, it was way too much for those tiny yards."

Although the development gave the impression of uniform-ity, Cele Roberts points out that the houses were not, in fact, identical. "The 1949 ranch house, for example, came in five dif-ferent looks, even though they were all basically the same house. The facades were different, some had high windows, some low. And the houses were different distances from the curb, they were slightly staggered." Still, in the early days there were no street signs, and one Levittown pioneer described finding her house by counting streets and houses "like finding your car in a huge parking lot."

Children were at the center of all the new suburban developments; they were the reason people moved to them and the developers understood this. One of Levitt's innovations was to place his kitchens at the front of the house so that mothers could watch their children at play while they cooked and washed up. So fecund were Levittown families that the development came to be known as the "Rabbit Hutch" and "Fertility Valley." Children were everywhere, playing and riding their bikes and trikes in relative safety on front lawns and curving sidewalks, far from traffic. They were also constantly in and out of each other's houses.

Clare Worthing, another original Levittown resident, points out that the very similarity of the houses was comfortable for the children. "I think they liked it that the houses were all laid out the same. For example, you always knew exactly where the bathroom was.

"On our block, there were five families who all had children roughly the same ages as ours. So we all grew up together as parents on this block and we covered for each other. One of the boys on the block was accident-prone and one day he broke his arm. His mother wasn't home, but one of the other parents who knew the family belonged to an HMO, took the kid over and got his arm set. By the time the mother got home that evening, the boy was waiting for her, all taken care of with his arm in a cast. If I was going to be late getting home, I'd just call a neighbor and ask her to keep an eye on my kids until I got home. That's very seductive. In order to live that way someplace else I would have had to have help."

In the beginning, at least, the suburbs did offer a kind of community to their inhabitants. Suburban areas were not yet linked to cities by public transportation and not many people had cars. Neighbors needed each other to share cars, do errands, and transport children. Cele Roberts waited a year to get a telephone: "This was still a rural area and they weren't prepared for this influx of people. We were on a waiting list, and were always going over to the neighbor who'd already gotten her phone to make calls."

Carol Freeman recalls the community of women in her suburb near San Diego. "It was a warm, boring, completely child-centered little culture. We sat around in each other's kitchens and backyards and drank a lot of coffee and smoked a million cigarettes and talked about our children. There was some competition, yes, but mostly we were young mothers and we were learning from each other and getting support from each other. We took care of each other's children, too, so that we were able to get away some."

Grace Crawford remembers how excited she was about moving to the suburban community of Richland, Washington. "You have to understand what we were coming from," she says. "We were living in a two-room apartment over a garage with our eighteen-month-old son and newborn twins. I didn't have an automatic washer, I didn't have any help. My husband would get up at 4 A.M. and make twenty-four bottles of formula and put them in the refrigerator and go to work. When he came home at noon the breakfast dishes would still be in the sink and I would have done nothing but bottling and burping babies. Kevin, my husband, never sat down without folding diapers.

"We used to call ourselves Hilda and Gilda, the friendly nursemaids. My sister was always saying, 'You've *got* to get a schedule!' and I'd just laugh and laugh. I got to be so efficient I could hold one baby in one hand, one in the other and grab the third with my knees. These children became my life. Kevin was working for the Army Corps of Engineers and would often be gone for three to five weeks at a time. I never complained. 'Whither thou goest,' you know. . .

"Then we moved to Richland and I thought I'd died and gone to heaven. Green grass, places for the children to play, good schools, a nice house, with an automatic washer and dryer and an Iron-Rite mangle—that was a real mark of status. We even had a car. But this was a government town, so the houses were all alike. The people were pretty much alike, too, and everybody was trying to achieve middle-class status. Everybody had to have the same things everybody else had, from appliances to hairdos. We went on the same kind of vacations, read the same books, we even had the same bubble hairdos. I have a picture of myself in a Lanz dress with a huge skirt, my hair in a bubble. You know, we also had something called a 'station-wagon dress'—it snapped all the way down the front so that you could put it on in a hurry and jump into the station wagon to go pick the kids up."

June Traven left Chicago and her job at an insurance agency with some reluctance when her husband, Ralph, was transferred to Florida. A trim sixty-year-old who runs her own travel business in Chicago, June still prides herself on her energy and flexibility. She was determined to make the best of her situation by treating it as a challenge:

"I think what made the move to Florida bearable was that it was an adventure—going to a new state, making new friends—this is what offset leaving the place I was used to, my friends, and my work. My big thrill was that my mother gave me a washing machine for Christmas. I really liked hanging the diapers and baby clothes out on the line, having my clothesline look neat, everything sparkling.

"I was determined to make homemaking represent a good job. I was continually painting, decorating, sewing slipcovers and drapes. By the second year down there, I was sewing all my own clothes as well as Susie's. And the cooking! I actually remember a recipe which called for making flowers out of mashed potatoes molded into Bartlett pears, with cloves for the stems, and glazed with egg whites. Well, you know, anything is a challenge until you've done it once . . . I kind of liked creating something special—up to a point. A lot of it was simple boredom. I needed something to do. And I was constantly trying to live up to some expectations about being a good mother and homemaker. After a while all this wasn't enough and I found this terrific black woman who would come in for a few hours during the week to look after Susie so that I could occasionally go to a meeting or something.

"I took a creative writing course, I took a speed-reading course. I joined the League of Women Voters—in fact, another woman and I worked out a whole reapportionment plan for the Florida state legislature. Of course, it never crossed my mind to actually get a job—even though we were pretty tight for money. And I was always home in plenty of time to have dinner on the table for Ralph when he got home. But Ralph was drinking pretty heavily by then, and doing things like not coming home till all hours, and then coming home drunk. I felt I was holding up my part of the bargain, but he wasn't holding up his."

Cathy Lee Shipley captures the euphoric quality of postwar life in an affluent Georgia suburb. On a scorching August afternoon, we sit drinking lemonade on her shady veranda in Macon, Georgia. Cathy Lee, who runs an expensive dress shop in Macon, reminisces in a soft, musical voice:

"All of our group, our friends—everyone was trying to piece their lives together after the war. The men in our group had been in the war in various services. We had all been wound up tight and then we were able to begin to relax. We were spoiling ourselves, spoiling our children, too. My daddy had a furniture store so he gave us a washer and then he gave us a television. We had this huge antenna, almost like a telephone pole in the backyard. If the weather was good we got something, but if not, we just had snow. We would be just glued to that set.

"We would get baby-sitters and we'd all go out every Saturday night—to eating places or to each other's houses or sometimes to the country club for a dance. My parents had a place over in Alabama and we'd go over there, a few couples together, and spend a weekend fishing and barbecuing. Then once a year we'd all go to the beach for a week, in a group of maybe ten, twelve couples. Eventually, we all got together and rented a couple of lots by the Chattahoochee, and the men went out and put down a concrete foundation and built a little shed where we could grill things. We had boats and we'd go waterskiing out on the river. We had a wonderful woman working for us, Ardella. She'd go with us when we went away. We'd just call her up and say, 'Ardella, we're goin' to the mountains this weekend, you want to come with us?' And she'd pack a little bag and go with us and then she'd be with the children if we wanted to go out on Saturday night. She loved going with us to these places."

Julia Harmon lived another kind of dream: the life of a woman married to a corporation man. After Julia and Chuck left their Quonset hut in Lexington, Virginia, they moved five times from 1953 to 1960, as Chuck rose in his company.

"All of the choices and all of the things we did were based on my husband's life, and his work, which was my life and my children's life. Each move was an advancement for Chuck, and his advancement was my advancement. This was our bread and butter. I rejoiced in Chuck's success, and I made up my mind that we'd make an adventure out of each move. And we did, especially when the kids were little. I sound like Pollyanna, don't I?" She laughs ruefully.

"There was also a great deal of entertaining—little dinner parties, big dinner parties, cocktail parties, barbecues . . . but it really was a good life—not too different from what I had anticipated. I was living the dream. As a citizen, I pitched in full metal wherever we lived. I was a member of the Junior League and whatever city we moved to, I had an immediate base, something to hook into right away. I'd usually end up at the art museum or teaching art classes or something like that. That provided an opportunity for me to meet people in my community.

"I felt extremely happy if everybody was happy: if I'd had a good dinner, and the children were scrubbed and happy and doing well in school and their clothes were clean and I was looking good when it all came together—that was pleasing, that was good. It was best when all these good things were happening for everyone else and I was managing it."

Julia's choice was not without its costs, however. She had willingly set aside her love of painting, and as we talk, a more complicated picture emerges.

"Chuck was away a lot, his work kept him traveling, so I was doing the major parenting, and that caused a little bit of tension between us at times. Sometimes I didn't feel he quite appreciated what I was doing, the contribution I was making. But yes, I felt valued, I felt loved, within the parameters of the way our life was structured. I had no glimmer of how else it could be. We both just took these roles for granted. Honest to Pete, I really think this was what I wanted.

"I never really abandoned art, you know. Of course, I never had a studio and I never could have worked while the kids were underfoot anyway. I'm a terrible night owl—I come alive at about nine o'clock at night. While Chuck was out of town especially, I would get out my materials and paint on the dining-room table. It was always my habit when I had anything I wanted to do to do it in the middle of the night—painting, drawing, sewing, making gifts for people. But it wasn't until we moved to a city where I could take good art courses that painting became a passion."

The toll suburban life took on women has been extensively documented by everyone from Betty Friedan to Marilyn French. Isolated in their child-centered enclaves, women struggled with boredom and frustration. But struggle they did, with varying degrees of success. Some managed to find ways to express their creativity within the framework of family life. Others, like Julia Harmon, stole time from their families to do things that interested them. Some turned to alcohol or prescription drugs to deaden their frustration or make the long days go a little faster.

Maggie Desmond abandoned her ideas about becoming an artist to marry her husband, Paul, a navy officer. The only daughter of parents who were somewhat Bohemian, Maggie saw marriage to Paul as a rebellion against her parents' values. In short order, she found herself in Jacksonville, Florida, on a navy base that had all the earmarks of a suburb. Maggie had trouble, at first, subduing her high spirits to conform to the role of navy wife.

"We women were all in the same boat, the officers' wives, and we bitched a lot, but we also had a kind of bond. We all had good minds and we got together and talked about everything. We thought it was terribly unfair that the men got all the glory. This was down in Florida and it was hot as blazes and we were festering our little brains out.

"There was this book called *Welcome Aboard!* and it was a manual for navy wives. We were all supposed to read it. When you arrived at a base you were supposed to make an official call on your commanding officer's wife. So we all put on our bathing suits and high heels and white gloves and hats and then, with copies of *Welcome Aboard!* under our arms, we went and called on our commanding officer's wife. Bless her heart, she opened her door and saw us and said, 'Oh shit!' She was very amused."

When Paul left the navy, he and Maggie, now a mother of two children fifteen months apart, moved to a Connecticut suburb.

"We flew up there with the babies and thousands of pounds of baby equipment. I was immersed in this round of work: wash diapers, make formula, clean, iron—I was still ironing Paul's shirts in those days—plan meals. I remember the *Better Homes and Gardens Baby Book* said you should feed your child his big meal at noon and by God I'd bake my little boy a potato, make him a whole dinner at midday. Paul needed the car to get to work, so I was cooped up.

"My one outing of the week was to go to the Safeway for groceries—we'd go in a group, a bunch of women, in a car pool. I had a tiny backyard which was hot in the summer, cold in winter. There was nowhere to go. It was at this point that I developed this depression, this listlessness. I wanted to sleep all the time. I went to the doctor because Paul and I both thought there was something drastically wrong. He just said he'd seen this before in women, but he had no suggestions. He gave me some thyroid pills and sent me home.

"After a while, I started trying to paint at night after the kids were asleep. You know, when you're kneading bread dough or hanging laundry up on the line, you feel you're somehow in the right place, that you're organically whole. You're at one with ancestors of women who have been doing these things. But if you try to paint a painting late at night when everybody's asleep, you feel the opposite, as if you're teetering on the edge of something. You feel you're in a place women don't go, that you oughtn't be here. I used to try to stay up—either to get the ironing done at a time when the kids couldn't mess it up, or to paint. If I was ironing late at night, I never heard from Paul, but if I was up late painting, he'd come roaring down with fire in his eye and tell me that I was ruining my health. What he really meant was that he wanted me up there with him, not doing this alien thing."

Dorothy Glenn, the woman who eventually left her husband because of their inadequate sex life, continually sought distraction from her suburban routines. She, too, had trained as an artist before marriage.

"I was doing a lot of reading about metaphysics and one day while I was rinsing out dirty diapers in the toilet, I thought, these things are incompatible. So I stopped the reading—I couldn': stop the diapers. When I had an hour I would just go and sit and look at the mountains and think. We would trade off taking care of the children, so I had one day a week when I could run around and do my errands. Sometimes I could work in forty minutes at the museum.

"I found ways of using my art—well, you really couldn't call it *art*, I suppose—in various artsy-craftsy ways. I loved Halloween, birthday parties, making decorations, costumes for the kids. I tried to do stuff around the kids—for example, I was on the Girl Scouts Council—until they spent two hours one day discussing paper plates. We organized a neighborhood association—of course, my husband became the president and I put out the newsletter. And I taught a little at the local YWCA, charm school stuff: how to sit and stand and walk across the room. We'd have these little fashion shows. My husband went back to school for his master's and I worked on it with him, did some of the research and typed it for him.

"I went and took a course in folk dancing at a local college because that was something I could do with the kids. Gradually, I did more and more physical activities. I could do folk dancing for hours. I used to go horseback riding. All that made me feel good. It was probably a sexual outlet."

In 1958 Christine Albrecht moved with her two young children to suburban Newton, Massachusetts, while her husband, Ned, finished Harvard Law School.

"I was feeling irritable and restless, so I started taking a writing class at Wellesley, and I took a religion class, too. And something started awakening in me that I had my own interests. Oh, I remember being so irritated at Ned because he had no idea about why I was doing this or what it meant to me. He would say, oh that's wonderful, dear. Suddenly I felt this passion in this writing class. It was so exciting and I felt as if nobody understood what I was talking about.

"We lived in one of these little communities that was filled with mothers and babies. In the winter we would get terrible snowstorms and you were really house-bound with small children. These women would show up at nine in the morning with their children and I would be furious. I couldn't actually say, don't come over—I was too nice for that. So I used to hide in the cellar where I had this little desk set up, and I wouldn't answer the door. That was the beginning of something. Something was wearing thin. During naptime I'd go down and write in the cellar. I became very strict with the children about banishing them, ordering them into their room so that I could have that little piece of time."

When Jill Morris moved to an affluent Long Island suburb, it was the fulfillment of a lifelong yearning for stability and rootedness. Jill's childhood had been severely dislocated by the Depression. After her father lost his job as a salesman, Jill's parents moved from state to state in the Midwest, looking for work and staying with relatives. Eventually her parents were forced to split up altogether.

Jill remembers standing with her husband in the doorway of their new house: "I had tears in my eyes as I watched all this stuff being delivered to *my house*—tables and chairs and beds and lamps. All I'd ever wanted was to be brought up in one house with a little picket fence around it. With stability and security and family, which I never had. I wanted to be like everyone else. That was my driving goal."

Five years and two children later, Jill found herself sleeping till eleven.

"Here I was in my nice house, twenty-seven years old, with nothing to do. I didn't know how to drive yet and we only had one car then, so sometimes I'd hitch a ride with the milkman downtown and bop around. We had help, a sort of family retainer who lived with us and did most of the housework. Eventually I found friends and started to do volunteer work— March of Dimes, polio, that kind of stuff. There were three couples that we were close to, and we raised our kids together. We'd take turns with the children, and we also took turns doing holidays—one of us would do Memorial Day, one would do the Fourth of July—we made family for each other!

"How I remember yearning for the moment when both my children would be in school for at least a few hours. All of us—I mean the women—took Dexedrine, and later Dexamil. My brother-in-law was a doctor and he used to supply us with Dexedrine and Seconal and phenobarbital. This was to have enough energy to get through the day. I didn't stop until the late sixties and I remember having terrible withdrawal symptoms."

As suburban families became more affluent, the sense of community that had characterized the early years dissipated. As long as you had only one car, you were dependent on your neighbors; a second car brought independence and isolation.

Eileen Hanley also saw the move to the suburbs as the beginning of the life she wanted to lead. The daughter of working-class Irish parents, Eileen had worked as a secretary to put her husband, Jimmy, through law school. When he was invited to join a good law firm, they were able to move out of their cramped Chicago apartment to a suburb north of the city.

"I was happy as a clam when we first moved to Winnetka," she remembers. "I loved my little house, loved decorating it, choosing the drapes and slipcovers. We were the first on our block to have kitchen appliances that weren't white, and that *matched:* we had an avocado-colored General Electric refrigerator and range. Very nifty.

"But once the house was finished I found myself very lonely. There really wasn't very much to do and the women on my block were all preoccupied with their children. I was trying very hard to get pregnant. It was around that time that I started drinking a little. Well, I'd always liked to drink, but I had cut back when Jimmy and I got engaged. Anyway, I decided to teach myself to cook and would spend hours poring over cookbooks, making these elaborate dishes like *coq au vin* and *boeuf bourguignon*—and sipping away on the cooking wine, of course. I did make it a point never to have a mixed drink during the day. But I'd meet Jimmy in the driveway when he got home at six with a martini in my hand. And he used to wake up in the middle of the night and find me kneeling next to my bureau drinking scotch out of a bottle I kept there. I did finally go to a psychiatrist and he told me, 'Your only problem is that you don't have children,' and that if I had a baby my drinking would stop. Which, of course, was what I thought, too."

Eileen did go on to have two children, but did not stop drinking until 1962. By that time, her drinking problem had become so severe that she had to be hospitalized for several months. She joined Alcoholics Anonymous when she came out of the hospital, and has not had a drink since.

Carol Freeman and I sit on the terrace of her apartment in a retirement community outside San Diego, drinking wine and watching the sun drop into the Pacific. She talks about her years in the suburbs with nostalgia tinged with bitterness.

"We did the classic GI thing. We put a down payment on a house in the suburbs before it was built and then lived with my mother while it was finished. You could get those tract houses for $11,000 to $12,000 with a porch. My husband was working very hard trying to get his law practice going. He had to travel a lot so I was alone a lot with little babies. I loathed it. My one outlet was that I got involved with the League of Women Voters—this was the only way I could talk to other adults. I was never a very gutsy person and the League seemed very safe, very rational, very moderate. I worked hard and did well and eventually I ran the thing. But I always felt there was something wrong with me that I was so unhappy in the suburbs.

"Later we moved out a little further. It was still a suburb, but we had a larger house that was a little more idiosyncratic than our old house. This was the time when people were very concerned about bomb shelters. This house had a large backyard, the largest plot on the block, and it had a swimming pool. Well, after we'd moved in, we were approached by the neighbors, who said, you've got the big backyard so we should put the bomb shelter in your yard. We thought this was dumb—we didn't think a bomb shelter was going to save any lives. And of course, no one was interested in sharing the costs of building this air-raid shelter! We did a lot of backyard entertaining—big brunches, swimming parties, barbecues. You were trying to live out this ideal of life in the suburbs, in a way, that you saw in *Life* magazines. But you always considered yourself just a little above it. You know, you had the Eames chair . . .

"But I have to be fair, here. As dissatisfied as I was, and as restless, I remember so well this feeling we had at the time that the world was going to be your oyster. You were going to make money, your kids were going to go to good schools, everything was possible if you just did what you were supposed to do. The future was rosy. There was a tremendous feeling of optimism. You were working for good causes, you believed that politicians were, on the whole, honest. You believed in this idea of good government and you believed you could have a part of it through political activity. You canvassed, gave parties for people to meet your candidate, distributed potholders with your congressman's name on them—and you felt that there was actually a correlation between your actions and the results. Much as I say it was hateful, it was also hopeful. It was an innocent time."

Chapter VII

Something to Fall Back On?

> [The factory wife] works, she almost always says, because she wants to buy something for the home, or to give her children a better education than she had, or for some other rationally satisfying reason. . . . [But] a great many factory wives work because, deep down, the wife-mother-homemaker role bores them and they get a greater sense of importance by entering a male environment.
> —*LIFE* MAGAZINE, DECEMBER 24, 1956

> I didn't think much about working. It was just something I had to do.
> —MARIA O'CONNOR

One of the great paradoxes of the fifties is that even in the face of a powerful domestic revival, women continued to enter the work force in ever-increasing numbers. In the first five years of the decade, the number of working women shot up from 16 to 22 million. The notion that work was something for women "to fall back on," a phrase that seems to have emerged in the fifties, presumed that work was a kind of afterthought, something a woman should be prepared to do in case something happened to her husband. The phrase ignored the reality that millions of married women worked because their salaries were needed to support their families.

In fact, the most interesting change in the female labor force after the war was the shift in the kind of women who worked. Prior to World War II, women in the work force had been mostly young and single, even though the number of working married women increased during the Depression. The explosion of war-related jobs brought huge numbers of married women into the labor force, many with school-aged and younger children. By V-E Day in 1945, the female work force had increased by 50 percent to nearly 20 million—and the majority of these workers were wives.

When millions of women lost their jobs after the war, they did not necessarily leave the work force. Instead, most were rerouted into clerical, sales, and service jobs—sex-segregated and low-paying. *Life* magazine, which only a few years earlier had been extolling women's suitability for war work like welding and crane operating, now justified women's predominance in "traditional fields" in stereotypical terms: "Household skills take her into the garment trades; neat and personable, she becomes office worker and saleslady; patient and dexterous, she does well on repetitive, detailed factory work; compassionate, she becomes teacher and nurse."

Nevertheless, World War II had permanently altered the face of the work force by breaking down barriers to the employment of wives and older women. The war forced the nation to accept, if on a limited basis, the idea of women working outside the home.

Marion Klinger was such an older worker. Born in Dayton, Ohio, Marion is a mild, pleasant woman of sixty-eight, whose bland amiability masks a streak of iron. Marion's family was hard-hit by the Depression. After her father lost his job, her mother's salary as a saleswoman was not enough to support the family, and Marion and her brother were sent to live with their grandmother in a small town in southern Ohio. We talk on the patio of the modest house in this town, where she and her husband have lived for over forty years.

"I always wanted to be a nurse. Don't know why, that's just what I wanted to be. Of course, I also expected to be married and have a family. There wasn't any place nearby where I could go to nursing school, so I went to a small liberal arts college for a year, but I didn't like it too much. Then Pearl Harbor came and everyone was going to work, so I decided I would, too. I went down with a boyfriend of mine to this ammunition plant near Louisville, Kentucky. They wouldn't accept him, but they took me because I'd had a year of college chemistry.

"This was during gas rationing and we were supposed to share rides, so I used to ride to work with a bunch of older fellows. They were all very nice to me, very gentlemanly. I worked in a lab where we were testing cellulose, I remember. There were a few other women working there and the men in the lab were nice to us, too. It was wartime, you know, and there was this feeling of everyone doing unusual things and pulling together.

"After about a year I decided to see if I could go to nursing school and I applied to Case Western in Cleveland. It so happened that was when they started the Cadet Nurse Corps, which paid for your education. I had just enough money saved from working at the plant to get to Cleveland and start out, and then the CNC paid the tuition and gave us a small stipend. And uniforms, we had very nice uniforms. That was all there was to being in the Corps—you just went to school."

Before she graduated, Marion renewed her acquaintance with an old beau from her home town who had been sent home from the navy to attend his mother's funeral. They decided to marry. "He was eight years older than I was and I liked him because he seemed dependable. I had some other men friends at the time, but I wasn't sure about them. With Jim, you knew you were going to be safe; you were on solid ground."

After they married, Marion finished nursing school while Jim finished out his term of service in Washington, D.C. At the end of the war, they moved back to the town where they had both been raised. Jim went to work for an insurance firm and they began their family.

"In 1952, when my daughter was five and my son was three, the local hospital called and asked me if I was willing to work. They were very shorthanded and said I could have any hours I wanted. I said I'd love to. We lived right behind the hospital, so it couldn't have been more convenient. I could look out the window and see my own backyard. And if the children needed me I could be home in a minute. And I had my mother-in-law to watch the children.

"My husband did have a hard time with it for a while. He felt I shouldn't work because it looked as if he couldn't take care of me. It helped that the hospital just begged me to come because they were so desperate for nurses. Later on I had an offer from a big hospital in Dayton, a good offer, but my husband opposed that. He felt it would take me too far away from the children. So I didn't pursue it.

"I worked part-time, about four or five hours a day at first. Later on, I worked the three to eleven shift. Jim's mom would come in from the farm and do her shopping and I would pick her up and bring her home and she'd cook dinner for the family and put the children to bed."

Although she refuses to see herself as a rebel, Marion's quiet insistence on working set her apart from other wives in her town, and her reasons for doing so have a distinctly contemporary ring.

"I didn't really think what I was doing was all that unusual. Most of my friends were staying home with their children, but I can't say anyone was critical about me working, at least not to my face. After all, they'd be playing bridge or playing golf and I wasn't spending any more time at the hospital. I just preferred nursing to bridge or golf. Working may have come more naturally to me because my own mother worked. I thought it was kind of nice for the kids and kind of nice for my mother-in-law, too. And to tell you the truth, I thought it made me a better person to get away from them some and to have other experiences."

Eva Banek was another older wife who went to work part-time when her two children were in school. Eva has strongly traditional views about family and takes great pride in the fact that she never allowed her job to interfere with her duties as a wife and mother.

"My husband was a bookkeeper and accountant and he made a decent living for me and the children. But I had outside family pressures—I had a brother who had returned from the army disabled and needed my financial support and a sick father-in-law, so I found it necessary to supplement my husband's income.

"I got a job as a home demonstrator for the Crossley Washing Machine company. The company would call me and tell me that Mrs. Smith had just been delivered a new washing machine and I was supposed to call her within a week to arrange to give her a demonstration. I made my own appointments between the hours of nine and eleven so that I would be home when my son came home from school. I traveled by bus and subway. I bought myself a little red guide book to the borough of Brooklyn, and taught myself how to get around to all the different neighborhoods. I was paid four dollars per demonstration, but the bus and subway fare was only a nickel or a dime and I had no other expenses. I spent approximately forty-five minutes in each home, so I usually couldn't do more than two homes a day.

"This was a new product, the Crossley washing machine. This was not a luxury item, it was a little upright machine, top-loading, that you could attach directly to your kitchen faucet, so it didn't have to have extensive plumbing. It was on rollers, so you could move it around. It was made for the poorer class of people who lived in apartments. My job was to show them how to attach the rubber hose to the back of the machine and snap it onto the faucet, and then I'd show them how to drain the water into the slop sink.

"I liked the job. Every time I went out on a demonstration I came home with another story about the people, how they lived, the families, the languages they spoke. Many of these homes were black and Hispanic, but I always felt safe. I befriended the children and I always had a little gang of kids around me. If I had to get into a certain building that I wasn't familiar with, these children would show me how to get in and they'd go with me. I had a little satchel with me for my equipment and I always carried some pencils and lollipops for the children. I wanted company in the elevators, you see, that way I felt safe."

Eva stayed at this job until her son started going to school for a full day. She had been a medical secretary before she married, and found a new job working for a doctor not far from her home.

"I worked from 5:30 in the evening to 9:30 in the evening, three days a week. I left my house at twenty after five and my husband came home at twenty to six, so the children were only alone for twenty minutes. I left the dinner cooked and ready, the table set—well, I had all day to do that. I think I made sixty dollars a week—five dollars an hour, it came to. I ran the office, greeted the patients and draped them, cleaned up after them. I also did X rays and blood, and I did the billing. I liked the work because I had a great curiosity—I always wanted to learn and I learned a lot working for this doctor."

Eva admits she probably would have worked even if she hadn't had family members to support—"just to be able to give my children those little extras, like a dancing class for my daughter." But she makes it clear that her willingness to work was contingent on being able to preserve the traditional gender balance in her family.

"I was very careful that there would be no disruption of the services, you might say, the cooking, the cleaning. We had our family evenings together every night. I could have taken a full-time job with the Department of Health with benefits and a better salary. I discussed it with my husband and I told him, if I take on this full-time job, I will be taking away something from you that you have to have. You are the breadwinner and I want you always to be the one who brings in the greater portion of the moneys. I will not take that away from you. To work full-time, I felt I would be taking away his manhood, his feeling of being the head of the household. I never regretted it. We had a good, loving relationship for thirty years."

The phrase "something to fall back on" also presumes that women would never *choose* to go to work. But one of the striking changes that took place during and after the war was the increase in employment among middle-class wives. Although their paychecks may not have been essential to a family's survival, women's earnings provided such "extras" as vacations, second cars, and college educations for the children. Many of these women also worked because they liked to work; in studies of working women at the time, a high proportion mentioned a sense of accomplishment, the stimulation of being with other people, and a degree of economic independence as benefits of their jobs.

Estelle Shuster went to work as a bookkeeper in 1950 when her daughters were eight and twelve. She's a small, elegantly coiffed and put-together widow of seventy. We talk in a quiet corner of the Brooklyn senior citizen center where she's a regular.

"I went to work because I was bored in the house. My husband was a CPA, he was never home, and when he was, it was the nose in his tax papers or the newspaper over the face. My mother thought it was scandalous that I went to work. And Arnie, my husband, said, what you're trying to do is make everyone feel as if I can't earn a living for you. Belittling, that was the word he used, he said I was belittling him by working. I said, I don't care how anyone feels, I have to get out of the house.

"I had a wonderful job. I worked for a big model agency in Manhattan. At the beginning I worked only two days a week, and later I worked four days a week. I never worked five days until after the girls were really out of the house. I took the train up to Fifty-seventh where the office was. When I got on the subway to go to work, it was like traveling into another world. Oh, the shops were beautiful, we had Bergdorf's, Bendel's, Bonwit's, DePinna. The women wore hats and gloves. Another world. At home, it was cooking, cleaning, taking care of the kids, going to PTA, Girl Scouts. But when I got into the office, everything was different, I was different. Well, this was a glamorous office. The girls were magnificent to look at, everyone was beautifully dressed. Very interesting people.

"I was making twenty-five dollars a day and it made me feel good. I had a reason to get up and get dressed in the morning. I had to go to the beauty parlor once a week. I managed the office. I handled the moneys, making out the checks for the models, making deposits, keeping the books. We'd go to the fashion shows, and to conventions where they used the models.

"Even the days when I was home, it wasn't so tedious because I had a release, an escape valve the other days. I had something to look forward to.

"I would come home by 4:30. The girls would come home at about three, and we lived in an apartment building so they would go to one of my neighbors' apartments or to a girlfriend's apartment in the building for an hour or so. We were a close-knit group in our building. Safety was the key. You never worried about them because everything was safe in those days. Most of my neighbors did not go to business, they stayed home, but they never said anything to me. After a couple of years, some of my neighbors started to go back to work as well.

"My mother never let up, she was constantly telling me that my children would be ruined. But after a while, I saw that Arnie started to be proud of me. He was proud of my accomplishments—the fact that I was able to run the household and raise my girls and still work. Now don't get me wrong, he didn't go around telling the world, 'My wife works.' I don't think he ever told his friends or business associates. He didn't advertise it, you know. But he couldn't really keep it a secret—if we went to a family function, what would I talk about? My job."

Interestingly, Estelle did not use her income for household expenses or even for family extras.

"The money I earned was for me, for savings, for independence. Anyway, Arnie was supporting us fine and it was important to him to pay for my clothes and the girls' camp. I spent my money on vacations, which my husband refused to go on. He just hated to travel. So I went with my mother or a girlfriend. And I did something else," she adds with a sly smile. "One of the models had a friend who was working down on Wall Street and every once in a while she would give me a tip and I would invest. So I made a little money that way over the years. I played the market. That was my little pleasure. It gave me a feeling of independence, that even though my husband was, strictly speaking, supporting me, I had this ace up my sleeve."

Work was a choice for white middle-class women like Estelle Shuster and Marion Klinger. For most black women, work was a central fact of life. In 1950, 57 percent of black women had jobs outside the home, compared to 37 percent of white women. And 42 percent of black women in 1950 were employed as domestics. Louise Daniels, who is now 60, began a lifetime of work at the age of 13. We talk in the living room of her tiny frame house on the north side of Kansas City, where she is continually interrupted by the seven children she is raising. They include nieces and nephews, adopted and foster children. Louise grew up in rural Arkansas. Her own mother was a domestic worker; her father worked at a laundry and had a small subsistence farm.

"I went to school up to tenth grade and I came out of school when I was about thirteen. I left home because I wanted to venture out on my own as a young girl. I wanted to see some other parts of the world and I wanted to see if I could make it on my own out there. I went on the bus down to Texas to work for a young white family and I stayed with them for a year and five months. I took care of their kids. They had a big farm out there, where people were chopping cotton. I was making about thirty-five dollars a week, and I had my room and board, so I saved my little money. And then I got tired and I came back home—that was about 1949. When I came home I had about five hundred to six hundred dollars that I had saved. I felt like I did real good on my own. I took that money and I bought some things I didn't have—you know, I wanted to live decent."

When she was fifteen, Louise decided she wanted to get married. "You know, as a young girl you heard everyone else talking about husbands, and so you wanted to try it yourself. So I went to a little town about fifteen miles from home and stayed with my auntie. This was where I met my first husband. I was working for another family, cleaning their house. They wasn't paying as much money as Texas—you weren't making no more than six dollars a week."

Louise's marriage lasted only a year because her husband

became violent. After he knocked her down when she was pregnant, causing a miscarriage, Louise's father stepped in and had
the marriage annulled.

"After that marriage was over I went with my sister and my
cousin to Ohio to pick tomatoes and do a little bit of everything. My cousin had a truck and we would make a kind of
motorcade and go around and say to people, we're on our way
to Ohio, you want to go and make some money? And people
would just jump aboard and they would join us. We made good
money there. That was when you started making good money,
around in 1950, '51. 'Course you had to work hard for that
money. I picked tomatoes and I picked cotton and I did it also
for the experience, me being young, I wanted to try everything.
I knew I had left school at an early age and I thought I had that
mother wit to be able to make it. I was determined that I would
go through all walks of life and meet all kinds of people and live
a good life, see how other people lived.

"We were living in these little plantation houses, shotgun
houses, we called them. You had a place for a bed and a little
kitchen and a bathroom. I did that for six months and I got
homesick so we came back to Arkansas. I stayed home about a
year, living with my folks and doing daywork and back to making six dollars a week.

"Then I decided to go to Hot Springs and I got me a job
working at this café, the Hollywood Capri, as a cook. By this
time I'd learned to cook pretty good. I'd go in at 6:30 in the
morning and I'd get off at 1:30 and then went back on at 2:30
and work till closing time. I was making about sixty dollars a
week, which was a pretty good salary and I was living in an
apartment. I had a bedroom and a living room and a kitchen,
but I had to share a bath with other people. I loved the work—I
love cooking, I love housecleaning."

In 1954, Louise went to visit her sister who was living in
Kansas City, Missouri, and liked it so much she decided to stay.

"My sister was doing daywork at the time for the family of this lawyer. She had taken sick and found out she had a tubeless pregnancy, so she had to stop working, and to keep her from losing her job, she asked me to take her place.

"Now this woman didn't want me to work but two hours a day, but she wanted me to do everything in two hours. And I tried to do it. And one day, I had just finished work and was walking down the street and this Italian woman called me: 'Hey, little colored girl'—you know, I was twenty years old—'hey, would you come to the fence?' And I said, 'Are you talking to me?' I looked around and I didn't see any little colored girl. So I walked up to the fence and this woman asked me would I like to work for her the rest of the day. And she had four sisters who wanted someone to work, too. I wasn't making any more than $3.00 a day, and I had to pay my carfare out of that. So when this lady told me she would give me $6.50 a day and carfare included, I jumped at the chance. That was good money.

"Those Italian ladies, I liked them, but they was always trying to get a little more work out of me. 'Louise, wouldn't you do this little ironing for me?' I'd say, 'No, ma'am, you want ironing, you can pay me extra.' And they was always pulling on me to tell about the other sister. But I never would do that, I knew better. I worked Monday, Tuesday, Wednesday, and Thursday for those four sisters from 1954 to 1971. Then I decided I was tired of daywork."

Louise continued to work at a staggering array of jobs including bakery worker, waitress, and factory worker. In her late forties, she went to work as an attendant in a nursing home, where she remained until she retired two years ago. She supports herself and her large household mainly on her Social Security, augmented by contributions from relatives. Louise seems to relish her years of work and gets a particular kick out of the range of jobs she has had.

"I always liked to work and try all kinds of different things. I didn't want to get in a rut. But I stayed on that nursing home job because I was getting ready to settle down and I liked the old ladies."

For young white women, one of the few jobs around that offered glamour, adventure, and travel was that of airline stewardess. Carla Vincent was lucky enough to land one of these highly sought-after jobs. In her Italian immigrant family, only her brothers were expected to go to college. In 1949, at twenty-one, Carla was working as a secretary in her home town of Omaha, Nebraska, and engaged to a man eight years older than she—kind, financially secure, and slightly boring.

"One day I saw an ad for an airline school in Minneapolis and I decided on the spot that I wanted to be a stewardess. I loved the idea of flying, and I loved the idea of getting far, far away. I was supposed to be getting married, but I kept putting this man off. Jerry, my fiancé, was a good person, really a wonderful man, but he was always telling me I wouldn't be able to do this or that after we were married. Great! I had to get away from this overprotected life, it was driving me crazy. Also, I had this great desire to serve people, that was the part of me that wanted to be a nurse. But I also had a desire to be independent and to see the world."

Carla went to Minneapolis, to the McConnell school for stewardesses.

"The course took six weeks and it was a lot of fun. We lived in this beautiful old mansion and went to school on the bus, from nine to five. There were thirty girls in the class, all in our twenties, from all over the country, all with different personalities. Like sisters, which I never had. You learned about airplanes, about altitudes, about serving people. The emphasis was on charming the passenger. You learned to walk with a book on your head—one book one day, two books the next. We learned makeup and how to do our hair. We all looked pretty much alike, we all had exactly the same makeup and the same hair-cut."

Carla digs out a recruiting ad with a photo of eight smiling, nearly identical-looking stewardesses, captioned: "The dream of every young man is to marry an airline stewardess!"

"When Jerry took me to the airport, he told me, whenever you're ready to come home, you just call me and I'll come and get you. Well, he didn't get a call and after a few weeks he came up to Minneapolis to see me and tried to get me to come home. I told him no soap. I was having a ball."

Toward the end of the course, the McConnell students were interviewed by representatives from the airlines.

"After my interview, which went very well, this interviewer, who was a woman, took me over to the window to look at the roots of my hair to see if I was dyeing. Then she asked me to lift my skirt so she could see my legs. I didn't like that. Plenty of the girls didn't get hired because they had bad legs, or bad complexions—if you had a hair problem of any kind, a weight problem, you wouldn't get the job. You were supposed to be natural. They were also looking to weed out the troublemakers. They didn't want girls who were too arrogant or too rebellious. You had to be willing to serve."

Carla was one of only ten girls hired by TWA, considered the most desirable airline to work for in those days, and went to Kansas City for flight training.

"Flight training was wonderful—I was with my friends from McConnell. You stayed in a hotel and went to training school every day for three weeks. Then you had three choices about where you wanted to be based. I wanted to go as far away as I could, so I put down Los Angeles first, then New York, then Chicago. I got my first choice, so six of us went out to LA. Boy, that was a trip I'll never forget! They put us on a DC-3 and it took us twenty-four hours to get from KC to LA with ten stops! Well, we were in pig heaven, we just thought it was marvelous.

We got off at every stop like immigrants, looking around the airports—Albuquerque, Santa Fe, finally we got to California and we were so excited to see palm trees.

"The six of us rented a house together out there. The pilots called us the 'sexy six.' They always looked at you in a sexual way. You know, you'd walk into the cockpit on your first day and they'd say, 'This is a test to find out if you're a virgin,' and they'd have a gyro and they'd make it spin, and then they'd say, 'Aha, you're not a virgin.'

"After a very short time, I started to find it all not so glamorous. We were at the bottom of the totem pole seniority-wise, so we pulled the worst flights. You were up and down, making all these stops, and you were always *in* the weather, never above it. Plus I was lonesome. My first assignment was Amarillo, Texas. I'd get up at six in the morning and get there at six in the evening and there'd be eight stops in between. My first time on that run I thought, well, I've got three days in Amarillo and I've got the captain and the first officer—they'll take care of me. It never occurred to me that I should set out and investigate the city myself. Anyway, we get to Amarillo, we're in a taxi going into town to the hotel and I'm thinking about all the fun we're going to have, and these guys say, 'Well, so long, kid, see you in three days, have fun.'

"That was a low ebb. I couldn't call home—my mother would have said, I told you so. Jerry would have said, I'll come right out and we'll get married. I called the hotel operator, practically in tears—I had to talk to *someone*—and she said, 'Oh, I saw you come in. Come on down here and I'll show you how to run the switchboard.' So I went down there and we became fast friends and she even introduced me to a nice guy, a radio announcer, who took me out around Amarillo and treated me very gentlemanly. So that was my Amarillo adventure.

"I was pretty disillusioned. After three months, I went to my supervisor and told her I wanted to quit. I think the emotional stress of separating from my mother and Jerry and starting this new life was beginning to get to me. Jerry would come out and visit me and he started to look pretty good. My friends were beginning to get married—some married pilots, some married men they met on flights. But my supervisor persuaded me to stay because she told me four-engine airplanes were coming in in a couple of months and I should hang in there because the flights would be smoother and there wouldn't be so many stops. She was right. As soon as we got the bigger planes I was transferred to the LA–Chicago flight—eight hours, nonstop. I did that route for years.

"The airline owned you. We got paid two hundred dollars a month and our uniforms came out of that. Of course, you could live on that, more or less, at the time. They were counting on your working for the glamour. And they had a quick turnover because girls kept leaving to get married—the average amount of time that girls stayed on the job was two to three years. They had all kinds of rules: if you got married you had to quit (and God forbid you got pregnant); you had to retire when you turned thirty-five. We just accepted this. We signed a contract. It never occurred to us to protest. Of course, we assumed we wouldn't want to work after we were married anyway, and we certainly wouldn't want to *fly* after we were thirty-five. Thirty-five, you were *old*. Of course girls were cheating about the marriage and even about having babies. They said they had hepatitis or some obscure disease and they brought in a note from their doctor.

"After we got organized and formed the union, people didn't quit so early. We fought the marriage rule and a lot of other rules about weight and age. But that wasn't until the early sixties.

"There were no rules against dating passengers. I wouldn't say it was exactly encouraged, but it wasn't discouraged either. The idea was never to have to buy your own dinner. Find a husband, that was the name of the game. That was why most of them joined. But I never wanted to get trapped like my mother. I saw that she never bloomed until my father died.

"In 1960, my friend Carol and I decided, we've gotta think bigger than Chicago–LA, we've gotta get to Europe. So I started flying international—I went to Italy, to Rome, and it was wonderful. I really loved my work. I loved getting up on that airplane, up over the clouds."

Carla was unusual in that she didn't marry until she was in her thirties. As she points out, most stewardesses stayed on the job about two years. In a 1958 cover story on stewardesses, ("Glamor Girls of the Air") *Life* explained: "The girls do not quit because their jobs pall on them but because, being so attractive, they soon get proposals of marriage. Sometimes their husbands are pilots or passengers. But mostly they marry men they knew back home." The fact that the airlines did not allow married stewardesses was not mentioned.

Maria O'Connor went back to work when her daughter was three because her husband couldn't provide for the family. Maria came to the United States from Italy as a war bride in 1945. At sixty-seven, she still radiates the fiery sexiness that made her friends nickname her "Sophia."

"I started work as soon as I got here, working as a nurse's aide in Bushwick Hospital in Brooklyn. It isn't there anymore, now it's a nursing home. I worked there for a couple of years and then my daughter was born in 1948. I took three years off, but then we needed money, so I went back to work. I didn't think much about working. It was just something I had to do. See, my husband had a gambling problem. He worked as a cab driver, but he wasn't reliable and money just slipped through his fingers. My sister-in-law lived in the same building, so I got a night job and she would watch the baby. I worked from eleven to seven. I'd come home by 7:30, feed the baby, clean her, clean the house. If it was a nice day, I'd take the baby out for a while. When she went down for her nap, I slept. That was my second job.

"When my daughter was six we moved and I took a job as a meat wrapper at Waldbaum's supermarket. I worked there thirteen years, full time. I was making about $125 clear, but that included overtime. My daughter used to come to the store right from school, the older girls would bring her, and stay with me until I was ready to go home at five. Or sometimes she'd go to one of my girlfriends in the building. Years ago you could be more safe.

"I had a couple of girlfriends whose husbands were doing well—one was an engineer, one worked in nightclubs—and they used to let me clean their houses. I wasn't proud. I really needed the money. That meant I could buy clothes for my daughter for school. Also, I had one Saturday a month off and on that Saturday, I used to take care of this older lady's house, clean and everything.

"At work, everybody was always making a remark, or touching you. Now they call it harassment. We had a lot of harassment from the supervisors, the managers. One time I bent down to pick something up and the manager put his hand on me. You know, you couldn't wear pants in those days, you had to wear a uniform, a dress. I was so mad, I had a cup of coffee in my hand and I threw it. The man ducked and the cup hit another young guy, but I didn't care, I yelled at him, 'You just keep your goddamn hands off me.' He says, 'If you don't like it, work somewhere else.' So he fired me.

"I took it to union for arbitration—that was the Amalgamated Meatcutters, Local 324. But this guy swore almighty God he didn't do it. And the girl that worked with me, she saw the whole thing, but she said, I didn't see anything. The union said he had to take me back, but I said, take your job. That was when I left Waldbaum's and went to work at a kosher butcher.

"Those years it was tough to be a woman on the job. If you didn't want to go out with them, they'd say you were a tramp, you were no good. Some of the girls, they'd feel like they had to go out with them. Now you sue them if they harass you. When I started out working at Waldbaum's, they used to say, come on, Maria, we have to go upstairs and get something from the storeroom. And then, moron that I was, I would go up there and next thing I know he's got me crushed up against the wall. So I say, stop it, take your hands off me and he says, oh, you can go work at the other store. Spiteful. You know, he was going to transfer me because I wouldn't let him get near me. So then I had to go to work at another Waldbaum's that was further away and I had to take the bus back and forth. Some of the girls never said anything because, you know, you need the job and you're afraid to make trouble. Then I would go home and my husband would start in on me about the guys at work. I'd say to him, 'If I leave the store at six and I'm home at twenty after six, when am I gonna have an affair?'"

Maria's story is a good illustration of the kind of harassment that used to be—and to some extent still is—a routine part of many women's working lives. Maria herself had a strong enough sense of her own bodily integrity to fight off unwanted advances. But, as she said, "Bottom line, you had to keep the job. I never minded the work itself. I just hated what you had to put up with as a woman where you worked."

Chapter VIII

Swimming Upstream

I'll never forget my father's response when I told
him I wanted to be a lawyer. He said, "If you do
this, no man will ever want you."
— CASSANDRA DUNN, 62

What do you want a law degree for? You have chil-
dren.
— A NEW YORK UNIVERSITY LAW SCHOOL ADMISSIONS
OFFICER TO A FEMALE APPLICANT IN THE 1950s

I don't think the ladies in the town accepted the fact
that I worked. That was the point at which I said to
myself, well, you're always going to be out of step
and you might as well face it.
— ELLEN RODGERS, 63, A CIVIL ENGINEER

Among the women I interviewed, a handful stood apart
from the rest—those who successfully entered male-dominated professions. It was unusual enough to find a woman
who had even a hazy idea of something she wanted to do by the
end of college; rarer still to find a woman whose desire for a
career or profession didn't wither for lack of encouragement, or
dissolve under the pressure to marry. But the women in this
group conceived a desire early on to be something other than

wives and mothers, and they were not deflected by marriage and family.

The fields they chose—medicine, law, engineering, and science—demanded a particular kind of drive and persistence precisely because these professions were hostile to women. A woman who tried to enter them was violating more than one taboo: not only was she insisting on an identity outside her role as wife and mother, but she was often refusing to stay within the physical bounds of home because these professions demanded her to be out in the world. She was also challenging prevailing ideas that women were innately unsuited to certain kinds of work. Such ideas gained currency in the fifties despite the fact that during the previous decade, women had shown themselves capable of handling a startling range of "unfeminine" jobs, from welder to lumberjack. But in the wake of the war, the need to make room in the work force for the flood of returning veterans dovetailed with an ideology that said women were better suited by nature and biology to the traditional work of homemaking and child rearing.

Why was the desire for this separate identity so strong in some women that they couldn't give it up—even in the face of institutional and cultural opposition? What was it in them, or in their circumstances, that didn't allow them to be distracted?

My sample is too small to be statistically meaningful, but the patterns that emerged are telling nevertheless. Three out of five came from families that instilled in them an expectation of independence and accomplishment, and in four out of five cases, the women strongly identified with their fathers. All but one had husbands who supported and encouraged their professional identities. The one woman who never married believes she succeeded only because she was unencumbered by husband and family.

Faith Merrill is a professor of pediatrics at a large university hospital in New Mexico. She's a tall woman of sixty-one, lean and flinty-looking. Her desire to become a doctor flourished without interference because of her family's geographical isolation.

"I'd known I wanted to be a doctor from childhood. My grandfather, who lived with us and whom I adored, was ill a good bit and I was concerned about his medical care and his longevity. We lived in southeastern New Mexico on an isolated ranch. I was also the only child in a family of adults—until I was ten, when my sister was born. And in that tiny town, the doctor was a woman who'd been there since 1937. I had women in my family who were educated and who had careers, so I grew up without ever having the idea that there were things women couldn't do. It was a tacit assumption that I would be a doctor—just as it was a tacit assumption that I would marry."

Following in her mentor's footsteps, Faith went to the University of Michigan for premed. In her sophomore year, she fell in love.

"I decided maybe I didn't want to be a doctor after all. I thought if I married this guy I wouldn't go on to medical school. I don't really know where this idea came from. I guess I didn't know any medical students at that time, so I didn't know if you could be married and be a medical student at the same time. I *did* know that medical school was going to be hard work, and suddenly I wasn't sure I wanted to do that. Suddenly it seemed more appealing to *not* work so hard and to have a different kind of life."

This was a moment I had heard described in so many interviews: the sudden wavering, the loss of conviction, the inability to remember exactly what it was you had wanted so badly or why. In the fifties, most women saw only two roads ahead of them: one lonely, difficult, and uncertain; the other, comfortable, predictable, and smoothed by loving companionship.

In Faith's case, two events converged to put her back on track. The man graduated and went to Europe, and at the same time Faith's mother became ill and she transferred to the University of New Mexico to be near home. The romance fell apart, presumably under the strain of separation. By the time she met her husband-to-be in her senior year, Faith had already been accepted at medical school, and her determination to become a doctor had reasserted itself more strongly than ever.

"Charlie was a hundred percent for my going on to medical school—and a good thing, because if he hadn't wanted me to go, I probably would have told him to forget it! At that point, with two more years invested, medical school was no longer an abstraction. I was determined to do this now. I think, in fact, that one of the things I liked—still like—about Charlie was that he was so supportive of my career. Of course, I did a lot of the housewifely things in addition to medical school and practicing medicine: laundry, cooked dinner, etc. But one of the reasons I don't feel furious and bitter about that stuff is that he helped me to do what I wanted to do."

Because the University of New Mexico had no medical school at the time, Faith went to the University of Colorado. In an unusual move for that time, her husband followed her to Denver where he worked as an insurance adjuster to support them both.

At the University of Colorado Medical School, Faith was one of eight or ten women of her class of eighty—an unusually high percentage. Sociological journals of the time commonly referred to the "traditional 5 percent quota on women [medical] students."

"In those days you did rotating internships and my first was in surgery, where women were in a very small minority. I didn't feel any particular discrimination, except that I thought I should have gotten an A in surgery and I didn't, and some of the men I worked with who weren't as good as I was did get A's."

Faith dropped out of the surgery program when she became pregnant. "I was going to go right back and finish after the birth, but I hadn't counted on . . . well, the 'maternal instinct.' When I saw this baby, there was no way I could go back to being exhausted all the time and not having any time for my baby. So I dropped out of the program and did some general practice with a fellow I'd interned with—one day a week."

Once again, Faith was at a point at which many women abandoned their career plans permanently. She stayed home for two years, had another baby, and tried to concentrate on raising her children.

"I was never very interested in being a perfect little housewife—cleaning a house is my idea of nothing to do. I wasn't exactly bored, maybe a little restless. I remember dragging my kids around a lot—around town, around New Mexico, on trips. I was the only one of my friends and neighbors who had something else I'd put on hold, something else I intended to get back to."

When her second child was three months old, a job opened up in the pediatrics department of a nearby hospital.

"Pediatrics had never entered my mind—it had not been well taught in my medical school and I didn't like it. However, when I was doing general practice and I'd come home at night and think about what I'd done during the day, what I really enjoyed was pediatrics. So I thought this job might be fun to try. And it turned out to be great fun. By this time I'd hired a woman who came to my house every day and ended up being with me for twenty-four years. That made all the difference. No matter how helpful my husband was willing to be, and he was very helpful, if I hadn't had the security of knowing I had this surrogate at home, I couldn't have done what I did."

Faith had extraordinary advantages: a family tradition of professional women, an early role model for the work she wanted to do, a supportive husband, and the financial resources to provide reliable care for her children. Still, she feels she constructed her career in what she thinks of now as a "female" way.

"I tried to do everything for everybody, so I became quite diffuse, rather than focusing on one area, which is the way you build renown in a career. I did things like going to clinics and working on the ward and, oh God, working on committees, instead of focusing on research, or developing a strong bibliography."

It's possible that what Faith calls her "diffusion" made her a more compassionate physician than her colleagues who were concentrating on building their reputations through academic achievement. Nevertheless, Faith maintains her approach made her "the persistent number two person in her department." Faith also acknowledges the costs of pursuing her career with a wry self-acceptance.

"I might have spent more time at home with my children," she reflects, then laughs and adds, "though I might have driven them bonkers if I had, because I was a restless, bossy, and controlling mother. So that might not have been good for them either. I used to tell my kids, 'You think I'm ornery, but you have to know that if I were not ornery I would be sitting in southeastern New Mexico on a near-bankrupt ranch hating some cowboy for trapping me in this awful life.'"

For Sylvia Beckman, also a physician, the idea of a profession came first, an early and intense reaction against her mother's life. Sylvia is an ophthalmologist who practices and teaches in the San Francisco Bay area. We talked in an empty classroom at a school for the blind where she donates time every week. A heavy, rounded woman in a silk print dress, Sylvia communicates a subtle warmth that is almost maternal. In fact, she has no children and has never married.

"The way I saw things, my mother was a slave to the house. She was always in the house, always cleaning or shopping or separating us from fighting, and it just didn't seem like a glamorous life. I'd go to the movies every Saturday and I loved those strong movie women, like Roz Russell and Joan Crawford. I wanted to be a pilot *and* a doctor. My mother's idea of a career was from the 'Perry Mason' show: she wanted me to become a legal stenographer. And she wanted me to get married and have children. She kept telling me how rewarding it was to have a family, and I would always say, 'I don't want any children.' I just never pictured myself as a mother."

Sylvia's family lived on Long Island, New York, and her father worked in the garment trade. He left early in the morning, came home late, worked hard. Sylvia's time with him came on weekends. "I used to go fishing with him on the pier or ice-skating on local ponds. I always thought the ideal thing would be to have a companion like my father for a husband—a friend you could do things with, but he wouldn't want any children."

Sylvia applied to and was accepted by Adelphi University. Although she already thought she wanted to be a doctor, when she went for her college interview, accompanied by her mother, she found herself in the office of the dean of nursing.

"My mother's notion was, 'You don't know anything about being a doctor. Become a nurse first and then if you like it, become a doctor.' This dean said to me, 'Well, what do you want to be, a doctor or a nurse?' What came out of my mouth was, 'I want to be a nurse.' To this day I'm not sure why. In a way I was trying to be practical. We didn't have that much money and I thought I could pay for medical school with a profession. You know, what women earned in those days was pathetic. One of my classmates worked in a bank and made two hundred to three hundred dollars a month. I had no artistic talent and I didn't like teaching, that was the other women's profession. What else was there? And then, I thought, what if I couldn't get accepted into medical school?"

For the first two years, the nursing and medical courses were pretty much the same. The last two years were spent at the hospital and "by then everyone around me was planning their weddings and knitting argyle socks. I thought they were selling themselves into slavery. I was trying to figure out how my courses could be applicable to premed."

But part of Sylvia was still holding back, trying to talk herself out of medical school. Perhaps a shadow of her mother's influence, perhaps because she knew how difficult that choice would be. "There was a time at the end when I thought, well, maybe I could do something in nursing. I knew I didn't want to be a bedside nurse, but I thought maybe I could get my doctorate and teach. At Adelphi, they offered a higher degree in nursing and I went and sat in one of the classes and I thought, this is ridiculous! It wasn't even challenging. So I went to the dean of the psychology department, and he said, 'Well, do you want to be a psychologist or do you want to be a medical doctor?' And I said, 'I want to be a medical doctor.' And he said, 'Well, go to the dean of the med school, for goodness sake, and she'll register you.' So I went and signed up for the courses I needed for med school." It took Sylvia four years working as a nurse to save enough money to put herself through medical school.

Sylvia applied to every medical school within a reasonable distance from her home and none would accept her. She remembers vividly her interview at Albany Medical School. "I'd traveled all day to get there, and I was anxious and it was a rigorous interview. At the end of the interview, that man said to me, 'You know, I don't know if I could ever recommend accepting a woman here. She'd have to be better than the best man . . . and even then, I'm not sure.' This was in 1957. You don't forget things like that." Sylvia was eventually accepted at the Women's Medical College of Pennsylvania.

"Of course, all this time my mother was hocking me to get married. She told me that the more education I got the harder it would be for me to get married. I did date a little, but since I was always either in school or working, I didn't have much time. One fellow I was dating in medical school, he was a veterinarian and he wanted to get married. I said, but you're going to be moving to Minneapolis, and he said, oh, you can quit and I'll take care of you. I said, 'Go.'"

Sylvia decided she wanted a residency in ophthalmology, which was difficult to get even if you were a man. When she got no response to her applications to various programs, her ophthalmology professor arranged for her to meet with one of the chiefs at Wills Eye Hospital in Philadelphia.

"We sat on a bench in the middle of the lobby there—I remember it looked like a train station—and he said, 'Do you plan to get pregnant or married?' I promised him I wouldn't do either. I felt like I was about ten years old. They gave me a year's trial in the research department and after that I could get a residency. Most people there, the men, had a three-year residency, but I had a four-year residency. I was only the second woman they'd ever accepted, and I was the only woman out of twenty men.

"I had a fellowship, so when I was finished with my work I'd have to go over to see how my research projects were coming along. I never, never goofed off. These guys were watching me all the time and complaining that I wasn't doing my work. It was hard enough to be a first-year resident, where you're the bottom person who gets kicked by everybody. I had no friends. My fellow physicians were constantly telling me I should switch to obstetrics or pediatrics, I should be home having babies, that a man could earn a wonderful living for his family in my place. Finally I was at my wits' end and I called my old ophthalmology professor and told him I didn't know if I could psychologically take this for another two and a half years. He said, 'You know, if you give up now I'll never be able to get another woman in there.' So I went on."

Even a young woman with Sylvia's determination to define herself through work was conflicted about pushing herself forward past nursing, the acceptable career, to medicine. Despite her contempt for her mother's life, her mother's values were almost powerful enough to derail her. In the end, her desire, combined with the timely encouragement of a mentor, helped keep her on course. Sylvia believes she could not have done what she did if she'd been married. Certainly it was the rare man—then or now—who could offer the wholehearted support Faith Merrill received from her husband.

Ellen Rodgers is an architectural engineer in Kansas City. Tall and rangy, her sandy hair unstreaked by gray, she looks much younger than the fifty-eight she claims to be. Ellen's demeanor is soft-spoken and diffident, but as she talks about her struggle to become an engineer, a steely determination emerges. When she was in seventh grade, Ellen's father, who was a civil engineer, brought home plans he was doing for a swimming pool for the local Boy Scout camp.

"At about the same time I happened to pick up a book about the Panama Canal. Watching what Daddy was doing, and reading that book—well, I just decided, by golly, I was going to be an engineer. I really wanted to build things. I told my father, who just said, well, if that's what you want to do. . . . He never really encouraged me. We were not really that close—he worked hard and he was gone a lot. But I had watched him and gone out with him when he measured. I think he was surprised when I came up with this idea. Mother was a little bit uncomfortable, but she didn't ever say anything."

In high school, Ellen took drafting and found herself the only girl in the class—an experience that would become familiar.

"I guess I got a taste of what it was going to be like if I wanted to go ahead. In the first place, you had to grit your teeth just to walk into that room, knowing that you stuck out like a sore thumb. I was shy anyway, so that was real hard. There were three groups of boys: those that ignored you, those that made nasty remarks, and then there were a few you could be friends with. I did learn to quit mouthing off a bit—that made it a little easier. But I also developed some friendships with boys I helped to get through school."

With the help of a Phillips Petroleum Scholarship, which she was eligible for because her father worked for the company, Ellen was able to attend Kansas State University.

"It was 120 miles from home and without the scholarship I doubt my parents could have handled my books and spending money as well as room and board."

At Kansas State, Ellen made a series of strategic decisions calculated to get her what she needed. She recognized immediately that because there were no women in most of her classes, the only way to have female friends was to join a sorority. She chose a sorority that had two or three architecture and landscape design students. She also sought out the handful of senior women in architectural engineering, one of whom was there on the GI bill.

"This group may have broken some ice for me. At least they were able to give me some advice, some feedback. For example, no one told you you had to make up for ROTC. All the boys had to do ROTC because this was a land grant college. If you were a woman in engineering, you had to make up eight hours in your sophomore and junior year. In all the other schools, girls just graduated with fewer credits than the boys. But in engineering, you were part of the group—but, of course, they wouldn't *take* you in ROTC because you were a girl! They were trying to discourage girls from taking the engineering courses. These older girls warned me about this so that I didn't get stuck in my senior year without those credits." Ellen also had to figure out how to gain access to the kinds of resources that have traditionally smoothed the academic path for men. "The guys could study together but I had to be back in the sorority house by ten o'clock. And we didn't have any engineering files in our house. You know, in fraternity and sorority houses, there were always files on various courses that you could review—old test papers and outlines. I didn't have any of that, of course. So I did cultivate some male friends in order to get input and to have people to study with."

Spending so much time as the only woman among men exposed Ellen to hostility from female students who were often dating her male classmates. "I was a smart, good-looking girl, so I guess they couldn't imagine why I was in those classes unless it was to get guys."

Although Ellen's strategy in most things was nonconfrontational, she did insist on wearing blue jeans to her surveying classes, in defiance of campus regulations against women wearing pants. This was a purely defensive measure.

"It was hell surveying on the campus. There was always somebody deliberately standing in front of your transit, or coming up and making smart remarks. Wearing a skirt would have just made it worse." Generally, however, Ellen tried to keep a low profile. "I found out at college that you could do a lot of things if you didn't make waves."

Ellen seems to have escaped the kind of crisis that threw many of her contemporaries off the track. For one thing, she was fortunate in finding a husband who supported her career goals. (Not that this was all luck. We can assume that, like Faith Merrill, she *chose* her husband for his ability to accept her as an engineer.) Timing was crucial as well. Ellen and Brian met and became engaged during her freshman year, but he went into the armed services for several years, while she finished college. This freed Ellen to concentrate on her work without distraction, while at the same time providing her with the social security of an engagement. "A lot of the girls thought I was nuts to be working so hard. Some of them were there looking for husbands, and they dropped out to get married. I had it made, in a way, because I was already engaged."

Ellen and Brian married when he returned and spent their

senior year at college together. During that year Ellen became pregnant and had a miscarriage. "I hadn't planned to have kids for a while and I was thrilled to find out that Brian didn't want them right away either. If I had thought we were looking at kids right at the beginning, I probably wouldn't have gotten married. So we were using birth control. Still, when I had the miscarriage I found I was terribly disappointed. I found out that miscarriages are . . . unsettling. We tried to have kids after that, but, truth to tell, I was kind of relieved we didn't. It didn't really bother me until I was almost thirty."

While Brian continued his pre-dental, Ellen looked for a job. "I went down to General Motors because they were advertising, and they said flat out, we don't hire women engineers. A lot of places didn't actually say it, but I got the message."

Through the good offices of a friend, Ellen eventually found drafting work at a bridge-building firm. She did well there and, as she moved up in the firm, her work became more complicated and challenging. When Brian was offered a dental practice in another town, Ellen left her job. This was the only time during our interview when Ellen faltered a little and seemed to express some regrets.

"That was probably the one thing . . . he was still looked at as the main breadwinner in the family—by me, and I don't know why. So I just went along with it. But I would have liked to have stayed."

By an accident of geography, the town to which Ellen and Brian relocated in 1957 turned out to be a kind of engineering hub, and Ellen easily landed a job in a small engineering firm.

"They didn't have any trouble with the fact that I was a woman—well, they were real busy and you were a warm body and they needed you—especially if you had some kind of training. This was a town of about twenty thousand and it was the jumping-off point to really western Kansas, so we did municipal work for all the little towns out there. Little bitty towns like

Leota, which was clear out almost to Colorado. They were putting in water systems, sewer systems, drainage ditches, that sort of thing. In the two years we were there I did miles and miles of powerlines."

"I don't think the ladies in the town accepted the fact that I worked. That was the point at which I said to myself, well, you're always going to be out of step and you might as well face it."

Ellen and Brian eventually settled in Kansas City, where she went to work for a firm that valued her, and carved out a successful engineering career for herself. She had her first and only child, a daughter, in 1961, when she was thirty.

Ellen was extremely fortunate to be one of the tiny minority of women in her field. The number of women in engineering, always minuscule, actually declined between 1950 and 1960, and in her specialty, civil engineering, the percentage of women dropped from 1.6 in 1950 to 0.6 in 1960. Ellen's success in negotiating her career undoubtedly owes a great deal to her style, which is easy-going and direct, but low-key. She says she learned from watching a woman colleague who "seemed to be able to blend in and not cause a lot of problems and still do what she wanted. She taught me never to come on with any kind of a sexual attitude. You know, from the handful of women I knew who were working in this field, I'd hear all these horrendous stories about fellows hitting on them. Men just didn't hit on me, whether it was because I stood five-foot-eight in my stocking feet and was a rather cool person to begin with, or what. And maybe the fact that I was happy in my marriage, it was easier to maintain a kind of neutral, friendly aspect." Nevertheless, she admits, without the steel under the velvet, she couldn't have done it.

"Every time I'd have to call vendors, for example, to get information about their products, I would have to start very aggressively right at the beginning by stating that I was an *engi-*

neer with this firm and I needed information. Because otherwise
I invariably got fobbed off because they assumed I was a secretary, or a housewife wanting information on some product. You
know," she sighs, "you can never completely let down—you
always have to have that little extra consciousness."

Cheryl Wolfe grew up in a family in which achievement was
both expected and encouraged. We talk in an empty conference
room in the prestigious Washington, D.C., law firm in which
she is the only black female attorney. A handsome, light-skinned
woman of sixty-six, Cheryl was born in Washington, the eldest
of two daughters of middle-class parents. Her father was an
insurance agent, her mother a teacher.

"They were both college graduates, so education was
paramount. My sister and I grew up knowing we were going to
go to college, that was just in our milieu. I had an expectation, I
think, that I would marry someone who could support me, but
I also assumed I would have some kind of profession that would
support me. I can remember my mother saying when I was a
teenager, I hope you'll never have to work if you don't want to,
but you should always be in a position where the choice is
yours, not somebody else's. So that you never have to stay in a
marriage because it's the only way you're going to eat."

Cheryl went to a prestigious, segregated high school in D.C.
called Dunbar. "This was a school that had only one aim in life:
to make its kids think that they could do anything, and to get
them into the best colleges in the country. In a way, we were
the beneficiaries of segregation because our teachers—primarily
women, but some men as well—were people who, twenty-five
years later would not have been teaching school, they'd be
working in corporations or something. So we got all these
teachers who were highly educated, and very highly motivated.
Out of my class of forty, we had kids going to all the major Ivy
League colleges—girls as well as boys."

Cheryl attended Wellesley in the late forties, where she was one of three black students in her class of roughly three hundred.

"They said there were no quotas, but there were never more than three black students the whole time I was there, so that struck me as pretty coincidental. Twenty-five years later when I went back, there were over one hundred black students in the class and they were desperately recruiting more. I used to always make a point that when I went to Wellesley it was before the big push: I guess I felt it diluted my own worth to have people think that I got in *because* I was black. I wanted people to know I was there when being black kept you *out*. Being Jewish kept you out, too, incidentally. There was always a fixed number of Jewish girls there, it never changed, although, again, they said there were no quotas. I should say that all three of us were also light-skinned. I don't know if this was a conscious thing on Wellesley's part, or just what they were comfortable with.

"Wellesley was a good experience. I turned out to be kind of a student leader—student government and all. I was part of a group of girls who lived together and were very good friends. There were some subtle things, though. One of these girls had a big debut and everyone was invited but me. She was embarrassed about it and said her mother simply wouldn't understand, and I told her I understood. Another girl got married and I wasn't invited to her wedding. Again, I understood, but it was hurtful."

Cheryl majored in political science, and through her political science professor, became interested in the law.

"I've since decided that this professor must have been a frustrated lawyer, because out of my class of about three hundred, there were about four or five of us that went on to law school. That was a very high percentage in those days, especially at a time when there was a lot of pressure to get married in a hurry."

Cheryl applied to and was accepted by Yale Law School, a

major accomplishment in 1948, when places open to women at Yale were sharply reduced to accommodate returning veterans. However, Yale Law had at least been admitting women since 1918; Harvard Law, by contrast, did not admit women until 1950, earning the dubious distinction of being among the last law schools in the country to do so.

At the beginning of her first year at law school in 1949, Cheryl was introduced to Art, a successful, black doctor practicing in New Haven. Within a few months they became engaged.

"Art was older—thirty-seven—and he had a lot of money. I think my head was turned. He kept giving me these little diamond presents—which I subsequently returned, incidentally! He was the kind of person I'd always thought I was going to marry, someone who could take care of me. But after a while I broke it off because I realized we just didn't have the same values. He was more interested in material things. I thought I cared a lot about humanity, and people, and social issues. And by that time I was meeting people in law school who had more my kind of values. I think also that his idea of a wife was more traditional than mine. He thought it was fine for me to go to law school, but he never expected that I'd actually *do* anything with it. I remember going out to meet his family in Detroit and his father said, why are you wasting your time in law school, why don't you two just go ahead and get married? But by then I knew I was going to do something with the law."

By then Cheryl had also become interested in a fellow law student, Steve Wolfe, "and this was a problem because he was white and he had zero dollars. I kept reassuring my mother that he had 'lots of potential.' We did not know what we were going to do with this relationship, which was perfect. I mean, we felt this was the right thing for both of us, but we knew the world wasn't going to think it was so perfect. I remember one of our professors suggesting we move to the Virgin Islands to live!"

In fact, Cheryl and Steve didn't marry for another four years

("We used to joke about how we were having the longest courtship on record"), by which time both families had become reconciled to the idea.

After graduation, Cheryl and Steve went to Boston, where she started looking for a job. "I was routinely rejected. I had a double liability and if I think about which liability was greater, I think being a woman was worse than any kind of race thing. You'd get, well, we don't want to hire a woman because—those were the days when they could actually *say it!*—we'll get you all trained and then you'll go off and have children and waste it all. And always, of course, they wanted to know if you could type and I just said no, although I knew how to type very well. I remember one great civil libertarian, a very prominent liberal guy, that everyone was just *sure* would give me a job. I spent the whole interview with him answering questions about my private life: do you have a boyfriend? Where do you and your boyfriend go on weekends? Then he went on to tell me about all the divorce cases he'd handled, stories in which he tried to shock me with sexual stuff. It was discouraging, but I guess I wasn't surprised."

Finally, with help from Yale, Cheryl landed a clerkship with a judge in Boston.

"After I clerked for this judge everything changed. He opened doors for me, wrote letters for me, and said, she's smart, hire her. He was my mentor. When the clerkship was over, I got a job with a Boston law firm right away.

"Once while I was clerking for him, the judge suggested I go use the Harvard Law library because it was the best law library in the area. So I went up there and Dean Griswold said I couldn't use the library because they 'didn't have any facilities' for me! I said, all I want to do is read the books, I don't want to use the john. Well, I went back to the judge and he called them and they let me in. Years later, I was in a position to retain a law firm to represent an important client. Griswold, by then, had left Harvard and was a partner in a firm we were considering. I went down to interview him and after the interview, I couldn't resist, I reminded him of this incident." Cheryl leans back in her chair, clearly savoring the memory of this moment. "He was embarrassed, of course, and it was a very satisfying moment. But you know, the funny thing is that at the time of that incident at Harvard, it didn't bother me because we just accepted things like that. We were conditioned, that was just the way the world was."

Although they lived separately in Boston ("in those days, it was unthinkable to move in together"), Cheryl and Steve were sleeping together by then and Cheryl became pregnant.

"Steve was living with the family of a good friend of ours. We went to them when I got pregnant and they were very sympathetic. I couldn't tell my own family. At that time, needless to say, abortions were not easy to come by. These people knew a psychiatrist and they arranged for me to have a medical abortion—one of those things where the psychiatrist says you're going to flip out if you don't have one.

"I often think how totally different my life would be today if I hadn't had that abortion. We were still working out the interracial thing and we weren't ready to get married. Also, I felt very strongly that I didn't want to have a marriage that was based on this. I thought that whenever anything went wrong, this would come up. Steve and I were in complete agreement. I've never talked about that abortion before. To this day I think only Steve and the two people who helped us know about it."

Cheryl and Steve also agreed that they wanted to wait a while to have children.

"An interracial marriage was a big step in those days, though, to tell the truth, I probably would have wanted to wait anyway. We also wanted to be sure we had enough money because it never occurred to me that I could continue to work while my children were little. We had our first child three years after we were married. We thought about moving to the suburbs and we decided to stay in the city. For one thing, we thought our kids would have a better chance of surviving in the city than in some suburb where mixed-race kids weren't so common. Also, I wanted to be in a place where, when I did go back to work I could be a cab or a subway ride away from the kids instead of having to depend on a train or a car. I had my two children nineteen months apart—I had them close together because that way I could get back to work faster."

Cheryl stayed home for the next four years, feeling restless, and spending hours in the park with "a psychologist, a math teacher, an insurance broker . . . watching the kids in the sandbox and planning our futures." As soon as her youngest child started nursery school at three, Cheryl went straight to her old firm and asked to work part-time.

"I sometimes wonder how I had the nerve to do this. My old boss wouldn't hire me on that basis, but he sent me to a place that would. I told them I wanted to work from nine to three and take school vacations, but that I'd take less money and I'd work through lunch. They said, okay, let's try it. As the kids got older, I worked longer. I ended up staying there for twenty-seven years."

Cheryl is fiercely proud of her achievements and reluctant to cede any credit for them to luck. At the same time, she's fully aware that having light skin in the fifties gave her a distinct advantage.

"Even at Dunbar, most of us who went off to Ivy League schools were light-skinned. And at Wellesley, for example, all my friends were quite aware of my background, but if we were going somewhere as a group, well, they were perhaps more comfortable because I looked the way I did. And later on, in my work, the edge may have been that people were confused about my race to begin with, but by the time they'd figured it out, they had enough confidence in me that it no longer mattered."

*   *   *

Anna Hellman's father was a renowned physicist who was at the heart of America's postwar romance with nuclear science. An only child, Anna spent her early years in Cambridge, where she roller-skated in the parking lot of her father's lab at Harvard.

"I was very close to my father—he was the person on whom I . . . well, I' won't say 'modeled myself' because I was the wrong sex to do that—but he was the person who was extremely important to me. No, he never said I was the wrong sex, but it was clear—you looked around you and you saw who the scientists were! I don't think it was conscious at that age, but I'm sure I noticed it at some level."

Anna's intelligence illuminates her face, which is bare of makeup. We talk in her utilitarian office in a prestigious eastern university. Behind her controlled, precise speech flicker glimpses of the self-conscious intensity of the brilliant, socially backward young girl she describes.

Anna's parents divorced when she was nine, and her mother remarried. In 1939, when she was eleven, they moved to Mount Lebanon, Pennsylvania, where her stepfather, also a physicist, was to head up a new explosives lab. Anna, who had been attending a private girls' school in Boston, despised her new public school ("self-righteous little snob that I was!"). Having skipped two grades, she was in the impossible position of being younger than her classmates, but light-years ahead of them intellectually.

"I was also way behind them—or in another world from them—socially. Here I was encountering this rather weird species called the opposite sex for the first time. And then there were the girls who used lipstick and nail polish and had no thought in their heads except attracting boys. I did well, particularly in mathematics where I had a very nice teacher who just gave me the book and said, go at your own speed. I didn't exactly hide my light under a bushel—I just didn't talk to anybody. I made no friends. Not one."

Unlike most of her classmates, there was never any doubt that Anna would go on to college and have a profession.

"When I was about ten or twelve, my father had a serious talk with me. He told me I should not count on getting married and having somebody support me, that I should plan to support myself and to be independent. That being the case, I should give some thought to what I wanted to do because it was much nicer to do work that you enjoyed than work that just earned you a living. There were some money troubles between him and my mother and I think he was not so happy when she stopped working."

By the end of high school Anna had decided to be a medical doctor, gravitating toward science but carefully carving out a separate sphere from her father's. She admits she may also have been thinking about her mother, who had gone to medical school in Germany but whose medical training had been permanently derailed by World War I. Her father insisted Anna attend Mount Holyoke. For one thing, she was barely sixteen when she started college; Mount Holyoke would provide a controlled environment in a lovely setting. Equally important, he had a high opinion of the science faculty at Mount Holyoke.

"All the universities had sent their best science faculty—the males, that is—into war work. But the science faculty at Holyoke were superb. They were typical women scientists, spinsters, most of them. They carried very heavy teaching loads, they did research during the summer and published. In many ways, they were in fact remarkably good role models because they were also enjoying life! They gave the lie to the notion that you had to get married and have kids and do nothing else in order to be happy. There were married women professors at Holyoke, but they were not the ones that I admired.

"The irony was that, not only did these professors not encourage and guide their students in the direction of professional achievement, they instituted a course called 'Marriage and the Family,' run by someone in the psychology department. I have a feeling that the faculty was told by the administration that the way to get higher enrollment was to make Mount Holyoke friendly to the idea that they were producing future wives and mothers."

Evidently obeying the dictum "do as I say, not as I do," 330 of Anna's graduating class of 350 got married immediately after graduation. Anna was one of the 20 who did not.

"I really did experience myself as weird. I felt like an outsider. I may have created the feeling for myself, but the reason I never smoked or played bridge was because the in-crowd did those things. The conversation was all about when so-and-so was coming home on leave and dates, engagements. When Miss Clark, who was the most famous of the chemistry teachers talked to me she said that, of course I would get married and have a family. I took a dim view of this idea at the time—I think my parents' divorce had left a sour taste in my mouth and I still didn't have a good grasp of how one went about dealing with the opposite sex. As time went on, though, I did begin to consider that I might combine marriage with a profession."

During college, Anna increasingly found herself drawn to nuclear chemistry instead of biology. "The sight of all the little fetuses floating in formaldehyde, or whatever it was, made me decide that I wasn't cut out to be a doctor." In 1949, there were only three suitable graduate schools for someone who had built a Geiger counter for her senior project: Columbia, Chicago, and Berkeley. Her father favored Berkeley, and under his aegis she was accepted there with a teaching assistantship.

Because Anna was still very young—only twenty—when she got to graduate school, she moved into International House, which was segregated into men's and women's sections. The work was exceedingly difficult and Anna had all she could do to keep up. "If there hadn't been some very nice guys in International House, I would have been sunk. These guys were kind enough to come into one of the lounges where both sexes were allowed to congregate to work on these problem sets so that I could join them. There I was, a teaching assistant, a very shy, socially awkward twenty-year-old teaching veterans and actually, I think I was fortunate to have that kind of student, because they had learned discipline and therefore they were there to learn and they didn't give me any trouble. What you have to realize was that I was very different from most of the girls in the sense that I was told that I was always very determined and that it projected itself."

Anna met her husband-to-be, a biochemist, in graduate school and they were married almost immediately. Anna is terse about Eric, from whom she has been divorced since 1966.

"It may seem a harsh thing to say, but I think a lot of Eric's attraction was his family. He came from a stable, traditional family. I very badly wanted someone to love and I liked both his parents very much. Plus he was good-looking and generally a nice guy. He was completely supportive of my work in science, so that was not a problem."

Nevertheless, when Anna got her degree, which she did in three and a half years, it was assumed she would stay in Berkeley until Eric finished. She laughs wryly about this.

"The inequality in the relationship was never exactly articulated. If, for example, I'd gotten a job offer from someplace very desirable, like MIT, there would have been enormous pressure on me not to take it."

In order to line up her options against the day when her husband graduated and they both had to find jobs, Anna wrote letters to a hundred universities large enough to have jobs for both of them. She received exactly one response, "A very nice Jesuit at Boston College who wrote me to say they would be charmed to have me on the faculty but unfortunately they were an all-male institution and this would not be possible."

Meanwhile, her husband, using the traditional route, activated an informal network of contacts through his adviser, landed a job at Columbia, and in the end, Anna too was hired by Columbia as a research associate in the chemistry department.

"They knew we were a couple, so I guess I benefited indirectly from the 'old boys' network' myself. The job was not what I wanted, but the job was specifically to work with Chien-Shiung Wu, who was the foremost woman physicist in the United States at the time. She turned me loose at Brookhaven, where I built a scattering chamber and did my own experiments. That was very exciting. We never talked very much, but she was responsible for my ability to start functioning as an independent post-doc in nuclear physics, which was a big change in my career. A year later the physics department picked me up as a research associate because it was so painfully clear that my interests were in nuclear physics."

When Eric was invited to become an instructor at Barnard, Anna was made an instructor at Columbia. (Nepotism rules precluded a husband and wife from teaching in the same department at most universities.)

At that juncture, three important events took place in Anna's life more or less simultaneously. Her husband was told that he would not get tenure at Barnard; Anna was told that if she stayed at Columbia she had a good chance for tenure; and Anna became pregnant.

"We'd always said we didn't want a child until we were established in our professions. This pregnancy was not exactly an accident, more like a relaxation of precautions. It wasn't a deliberate attempt, but Eric wanted to start a family and I sort of drifted into it. I closed my mind to the whole thing. I can't say it was completely an accident . . . and I had no idea of what having a child would be like. Eric got a job at MIT. Both my husband and my father were of the opinion that I should not stay in New York City bringing up a child by myself, and so quite a good deal of pressure was brought to bear that I should leave Columbia. I was not at all pleased. If it had just been Eric, I probably would have stayed at Columbia. But the fact that my father really didn't think that I would be able to cope, well, that clinched it."

Evidently the possibility of Eric staying in the New York area to accommodate Anna never occurred to anyone. Anna and her husband relocated to Cambridge, where she was offered an assistant professorship at another university.

Anna's daughter was born in 1958, her son two years later. She was able to teach and do research due to the services of a lively and competent young German woman. It was not until the young woman left to get married herself that the full weight of managing a profession and a family descended on Anna. When her son developed a severe diaper infection in the care of an incompetent baby-sitter, Anna went to her ob/gyn in despair.

"I had been reading all this stuff about the female role and how important it was to accept it. In fact, when I went into the hospital to have my son I took along an early version of Dr. Spock which was all about how the mother should stay home. There I was about to start as an assistant professor, reading that I should stay home. All the mothers I knew were staying home. I was shaken by all this and poured it out to my doctor and said I thought maybe I should quit work because I was so discouraged and worried that they weren't being properly taken care of. I was very fortunate in this man because he sent me to a psychiatrist, also a man, who was very atypical of the times. The psychiatrist asked me about my symptoms and suggested that I should apply the same intelligence that I applied to my work to getting adequate child care. He said he thought I would do my children more harm than good by giving up my career and staying home."

Eventually Anna and Eric did find a satisfactory baby-sitter, but the ordeal took its toll on Anna's career. She was not promoted to a tenure track and took a position as staff scientist at another institution where eventually—and not without considerable struggle—she became a full professor.

"I made the mistake of discussing my child-care problems with my colleagues," she explains with an edge of bitterness in her voice. "A few years after I left, I ran into a man who admitted he'd been partially responsible for my not being promoted. He said, 'But Anna, you were talking as if you were nonfunctional!' Well, I clearly *was* functional, but they didn't look at what I was doing. If a man goes and talks to his colleagues about his prostate cancer or whatever, they are sympathetic and supportive. If a woman says she's having trouble getting good child care, they view this as crippling.

"I felt defeated at the time, but I also thought my life would be easier if I just did research and took care of my children. In retrospect, it turned out to be a good move. My research wasn't diluted by committees and teaching and I was fortunate in being principal investigator in a team experiment that turned out to be interesting and important. This led eventually to my becoming a senior research scientist, which at this institution is the equivalent of a research professor."

In a sense, as Anna freely admits, it was not until the early sixties that she came face-to-face with the limitations of being a woman in a bastion of male privilege. Until then, she had been insulated from the problems encountered by other women.

"Being my father's daughter gave me a unique freedom to make choices," *Something to Fall Back On?* hat I could do whatever I wanted to do was unchallenged for a long time. It gave me an unreal approach to life, and an unreal idea about the realities of women in science."

Like Anna Hellman, all the women in this group were blessed with exceptionally good fortune: support from a parent or a husband, the critical intervention of a mentor, accidents of timing, geography, or economics. But the very extraordinariness of their circumstances and personalities underscores how difficult it was for the average woman to attempt to step outside her prescribed role. And even so, we see these five women maneuvering and negotiating, calculating and strategizing, dodging and weaving to get where they needed to go.

Their stories illustrate how precarious their luck really was. Because they were essentially swimming upstream, against the current of public opinion, and without institutional or cultural supports, they were always in danger of being diverted from their course. If Faith Merrill had married her first college sweetheart, if Sylvia Beckman had listened to her mother, if Ellen Rodgers hadn't miscarried, if Cheryl Wolfe had married her New Haven doctor, if Anna Hellman hadn't found a good baby-sitter . . . at these moments you can feel the tug of the mainstream.

Not every woman in the fifties wanted to practice a profession as these women did; many were content to be wives and mothers. Others chose to work in fields that were hospitable to women like teaching, social work, nursing, or fine arts. But what of the ordinary women without exceptional resources, whose desire, talent, and energy was wasted? For every woman like these five, there were many like Jane Hunter, whose doctor persuaded her to give up architecture because it would destroy her health, or Bridget Moran, who felt compelled to choose between doing mathematics and having a family. Women whose determination faltered in the face of a husband's opposition, or an institution's hostility. Women who simply couldn't see how to manage the work and the children and were unwilling to forgo the latter. They had to make a choice men never have to make, between a family and meaningful work.

Chapter IX

The Silence

In my second year of nursing school in 1951, I roomed with an older student and we had a relationship. This was definitely a sexual relationship. I'd never known anyone who did anything like this. And yet, I knew what to do, how to be with her. There were other classmates who were also having relationships, everyone knew and no one spoke of it. We never, never used the word "lesbian." I was happy with this woman but there was so much about it that could never be expressed because of the silence of all my friends, and everyone in the school. When I graduated, I walked away from this woman and never saw or heard from her again.

—AMY STEEL, 60, WHO SUBSEQUENTLY MARRIED, HAD A CHILD, AND LIVED AS A HETEROSEXUAL FOR TWENTY YEARS

It has never been easy to be a lesbian in this country, but the 1950s was surely the worst decade in which to love your own sex. All the more so because the war years had seen a sudden opening up of opportunities for gay women and men to be with each other. The rigid sexual mores of the Victorian era had in fact begun to disintegrate during the twenties. The ideas of Freud and Havelock Ellis, popularized by mass culture magazines, promoted an increased acceptance of heterosexual sex as a healthful activity necessary for human fulfillment. Victorian ideals of female purity and asexuality were giving way to the notion that women had a legitimate interest in sex. Arguably the most revolutionary development of all was the introduction and widening availability of birth control. Not only did this phenomenon imply an acceptance of female sexuality, it made possible, for the first time, the separation of sexual activity from reproduction.

Although this trend of sexual liberalism primarily benefited heterosexuals, it had a kind of trickle-down effect on homosexuality as well. By the thirties, what historians John D'Emilio and Estelle Freedman call "the resources for naming homosexual desire" were slowly expanding. In American cities, at least, homosexuals were finding ways of coming together. And images of gay men and women, albeit often distorted, were beginning to seep into the culture. (Paradoxically, the growing acceptance of psychoanalytic ideas, while opening up discourse about homosexuality, also furnished labels like "perversity" and "deviance" which were used to condemn homosexual activity.)

World War II broadened the erotic horizons for gays of both sexes dramatically and almost overnight. Men and women who joined the armed services were thrown in with their own sex in unprecedented numbers. Women who migrated to the cities for war work found themselves living and working alongside large numbers of other women for the first time in their lives. As D'Emilio and Freedman point out in *Intimate Matters: A History of Sexuality in America*, "For some, their wartime careers simply made more accessible a way of living and loving they had already chosen. For others, it gave meaning to little-understood desires, introduced them for the first time to men and women with similar feelings, and allowed then to embark upon a new sexual road. Truly, World War II was something of a nationwide coming out."

The momentum of this newfound freedom—and I use the word in its most relative sense—continued briefly into the postwar demobilization period. Gays for whom a new world of sexual and emotional experience had opened up were unwilling to retreat to the isolation and loneliness of the prewar years. Gay bars had begun to appear in many cities and a lesbian subculture, albeit limited and discreet, had taken root. A woman's diary in the Lesbian Herstory Archives speaks of going into a working-class lesbian bar in Columbus, Ohio, in 1955, a bar that evidently had been serving the community for some time. In fact, the first two national organizations for gay men and women, the Mattachine Society and the Daughters of Bilitis, were founded in the early 1950s.

It was inevitable that, as homosexuals emerged more visibly on the American landscape, they became a focus of Cold War anxiety. There was already great concern about the ability of returning veterans to adjust to domestic life after the trauma and excitement of their war experience. Even before the end of the war, in fact, experts were raising fears about the mental hygiene of American servicemen. In his 1946 book, *Their Mothers' Sons*, psychiatrist Edward Strecker, who had served as adviser to the army and navy surgeons general and the secretary of state, warned that the armed services were being flooded with "psychoneurotics." Army and navy NP (neuropsychiatric) wards, he declared, were crowded with immature, exhausted weaklings whimpering for their mothers and refusing to return to battle. Even more despicable, in Strecker's view, were the nearly three million men who did not serve, in whose numbers he included "draft dodgers," as well as men rejected at induction or discharged for psychiatric reasons.

The *Kinsey Report*'s finding that over a third of adult American males had had homosexual experience seemed to confirm the notion that homosexuality was spreading like a canker throughout the population. Fears of perversion merged with the growing hysteria about Communism, which was thought to be sapping the moral strength of the country. In *Homeward Bound,* Elaine Tyler May explains the reasoning that linked these two anxieties: "National strength depended upon the ability of strong, manly men to stand up against communist threats. . . . According to the common wisdom of the time, 'normal' heterosexual behavior culminating in marriage represented 'maturity' and 'responsibility'; therefore those who were 'deviant' were, by definition, irresponsible, immature, and weak." Such men, the thinking went, not only weakened the moral fiber of the nation, but were vulnerable to sexual blackmail by Communist infiltrators of both sexes.

If a strong, traditional family with a father at its head was the cornerstone of the nation's mental health, then homosexuality, with its implicit separation of the erotic from the procreative, was perceived as a threat. Female homosexuality offered (and still offers) the most profound challenge to the family. A lesbian not only rejected the sanctified role of wife-and-mother; she was a woman whose sexual satisfaction did not come from a man.

The effects of this antihomosexual hysteria were concrete and devastating. Homosexuals were a convenient target because, trapped by their fear of exposure, they were unable to fight back. In April of 1953, newly elected president Dwight D. Eisenhower issued an executive order banning homosexuals from all federal jobs. The armed services discharged thousands of men and women practically overnight, some simply for displaying homosexual "tendencies." Corporations and state and local governments took their cue from the White House and subjected millions of employees to surveillance and loyalty-security investigations. Local police conducted crackdowns, raiding gay bars, and arresting and often beating hundreds of homosexuals. Local newspapers frequently published the names, addresses, and places of employment of those arrested. Lesbians had perhaps the most to fear during this period because, as women, their employment opportunities in the Cold War economy were already limited.

As an army veteran, Cam Donahue was in a position to fully experience both the "nationwide coming out" of the war years, and the brutal crackdown of the 1950s. At sixty-four, Cam is about to retire from her job as a lineswoman for the phone company. A rough-and-ready character with close-cropped gray hair, she's not much given to introspection, but she's a riveting storyteller. She was born in Minneapolis to a show-business family that criss-crossed the country doing musical comedy and vaudeville. In 1936, when Cam was ten years old, the family settled in Los Angeles.

"In 1942, on my sixteenth birthday, we went to the Brown Derby. We were sitting at a table and my dad was talking to some guy he knew in show business and a gorgeous woman walked by. This guy says, 'Well, there goes the Queen of the Lesbians.' Something happened to the back of my neck and I turned right to my mother and asked her what a lesbian was. She just said, 'Oh, it's a woman who loves her own sex.' That's all. End of conversation. By the time I hit seventeen I was picking out who was and who wasn't in high school. There was this girl named Fay and she was real butch. She had her hair cut in a dutchboy bob and she wore pants all through high school. I wanted to hang around with her, but she lived pretty far from me so it wasn't easy.

"One night I ran into a couple of girls from my class at the movies. I sat with them and the two of them were holding hands during the movie. They looked at me and I looked at them and I just smiled. I think I understood something. It seemed natural to me, somehow. After the movie I drove them home and we never discussed it.

"I dated a little in high school. This was wartime, so I went out with some sailors and soldiers and marines. Couldn't wait to get home, though. I just knew that something wasn't right. I think that a lot of the gay women who went out with servicemen in those days, it was the uniform that attracted them more than anything. We may even have identified with the uniform.

"Once I started to be old enough to use the car, I used to drive around, exploring. I found a café in LA called the If Café. It was a lesbian place, and I used to park the car and sit in front of it for hours watching who went in and who came out. This must have been in about forty-five. I was fascinated, but I was afraid to go in. After doing this for six months, I finally worked up the nerve to walk in, had a drink at the bar, spoke to no one, and walked out. I was so scared. In those days you had nobody to talk to, ask questions, or even read. People were so ignorant: when my aunt found out I was gay, she said, 'Oh, you're an ass-kisser.' Really. That was what she thought it was."

It wasn't until Cam went to work for the navy in 1945 that she met any lesbians. She chose the navy because her brother was a sailor and she liked the sea, the ship, "and the uniform."

"I was a civilian worker, a forklift driver down on the piers. The first person I met there was a girl we called 'Legs'—she was very tall and thin. She introduced me to a few people. I met this woman called 'Father Dolan,' her real name was Liz Dolan, God knows why she wanted us to call her 'Father.' Anyway, we all used to hang out at her house and talk, about eight of us. We talked about poetry and books and movies. We used to go on picnics down at the beach and get drunk and run around. It was the beginning of close friendships. And yet, we were sort of holding back.

"That's when I met this woman Ethel, a real dynamite woman, and we ran around together for about five years. At that time there wasn't an atmosphere of fear and secrecy. Because it was wartime, women were running around together anyway, because there weren't that many men available. Now, a few in our crowd were pretty obvious-looking dykes, but the rest of us, including me, looked regular—our hair was long, we wore dresses and makeup. But in California in those days, everybody wore pants a lot anyway."

Cam and Ethel moved to Sacramento in 1949 where they lived together and worked for the department of motor vehicles. When their relationship ended in 1953, Cam signed up for the army.

"I went through basic at Fort Lee, Virginia. Now when I walked in there, it turned out *everyone* was gay! My captain, my first sergeant, right on down. Man, I was like a kid in a candy store. I went berserk. And I was the supply sergeant: I met them first! They had to come to me to get their supplies. In basic, I was still more or less observing what was going on. Then I went to my first station—that was Fort Ritchie, in the Pennsylvania mountains. It was the kind of town where they pulled the chickens in at dark, that's how bad it was. So the only place you could go was the PX and the bars. That was the first time I ever saw women dancing with each other, in these country bars.

"Now when I first saw my captain, when I hit the post, she was playing baseball. She misses a fly ball and she says, 'Shit!' Later I see her on duty and it turns out she's my captain. We got pretty tight, she and I, and we used to neck in the dayroom, that's how open things used to be.

"But then we got this new lieutenant and she began to be real RA (regular army) and things began to get a little hot and heavy. This was 1955–56. I now think they might have brought her in to clean out the post."

In fact, specifically anti-lesbian screening policies had been in place in the WAC (Women's Army Corps) since 1944. But the need for personnel during wartime was so urgent that this rigorous screening was never implemented. After the war, however, in keeping with the drive to encourage women to leave the work force and resume their domestic duties, women in the military were also expected to return to civilian life. Those who chose to remain in the military or actually enlisted during this period came under suspicion of homosexuality. Lectures were instituted within the services that portrayed lesbians as "exotic and dangerous perverts ready to seduce any woman who was young and naive." As the anti-homosexual campaign gathered momentum in civilian sectors, the armed services also conducted increasingly frequent purges of its ranks. According to historian Allan Berube's calculations, the discharge rate for homosexuals tripled during the postwar years from 1947 to 1950, and remained at that level throughout the 1950s. And a secret navy report acknowledged that by the mid fifties the discharge rate was "much higher for the female than the male."

Pat Bond describes this period in *Long Time Passing: Lives of Older Lesbians:* "Every day you came up for a court martial against one of your friends. They turned us against each other. When I was living it, I didn't have any idea why they were doing this to us. I only knew they were throwing us out of the army with dishonorable discharges." Bond herself married in order to protect the woman she was involved with and get out of the army legitimately. She adds, "They sent five hundred home for dishonorable, but a lot of them got off because the Attorney General's office looked at it and said, 'Come on, *five hundred?*' What they didn't know was that all five hundred were dykes."

At Fort Ritchie, Cam Donahue and her friends began to feel the pressure. "They started watching us very carefully and following us. We called them Uncle CID—the criminal investigation department of the army. Then one night about four of us were in my car, parked, drunk and necking, and the local police found us and reported us to the MPs. So we were put on reserve duty. One day I decided to go out and clean out my car. Well, the minute I got the car open they swooped down on me and started to search it. See, they couldn't go in my car as long as I didn't have it open. They were looking for incriminating evidence of homosexuality. But I never kept letters, and I never put my return address on my envelopes. And I used to mail my letters off-post. When I got my mail, I'd go in the toilet, open it, read it, and flush it right down the toilet, right then and there."

Cam Donahue herself was kicked out after two other women went AWOL and left behind letters mentioning her name, among others.

"After I was caught, they interrogated me for two days. I was talked to by these two men and they were pretty crude: 'How do you like it, inside or out?' they'd ask me. I was disgusted. And I was scared shitless. They weren't really asking me for information, they were trying to intimidate me, and along the way, they got their jollies off. Then they sent me along to this psychologist or psychiatrist or whatever they had. I go in, I sit down, and for an hour I don't think we say five words between us. He just sat there and stared at me as if I was a specimen under glass. And then he writes this report stating that I am definitely a homosexual all the way. So now they threaten you by saying they're going to tell your parents. Well, this works if you're eighteen or something, but I was thirty-two. I knew I was getting out with a dishonorable discharge. They were redlining me, too—that means no pay. All they gave me was a ticket home."

After she was discharged from the army in 1957, Cam and a friend drove across the country to California. On the way, they stopped for a night in New Orleans. "Now both of us are in pants and we're from New York. We went to dinner at a fancy restaurant and had Oysters Rockefeller, and as we're walking back to the car, we hear, 'Hey, you two!' We look around and there's this policeman standing by this paddy wagon and the next thing we know it's 'Get in!' We were arrested—for *vagrancy!* Now we've each got over a hundred dollars on us, which in 1957 is a lot of money. They send us up to night court and we have to sit through all these cases—attempted murder, murder, theft, prostitution, rape. And us. I was scared, seeing as I'd just been kicked out of the army for homosexuality. But real calm, we tell the judge we're on our way to California, we just stopped off in New Orleans for a meal, and he dismisses us. We later found out New Orleans was particularly hard on lesbians because the mayor's wife had been 'taken away' by some lesbian—that's how they said it. She left him for some dyke."

Cam had hoped to see her father and brother in California—her mother had died in 1954.

"Back when I joined the army, my father had written me a letter saying he didn't want to see me again unless I got rid of my 'fairy nice friends.' I wrote him back immediately saying, 'Don't worry, you don't ever have to see me again. As far as you're concerned, you only have a son. I'm dead.' If I'd waited a couple of days to mail that letter, my temper might have calmed down, but I mailed it immediately so I was committed to it. I tried to contact him when I got out to California, but he didn't want to see me. I never saw my father again. He died in 1959.

"My brother didn't want to see me either. He made it known to me that he didn't like me coming to his home when he wasn't there and being alone with his children. He had five kids, and I knew if one of 'em turned out gay who was going to be blamed. He told me, 'When you come to my house you have to act and dress like a lady.' I thought to myself, 'Fuck you, George.' I left California and didn't see my brother again for seventeen years."

Back in New York, it was now 1958 and Cam went to work for an insurance company. "This is when I really felt I had to be looking over my shoulder all the time. I had a male co-worker, Dave, who was also gay. We became good friends and my new lover, Anne, and I would pal around with Dave and another guy she knew, and take pictures and stuff—to distract people from thinking we were gay.

"In the bars in those days, if the cops walked in, you flipped the lights and people would step apart from each other. If you kissed someone or touched them in a bar in the fifties, they would throw you out. We used to have a place on Sixth Avenue in the Village called Pam-Pam's. We'd mill around in the street out in front of the place and make noise and all, and the cops would always come along and tell us to move on. Oh, we'd give 'em a fight and they'd throw us forcefully into the squad car. You had to have three pieces of female clothing on. So we all wore bras, female pants—that meant pants that closed on the side instead of flyfront—and girl's shoes. We used to have an outfit we called 'Balboas'—this was a light blue denim jean with a matching jacket with a ribbed wrist and collar, and then we'd wear light blue canvas boat shoes. That was your 'Balboas,' that was dressing up."

There's a part of Cam that clearly relishes her history as an outsider, part of a beleaguered, outlaw community. Although her toughness and bravado are convincing, as I was leaving she revealed something darker:

"You know, when I first started out in gay life I was a hot son of a gun. There was a fire in me all the time and I thought there was something wrong with me. You hear this word, nymphomaniac, and I thought I was one of them. I hated myself for a long time. None of us *knew* anything!"

Despite the confusion and self-hatred, Cam and her friends participated in a vital chapter of lesbian history—the breaking open of silence and isolation. World War II created the special circumstances that enabled them to come together and experience themselves as a community.

And even though the fifties brought a brutal slamming of the closet door, the groundwork for gay liberation had been laid. Writer and lesbian activist Joan Nestle believes that in some ways the oppression of the fifties may have strengthened the movement more than the freedom of the forties: "My own theory is that the stronger the oppression of sexual desire, the more profound is the sense of community. Women had to fight with their fists to be in those bars in the fifties. That experience of *taking space* is what gave birth to gay liberation."

Lesbians who had lived through the forties were in a stronger position to weather the fifties—especially if they lived in urban areas. But younger women raised in the isolation of small towns and rural communities had to struggle alone with their lesbian feelings.

Helen Schumann, fifty-two, was raised in a small town in Pennsylvania, where her father was the foreman of the local shoe factory. Her mother, one of seven children in a coal-mining family, had managed to escape and had worked as a nurse in New York. At the age of thirty-five, feeling that she'd never have another chance, she married and became a housewife, but she was determined that her daughter should escape the town. Helen is a psychologist who practices out of the home she shares with her lover, Gloria, in a college community near Philadelphia. We talk in her wintered-down garden on an unseasonably warm November day.

"My mother started landscaping our yard for my wedding when I was about ten," Helen remembers with a pained laugh. "She started early so that the plantings would be mature when the time came. She used to describe my wedding to me before I went to sleep, like a bedtime story: 'You'll come down the front steps and out through this door into the yard . . . there'll be bridesmaids carrying baskets of flowers . . . ' I felt embarrassed and guilty. We were very close and I wanted so much to be the person she wanted me to be.

"I'd started feeling different from other girls when I was about eleven. I felt a depth of attachment to my friends that I knew they didn't feel. I didn't feel comfortable with other kids in general because they were too rough. But I had a boyfriend at home starting in seventh grade. We'd gone to grade school together, and we started 'dating,' if you could call it that, at twelve. He was different from the other boys in town because he was an artist and he had a good sense of humor. It was a pretty platonic relationship, but it was a relationship. He was kind of like insurance, a safety net. My parents liked him but they didn't approve of him. He turned out to be gay, too, so I guess we were being insurance for each other.

"My mother sent me to a girls' boarding school at twelve so that I could get into college and get out of town. At boarding school I still felt inferior to everybody. They all seemed so much more comfortable with themselves. The headmistress periodically called me in for little talks. She would say she'd noticed that I was getting very close to someone and she didn't think that was such a good idea. I was already freaked out about my own feelings, so I wasn't going to ask her to spell out what she meant. I developed this magical thought that if anybody ever said *the word*, that would make it true—the word *lesbian*, or *homosexual*. So I was terrified all the time. As long as the outside world didn't accuse me, that one last piece hadn't fallen into place, and there was still hope that it wouldn't.

"Wellesley was where it finally happened. The word was used. In my freshman year, 1954, I became close friends with a woman from Kentucky. We weren't lovers—the very *idea* of being lovers was so far from me then. I wanted so badly to be normal. But this woman and I had a lot in common and we were really good friends. We'd planned to live on the same floor our sophomore year—now, we didn't want to *room* together, but we wanted to be near each other. When it got to room drawing—freshmen are always at the bottom of the draw—it turned out that the only way we could even be in the same dorm was to room together. So we said OK, thinking that maybe something would open up and we could get separate rooms.

"That summer, two days before I left home to go back to

college, I got this letter from the Dean of Students saying that we'd been switched and my friend had been assigned a room in another dorm and I was to come see her as soon as I got to school. I knew something was up—I always thought something was up anyway because I was living in fear of someone finding out.

"So my friend and I went to see the dean and she said, 'You have been separated because sometimes it happens that girls are too fond of other girls.' So now someone had said it. She also said that 'everyone in your dorm knows this and is upset, your housemother and the house council.' So I thought people had been watching me all the time. I was just destroyed by this.

"My mother had driven me up to college and when I came out of that meeting, I was in tears so I had to tell her what was wrong. Her response was, 'How could you do this to me?' This pretty effectively ended our relationship for a number of years. Meanwhile, my friend and I decided we'd better never speak to each other again. Interestingly, I found out later that this dean was a lesbian herself. I think some of those women were more oppressive than straight women because of their own fear of exposure."

Helen's experience at Wellesley confirmed her worst fears. She spent the rest of her time at college in virtual isolation, unable to share her feelings with anyone.

At graduate school in Indiana, Helen continued to be tormented by her desire for intimacy with women, her fear of exposure, and self-hatred for what she felt were "abnormal" desires.

"At around that time I started thinking seriously about killing myself, which I thought about on a daily basis until 1961. I kept thinking, I can't live like this, I can't *be* like this. I kept falling in love with people at school and not being able to show it. During this period my mother was sending me a stream of letters, tightly sealed with Scotch tape, advising me how to dress and act so that people wouldn't think the wrong thing about me. She called me a couple of times a week to find out whether I was dating, who I was dating. As it happens, I *was* dating some guys—I was still half-heartedly trying to persuade myself to be heterosexual—and one of them, a professor in agriculture school, had been threatened by his department head that he might be fired if he didn't get married soon. I think he was probably gay himself and that's why I felt safe going out with him. But there was absolutely no trace of a gay underground, I never heard word one about anyone having homosexual affairs at Purdue. Just silence. So I felt totally alone with my feelings.

"It wasn't until 1961 that I stopped thinking about suicide. I remember getting to a point of sheer misery, sitting in my room and saying to myself, 'Either do it now, kill yourself and be done with it—or start living. Change your life.' And I decided to change my life. So I went into therapy and began the process that, years later, led to coming out."

Helen's terror of hearing "the word" reveals how she had made the silence part of herself. The lack of words or images of homosexuality, and the potent ideas about "normalcy" that pervaded the culture, made it almost impossible for lesbians not to internalize the belief that their erotic longings were perverse. Helen's conflict became so intolerable that it drove her to begin the process of coming to terms with her lesbian feelings. Gradually, she was able to carve out a life for herself as a gay woman. For many other women, their first lesbian experience in the fifties was sufficiently traumatic to make them repress their homosexuality for decades.

Jill Morris, the woman who wept as she watched her furniture being carried into her new suburban home, struggled for years with her lesbian feelings. In her case, these feelings were in sharp conflict with her powerful need for family and roots.

"I started thinking about girls when I was around fifteen," she says. "I read *Well of Loneliness*—the only book there *was* to read—with a newspaper wrapped around it. At the same time, I did all the usual stuff, I was necking on the backsteps with neighbor kids when I was twelve, I had boyfriends in high school, and belonged to a whole heterosexual group in Missouri. And then the war started and we'd go to the Jewish USO and dance with servicemen.

"I don't remember feeling conflicted about my feelings for women at first. I wanted friends, I wanted sisters. I hated being an only child. I was very isolated and alone out there, with just my mother and my grandfather. I wanted *family!* I didn't think seriously about my feelings for women until I got involved with this woman in college. It was my freshman year at the University of Wisconsin and it kind of just happened. We were very naive, and suddenly something was going on between us that was very, very strong—we thought we'd invented it. We used to act openly affectionate right out in the common room. We couldn't keep our hands off each other. I remember going to her parents' house and going into the bathroom and lying on the floor making love. All kinds of crazy, exciting stuff.

"I guess everyone was talking about us. I transferred dorms at one point and somebody asked me where I'd lived before and when I told her, she said, 'Oh, we heard there were a couple of lesbians over there!' Eventually we were reported to the dean of women, who was known as Black Mariah. We walked in to talk to her hand in hand, and I lied and said these people who'd reported us were just jealous because we were such good friends. She fell for it. I was terrified that my mother would find out. Then my friend went home for Thanksgiving and when she came back she told me she'd met a boy and she was going to get married. I was stunned. I felt abandoned. But, you understand, I felt so guilty about what we were doing, that I accepted this as the right decision. I was even a bridesmaid in her wedding, that's how crazy it was. That wedding was a nightmare."

Jill succeeded in repressing her lesbian feelings until her senior year when a woman approached her sexually. "I found it exciting and stimulating and I didn't want it, so I went to the college psychiatrist. This guy was doing some kind of study on homosexuality and he labeled me obsessive-compulsive. That was not very helpful."

After college, Jill moved to New York City, still struggling with her sexual identity. She tried sleeping with a man she liked, determined "to find out once and for all what the fuss was about," but found it uninteresting.

"Meanwhile, I had this marvelous memory of passion with this woman. In New York I had a group of friends, some of whom were lesbians and some were not. I made some overtures to women and was turned down—these were, of course, straight women, so they were bound to turn me down. I must have felt conflicted about my identity, but I don't remember it. I do remember thinking always that the goal was marriage, always marriage, whatever else you felt."

Jill became engaged to a psychiatrist, the son of a friend of her mother's.

"The night I got engaged to this guy I knew it was wrong. But my mother was writing me these letters, she was all excited. I remember this incident: I'd gone to Long Island on my vacation with a bunch of women friends and we were having a wonderful time. Then this guy, my fiancé, decided to come up for *his* vacation, so I had to move out from where I was staying with them and move in with him. I wasn't happy and the sex was awful. Finally I said no, and broke it off. This guy was furious, told me I was highly neurotic and picked out a psychiatrist for me to see. In fairness, I *also* thought there must be something wrong with me that I didn't want to marry this wonderful guy, this doctor, who was already close with my family.

"So I started in therapy in 1950. The psychiatrist was a

woman and it was agreed that my problem was: why had I broken up my engagement with this wonderful man, why I had
these feelings for women . . . and some ambivalence I was beginning to feel toward my beloved mother."

Three months later, Jill was married.

"I had met this man at a party. He was good-looking, sweet,
six years older than me, and in the clothing business. He was
solid. He had all the necessary ingredients. And he made me
laugh. We liked each other a lot. And he was sexually experienced, so that part was OK, too. We took a trip out west
together—I was going to visit my mother and he had business
out there, and while we were out there we just impulsively
decided to get married. We were both ready and we just
thought, why wait? The minute I got back to New York I quit
therapy. The therapist and I both accepted that now that I was
married I didn't need to come any more."

Jill settled into life as a suburban housewife, her lesbian feelings "simmering, but very much underground. We did some
sexual experimentation during that period. We'd go on vacation
with this other couple and switched partners with them. It was
kind of fun. But my gut feeling was I'd rather have slept with
the *woman* of the other couple than the man! I didn't pursue
any feelings toward women, I still felt these impulses were
wrong and bad."

In 1957, after the birth of her second child, Jill went back
into therapy.

"I don't remember exactly what my symptoms were . . . oh,
wait, maybe I do remember. There was this woman. We'd
become friendly with this couple, and I had become infatuated
with the wife. She used to come over to the house and stay and
stay and stay. I finally confessed my feelings to her, and it turned
out she was trying to get close to me in order to get to one of
the men in our group, a man she wanted. So I was conflicted
and hurt. I guess I was worried about these feelings. I had

everything—these beautiful children, a nice, really nice husband, a house—why was I depressed? Something was wrong, something was missing. I remember my therapist kept saying to me, 'But look how far you've come . . . you have this marriage, this family, a home. You've made a success.' These were the signposts of maturity. In the meantime I continued to be unhappy—and to *worry* that there was something wrong with me that I wasn't satisfied, that I wasn't enjoying this life. I guess I was always struggling with an identity."

Jill and her husband divorced in the mid seventies. She and her lover, Nancy, now live in the same suburb where Jill raised her family. Their small, comfortable house is full of photographs of both their families at various stages. Jill's satisfaction and pleasure with her life are palpable, and it occurs to me that time has allowed her to have the best of both worlds: a heterosexual marriage and children, followed by this relationship which satisfies a different need. For if Jill had been able to accept and live out her lesbianism earlier, she might never have had children of her own. And given the economic and socially marginal lives of most lesbian couples in the decade, she was unlikely to have found the stability and rootedness she craved with a woman.

It was difficult enough to be a lesbian in the fifties, but to be a lesbian mother who wanted to keep her children was virtually impossible. Such a woman provoked society's violent disapproval, backed up by full force of the law. Even people who might have viewed a lesbian with a kind of laissez-faire attitude—as long as she lived alone and kept to herself—were horrified at the idea of a homosexual living with small children. Lesbians still find themselves in fierce custody battles, of course, but the virulence which characterized public attitudes toward homosexuality in the fifties made it impossible to win a custody suit. Many women simply relinquished their children, rather than subject themselves and their kids to the excruciating publicity of a trial. The peremptory cruelty with which Karen

Oswald's children were taken from her was typical of the time.

A slight, fragile woman of fifty-six, Karen sits uncomfortably on the edge of the sofa in her small Queens apartment and speaks in a barely audible voice. She tells me she has never told this whole story to anyone before and isn't sure she can tell it now. Occasionally she interrupts herself, saying brusquely, "I don't want to talk about this." There are times when she is unable to go on, and we sit silently until she can speak again.

Karen was born to Polish immigrants in Chicago. Her father was a "dancing master"—he taught ballroom dancing and managed dance studios—her mother was a waitress. Karen and her father were close. He taught her to dance and took her with him to taverns where she would dance and he'd pass the hat. When Karen was ten, her parents separated and she didn't see her father again until she was an adult.

At fourteen, before she had finished high school, Karen became pregnant. "I never thought about abortion—I didn't know it existed. I didn't even know how babies came out of a woman's body. My mother more or less disowned me when she found out I was pregnant, and my father was gone. There was no one to talk to about this. So I got married. My husband was a Greek immigrant, and we lived with his family. The mother was illiterate. Everyone in the household worked—the mother, the father, my husband's sister, and my husband. I was the one who stayed home and did the housework and the cooking. I wanted to finish school by taking correspondence courses. But my mother-in-law vetoed the idea. She felt I had enough to do taking care of the baby and the house. I think she also felt uncomfortable because she herself didn't read or write."

After two years, during which her husband was physically abusive to her, Karen divorced him and married an older man, a psychologist. She did not bring her first child into this second marriage, and when I ask her about this, her eyes fill and she indicates with a wave of her hand that she won't talk about this.

Max had promised Karen that after their marriage she could return to finish high school.

"It didn't happen that way because I got pregnant almost immediately. I tried to give myself an abortion by taking something someone had told me about, but it didn't work. I didn't want to marry him, really. But I didn't have any goals. It never occurred to me to have a goal. But I did so want to go to school."

Karen and Max had two children, and while she was pregnant with the second child, Karen persuaded her husband to let her attend a pottery class two evenings a week while he stayed home with their daughter.

"That's when I met Marge—she taught this class. She was about seventeen years older than me, a very charismatic person. I was very shy. I felt comfortable with her. In my first marriage I had suffered a lot of physical brutality. And with this psychologist I was suffering a different kind of abuse—more mental. With Marge I felt safe for the first time. She was the first one who ever treated me as a complete person, which was sometimes almost startling.

"She was a lesbian, but that word wasn't in my vocabulary at all. I knew nothing about homosexuality. My sexual feelings for Marge grew over a period of time. We'd sometimes go and eat after working in the shop and go and visit other galleries. Once we took a trip together to Wisconsin and we stayed in a homey kind of hotel on a lake. I don't remember how I explained this to Max, how I got away to do this. That was when Marge and I first had a physical relationship. It was overwhelming to me because I'd never felt sexual desire and feelings of love together in that way before. Before I had been just more or less there during sex. But not as a whole person.

"Max never suspected about this relationship. I don't think he could have even imagined it. Max was the kind of man who would ask me to come all the way across the room to close a window which was six inches behind him. His entrance into a room made me feel as if I was being crushed. It was difficult to breathe."

A year after Karen and Marge met, Karen left Max and, taking the children, moved in with Marge, who lived in Lake Forest, about thirty miles outside Chicago.

"I had a truck come during the day and move the things I needed for the children. Max was incensed, But I think he thought I'd be back. I don't think he understood yet that Marge and I had a physical relationship."

A few weeks later Marge and both children came down with a serious virus. Karen was unable to cope alone and, in desperation, sent for Max, who brought Karen and the children back to Chicago. A few months later, she left him again.

"This time I took the children to a caretaker from some kind of agency. You understand, I had no relatives and my mother had removed herself from my life."

Karen and Marge moved to southern California, where they both got jobs, Marge at Douglas Aircraft and Karen in an insurance company.

"We rented a very nice house, and our idea was to establish a life out there and then send for the children. We were homebodies. We had a fireplace and liked to stay home in front of it. We went to museums. We were happy. I never had any self-consciousness about our relationship. Marge had a circle of friends there and no one ever made us feel uncomfortable or weird. But I had been so isolated from normal socialization processes. I just didn't have an awareness of society and its norms at the time. Among these friends, we were perfectly acceptable."

It was when Karen tried to bring her children to California that she began to realize the difficulty of her position. Max had found the children and taken custody of them. Karen consulted a famous California divorce lawyer, who advised her that her only chance of getting custody was to kidnap her children and bring them to California. Karen flew back to Chicago intending to carry out this plan, but Max refused to allow her to see the kids.

"I experienced this as a kind of death. This is when my life started to get torn up. I've never spoken about it before. When I went to Max to talk about a divorce, he said that if I attempted a legal battle for the children he would have my daughter, Miriam, testify that she had seen us in bed together. This wasn't so. We were never in bed together unless we were alone. Other people, friends, told me that this could ruin my daughter's life, and that in a court of law I would be in a weakened position because of this.

"I don't remember much about the divorce, but this was the upshot: Max got custody of the children and I was told I could reopen this matter when I had established a home that was suitable to bring children into. I think even my lawyer believed that Miriam had seen Marge and me in bed together, and he said it would be disastrous to take that chance. The fact that their father was a professional man, a psychologist, an upstanding member of the community, put me at even more of a disadvantage. I had no education, no job, and I was living with a woman in an unacceptable relationship."

In a desperate effort to establish a "normal" family life, Karen married a Czechoslovakian immigrant who, in return, would obtain U.S. citizenship. The marriage lasted only a year. Meanwhile, the emotional strain of the events surrounding Karen's divorce and custody battle had taken its toll on Marge, who was hospitalized with a nervous breakdown. And when Karen realized that she was probably never going to regain custody of her children, she suffered a breakdown herself.

"I just stopped moving. I had a terrible fear of making any physical movement at all. At the time I had no place to go— Marge was probably still in the hospital herself. So my doctor had me commit myself to a state mental hospital. I had seen the movie called *The Snake Pit* and it was exactly like that. You had to carry your possessions with you in a bag at all times because if you left anything anywhere it would be stolen. I slept in a room with two hundred people, with two attendants at the door. There were a lot of classes, all of which, of course, I attended, always trying to get that education. In order to get out I had to go before a board—just like in *Snake Pit*. I remembered from the movie that she couldn't get out until she could recite her social security number by heart, so I had taken care to memorize my social security number. I knew how they wanted me to present myself in order to get out of there."

After Karen was released from the hospital she returned to Marge, who had by now recovered and returned to Chicago, and they lived together for ten years. Although Karen never regained custody of her children, she was eventually allowed to visit them on weekends.

There are some gaps in Karen's story, some questions she's unwilling or unable to answer. It's as if she's purged her narrative of distracting details and ambiguities. But even allowing for oversimplification, the outlines of her story are tragic. She was a woman in oppressive circumstances reaching instinctively for a relationship that would nourish her and give her pleasure.

"For both of us, this was the most complete relationship we'd ever had: we were friends, we were two human beings who cared deeply for each other, we were sexual partners. But the message I got from everyone around me was that this relationship was so unacceptable that it would damage my children. I didn't feel like a criminal. But I felt people thought I was a criminal, to leave my children and to go live with a woman."

Gay women still lose custody of their children too much of the time. Joan Nestle estimates that today a lesbian has a sixty-forty chance of keeping her children. Though still not acceptable, these odds are far better than they were for lesbians in the fifties. Karen Oswald and women like her were the victims of a monolithic consensus that lesbians were "unnatural," and that their influence on children could only be injurious. A lesbian fighting for custody today has a community behind her, lawyers eager to argue her case, and a body of public opinion in at least a segment of the population that supports a lesbian's right to keep her children.

No longer shrouded in invisibility and silence, lesbianism now has a face and a voice. The material difference this makes in people's lives is incalculable. The existence of lesbian books, bookstores, newspapers, and presses means that lesbians can find their experience and sexuality represented in words and images, their history restored to them.

The isolation of the fifties has been replaced by community. Lesbian institutions and social organizations are listed in the phone books of every city; lesbian guidebooks direct women to places and organizations that will welcome them. A communications network provides lesbian therapists, doctors, and attorneys.

The powerlessness that goes along with invisibility is yielding, slowly, to the beginnings of political clout. Lesbians serve as elected officials and are increasingly visible in public life. Lesbians and gay men are even perceived in some cities as voting constituencies that must be served. Laws have been passed banning kinds of discrimination that were taken for granted in the fifties. Surely the most spectacular symbolic answer to the silence and invisibility of the fifties is the spectacle of thousands of lesbians marching triumphantly through the streets of America's cities on Gay Pride Day.

Chapter X

Which Side Are You On?

When I was at the University of Michigan in 1955, a Pete Seeger concert got canceled at the last minute. Rumors were flying all over the campus that it was because of Pete Seeger being a Communist. We all shook our heads and murmured—whined, really— "Oh, that's not fair." That was all. Just, "Oh, that's not fair." It never would have occurred to us to do anything about this. The idea of protesting anything simply wasn't in our repertoire. We accepted everything.

—RONNIE HOFFMAN

All those years our house was the central meeting place for our group. Every meeting, every party, every visiting CP fireman was put up at our place. I always hated it.... "Who the hell does all the work?" I'd yell. "While you sit on your ass making the revolution, I'm out there in the kitchen like a slavey. What we need is a revolution in *this* house...." And it was like that to the very end. We always had a houseful of Party people, and organizers, and, finally, FBI agents."

—VIVIAN GORNICK,
THE ROMANCE OF AMERICAN COMMUNISM

In the 1950s, few Americans were giving much thought to society's wrongs and how to right them, most were turned inward, absorbed in their private lives. They were preoccupied with raising their families, finding and building homes, and acquiring the consumer goods they'd been deprived of during wartime. It was a time of hunkering down, of closing ranks. When they thought about the future, it was defensively: the future was something to be safeguarded, made secure, above all. If they looked out at the larger world, they saw things that made them nervous: the Russian H-bomb and Euro-Communism, which Illinois senator Everett Dirksen called "this red tide . . . like some vile creeping thing which is spreading its web westward."

The fear of enemies without was easily manipulated by demagogues like Senator Joseph McCarthy into a near-hysterical feeling of subversion within the country. But in fact as early as 1947, three years before Senator McCarthy began his anti-Communist campaign, President Truman created a federal loyalty program which called for the dismissal of any federal worker associated with a list of tainted organizations. Thousands of federal employees were fired and hundreds more were intimidated into resigning. State and local governments jumped on the bandwagon, instituting loyalty oaths of their own, and purging employees who refused to sign them. Jill Morris, who was working in the Department of Welfare in New York City in 1949, remembers:

"They passed around this thing at work. On one side was a loyalty oath and on the other side of the paper it said you volunteered for twenty-four hours of civil defense duty. Well, *a*, it didn't make sense to me to be forced to volunteer for anything, and *b*, I didn't believe in the loyalty oath. I wasn't all that political, but I guess I had instincts. In college I had been a member of the interracial club. There were six of us and we met in the Unitarian church. Our big activity was, we demonstrated about the fact that the college football hero, a black guy who was routinely carried on the shoulders of his teammates after games, couldn't get a hamburger at the local steak-and-shake. So my basic sense of justice got activated and I refused to sign this thing. Well, one night I open up the *Journal American* and there's a headline: 'Commissioner of Welfare Fires Rotten Red Apples,' and there's my name and address, big as life. About two dozen people were fired from my office on 125th Street. No benefits, nothing. Eventually I had to go back up to the welfare office to get the two weeks' vacation pay they owed me and I had to sign the damn thing because I needed the money so badly."

Drawing on what historian Bernard DeVoto called "a hash of gossip, rumor, slander, backbiting, malice and drunken invention," the FBI destroyed reputations and lives. An accusation alone was enough, not only to get you fired from your job, but "blacklisted" from other jobs in your field. Individuals and groups that publicly protested these abuses automatically came under suspicion themselves.

Alix Berns's family fell victim to the anti-Communist witch-hunts in 1948. "My father worked for the 'Voice of America,' and while I was in high school, he lost his job. When this happened it wasn't discussed a lot, even though life changed pretty dramatically. My mother took a full-time job. My sister and I were pretty hazy about what was really going on, but there was this sense that something terrible was happening and that we all had to pull together. We weren't that unusual—there were known Communists in our neighborhood—they were considered exotic and interesting and just a little more liberal than the rest of us. But I didn't know anybody else that this kind of thing was happening to. I assumed my parents weren't talking about it because it was so terrible they were ashamed, but in fact, they explained later, they were just trying to keep us from being frightened and worried.

"We knew we had to be very careful around the house so as not to add to father's stress, to behave ourselves. My sister remembers that my mother tried very hard to keep us from going into the room where the television was, where she was trying to keep an eye on what was happening in the hearings.

"Years later, my father told me the whole story. Evidently he had been denounced by one of his co-workers. There was a loyalty hearing and he was cleared. Then there was another hearing, but this time there was no decision for nearly a year, and by that time the atmosphere at work was very uncomfortable, with this thing hanging over him. McCarthy was gathering steam by then and he knew things were going to get worse. He was sure he would eventually be fired, so he quit. He was really driven to quit. They never knew if he would have to appear at the hearings, if he would be on television, and what kind of humiliation that would be for us. And in fact, he *was* summoned to the McCarthy hearings in 1951, but it turned out he didn't have to testify—just by a lucky fluke. What this was all about was that he had been one of the founding members of the Newspaper Guild and had been involved in organizing strikes. This was just the kind of thing the witch-hunters were looking for. The FBI were all over the neighborhood asking questions about him. They evidently asked our downstairs neighbor whether she'd ever seen any black people at our house. In fact, one of Mother's colleagues at school, a French teacher, was black, and had been over to dinner several times. So that was one of the pieces of evidence they had that my father was a suspicious type.

"This period had a profound effect on me. I learned how someone very strong and powerful, as I thought my dad to be, could be affected by events outside their control. I saw my dad change and I began to feel I had to be the strong one. I was the firstborn—the son, if you will, the one always admonished to take care of your sister. So I was feeling very protective of everyone. I knew I had to get my act together. I think this was when

I started getting good at school. It became clear that there would be no money for private college, so I went to Queens College. My friends at college would be drinking and playing bridge, but I felt I couldn't be that frivolous. It was a loss of innocence in a way. I began to feel I wanted to be my own boss. I didn't want anybody to be able to come in and take my job away or control my life in any way, the way they had with my father."

The anti-Communist hysteria infected communities, neighborhoods, institutions, and industries. The witch-hunts reached grotesque heights during the House Un-American Activities Committee's hearings on subversion in the entertainment industry in the late forties and early fifties. People who attended funerals of colleagues and friends driven to suicide or early death by the persecution found themselves subpoenaed to testify before the committee.

Between 1950 and 1954, when he was formally condemned by the U.S. Senate, Senator McCarthy had carte blanche to conduct his devastating campaign. By 1954, however, public opinion was beginning to turn against him, soured by the nationally televised spectacle of the Army–McCarthy hearings. Dorothy Glenn remembers watching the hearings in her suburb:

"A friend and I would arrange the day so that we'd get all the children sleeping at the same time so that we could listen. We weren't particularly liberal in those days, in fact, we were all pretty conservative. We even knew a couple of people who ended up in the John Birch Society. I was genuinely worried about the Russians—I remember having dreams about the bomb. But we thought McCarthy was crazy. We were overjoyed when Welch finally started cutting him down."

Tyler Barrett was also disturbed by McCarthyism and concerned about other social issues, but felt reluctant to voice her opinions openly.

"I was so aware of not fitting in. I'd been in Europe when

McCarthy got started and had a different slant on him from the people around me. I thought he was a joke, despicable. I was also beginning to be aware of the Civil Rights movement, enough to get involved with Urban League kind of stuff. But I was afraid to go down to the John A. Brown company and sit in on the lunch counter because I knew that would offend my family and friends. I'm ashamed of that now. I knew I was seen as a woman of strong opinions, who should know better because she's 'one of us.'"

When Angela Barone moved to Levittown, she wanted to do "something more than just the usual kaffee klatsch, so I got involved with something called the Committee to End Discrimination in Levittown. There was a whites-only clause in the covenant, you know—it was a *policy* not to admit blacks. In 1950, someone from the NAACP—maybe Roy Wilkins?—was speaking at someone's home and I went. The group seemed to be highly motivated and the idea was to find a house for blacks to move into, they'd check around the area and be sure it wouldn't start a conflagration. That seemed rational. At the time, my husband was working for a company where he needed clearance because they had defense contracts. So he was a little concerned because this was the kind of group that would often attract Communists. I promised him faithfully that if I saw any indications of that, I would leave immediately. They finally did find a house for a black family to move into, but they didn't do their job properly and there were problems. People were getting calls at all hours of the night, people had nails put in their driveway. It was very unpleasant. Then more people started joining and some people took over and the focus seemed to change to publicity. I felt these new people were using the committee for their own purposes and I left."

In this climate, anything that smacked of a concern for the common good or for social justice was viewed with suspicion. Indeed, the very words "social" and "common" set red flags awaving in many people's minds. Religious leaders Billy Graham and Norman Vincent Peale even made public statements decrying social activism. To live a political life in this atmosphere was, ipso facto, to go against the grain of American society. At best, you might be part of a tiny, beleaguered community bound together by shared ideals and goals. At its worst, this life was secret and embattled, pervaded by the fear of discovery.

Ruth Friedman was an ardent young Leftist in the 1940s. Her story is a paradigm of the journey of a woman activist from the heady excitement of political life in the forties to the life of a fifties housewife, circumscribed by gender and chilled by the fear of discovery of her Communism. Tiny and energetic, Ruth shows no signs of yielding to her seventy years. We talk in the dark but cozy clutter of the apartment on the upper west side of Manhattan, where she and her husband Ben have lived for twenty years.

Ruth grew up in a small New Jersey community where hers was one of only three Jewish families in town. Her father was a building contractor and a compulsive gambler who lost everything in the crash. "We had oriental rugs and a Steinway grand in the hall and almost overnight it was all gone," remembers Ruth. "However, my father still had these incredibly crazy, bourgeois ideas. I did quite well in high school, for example, and could have had scholarships to any college I wanted. I wanted desperately to go to Barnard. But my father's view was that we didn't accept scholarships—that was like charity. So I ended up going to City College."

For several years Ruth worked as a dental assistant during the day and attended City College at night.

"Those years were awful. I made ten dollars a week and gave nine dollars to my mother. Luckily I had to wear a uniform all day because I had only one good dress for two years and it would have fallen apart. We were having a hard time finding a place to live because we couldn't pay the rent, but my father got hired as caretaker of this magnificent, empty whitestone mansion on Fifth Avenue. We lived in the basement with almost no furniture."

In 1941, Ruth transferred to the uptown branch of City College and her life changed almost overnight. "One of the first nights I was there somebody asked me to join the American Student Union and I did. I was feeling very bitter about my father and everything that had happened to our family. So when this guy at college started talking about how the system—capitalism—works and what it does to people, it gave me a way not to be angry at my father. It enabled me to see that it wasn't just that he was weak, but that this is what the system does to people. I became completely immersed. It was a new life! Suddenly I started to meet people and go out and be the Belle of the Ball. After one semester I was asked to become the president of the uptown ASU and the next thing I knew I was out there making street-corner speeches. I'll never forget the first time—it was on the corner of Convent Avenue and 137th Street and I didn't know what the hell I was talking about but I did it."

At about this time, Ruth also went to work as a file clerk at Columbia Pictures. "That was the beginning of my organizing career. The United Office Professional Workers, the UOPW, was just starting to organize there. I remember signing my first union card in the toilet at Columbia Pictures—I was one of the first five to sign. That was a wonderful, exciting period. We were all totally involved in organizing this union and they were marvelous people. Most of them were Communists, visionaries, very bright and knowledgeable." When Ruth was promoted to screen reader, she also became a union shop steward for five hundred workers. After a year or so, she left Columbia and went to work for the UOPW.

"I was going out with Ben by now, and right after the war started, he was drafted. We got married two weeks before he shipped out and then I didn't see him for three years. They sent him to Europe and he was in the Battle of the Bulge. I never expected that he would ever come home in one piece.

"During those war years, life was hard, but everyone was up. We were hopeful, we were fighting Hitler, and there was an esprit that carried us along. The union had a lot of victories, we'd organized the whole screen industry in New York.

"My mother had gotten fed up with my father and his bad debts and she, my sister, and I moved to a furnished room on 111th and Broadway. They were these big old apartments which had been divided up into rooms. We shared a kitchen with seven other families. My mother slept in one bed and my sister and I shared the other. Our bed was always warm because we worked separate shifts: she was working nights at Western Electric and I was working days. So when she got up, I got into bed and when I got up she got into bed. We used to have Communist Party branch meetings in that room on Sunday mornings, after my mother went to work. Our room was separated from the next room by French doors and on the other side of the doors was a young couple, and while we were having these serious, high-minded meetings, this couple would be screwing their heads off and yelling with passion. It was a wonderful, hopeful time. We were sure we were going to see socialism in our lifetime."

When Ben came home from the war in 1946, Ruth quit her job at the union and went to work for the first in a series of Jewish organizations.

"With Ben home, I didn't want to work one hundred hours a week any more. But we were both deeply involved in political work during that period. Ben was active in the teachers union and I was active in the American Labor Party. I was back speaking on street corners and someone inscribed a book to me as 'La Passionaria of Washington Heights.'"

Ruth and Ben put off having children for three years. Life was busy and hectic, full of meetings, election campaigns, and organizing drives. "Then we just did it—we didn't talk about it much. What's to discuss? We were married so we should have babies. I'd always assumed I'd have children, even though I never had any particular feeling for children. I'd had no contact with kids and wasn't eager to be with kids. I think if I were twenty-two now maybe I wouldn't have children. But in those days, for us and for most of the people that we knew, to think about yourself, to introspect about how you were feeling, you just didn't do it. You thought about humanity, the whole world that you were going to change.

"So we started to build a nest—we bought all this furniture that you see here. David was born in 1949. Oh, that was a classic situation—I remember being left alone in this room in Beth Israel for about ten hours in labor. Then I was given an anesthetic, and I was out, so that was that experience. Breast-feeding I wasn't interested in—I was anxious to get rid of my body then.

"We were living in this little apartment in Washington Heights, and we gave the bedroom to David and we slept in the living room. I stayed home after David was born, of course. Nobody thought that you could leave infants unless you absolutely had to. Suddenly my life was so different. I couldn't work, couldn't do my political stuff, couldn't even make phone calls without being interrupted. I loved my baby, but it was always mixed with resentment at the interference. Here was something, somebody I couldn't control. If he cried, I had to do something about it. I always felt I was withholding part of myself out of resentment. David was a colicky baby, couldn't be consoled. I remember putting him in his carriage to soothe him, rock him, and then, when he wouldn't stop crying, I'd find I was rocking the carriage more and more violently. I was so desperate for him to stop. Of course I loved seeing him grow and develop, but to tell you the truth, I never really felt I was doing this wonderful, creative thing. I always tried to work at something—like selling World Books or Avon products."

When David was a year old, Ruth and her family moved to Queens Village, a veterans co-op that Ben, as a GI, was entitled to live in. Their daughter, Sarah, was born in 1952.

"We were all young families, and we had garden apartments around a big courtyard, and the children were always out there. There was lots of activity, lots going on. We had a big group of neighbors who were progressive, and we had a very active community council. Those were the McCarthy days, the Rosenberg days, and I even remember that the community council passed a resolution in support of the Rosenbergs. I remember going out in the mornings with my daughter in the carriage, taking David up to nursery school and pushing the carriage around collecting money and signatures for the Rosenbergs. That was the time when we had to get rid of all our books, all our political books. Not everyone in that co-op was progressive—for example we had a neighbor, a conservative Catholic woman, who was always in and out of our house. With Ben teaching, we felt extraordinarily vulnerable. He was meeting with a Party cell within the teachers union and we were genuinely afraid that he could lose his job."

By the time Sarah was born, Ben had begun work on his doctorate, which meant he was rarely home. "There was no discussion about which one of us would go on for further education. It was just taken for granted that it would be Ben—taken for granted by both of us. It wasn't until some time around the late fifties that I began to feel unhappy being at home alone with the kids and seeing that Ben was advancing himself intellectually and in every way. He was *out there* and I was *in here*. I remember once looking down into the courtyard and seeing my neighbor Louise getting into a car. I had not yet learned to drive—we only had one car and Ben used it. I had a kind of epiphany, I guess. I said to myself: first, I have to learn to drive and then I have to get the hell out of here. I started to think about going back to work."

By the time Sarah was able to start nursery school, Ruth had learned to drive and landed a job as secretary to the director of Hillside Hospital. "When I first started back to work, there was a regular chorus, when I left in the morning, of *tsk tsk tsk* all around the courtyard. I was the only woman who went to work in that development, even among those progressives. They were staying home with their children. People would say things to me, they would allude to the fact that 'you're never around.' There was not a morning that I went out that I didn't feel conflicted about going. Not conflicted about *wanting* to go to work—I *knew* that was what I wanted. But about whether or not it was the right thing to do. The image that's engraved on my mind about the whole working experience is Sarah, age five, sitting on the curb where the nursery school bus had left her off, waiting for me to come home. I still wonder if it was the best thing to have done. . . . I know it was the best thing for me."

Even this progressive community was not immune to fifties values when it came to sex roles and family. People who were prepared to challenge almost every other shibboleth of mainstream America did not question the assumption that a woman's role was to bear and care for children, the man's to win the bread. Ruth Friedman herself accepted the imperative to give up her job and the political work she loved and turn her entire attention to family life. And when she did eventually go back to work, her decision was as roundly criticized in her progressive community as it would have been in any suburban enclave.

The change in their life and relationship from the forties to the fifties was dramatic. In 1942, they were two independent, committed young people living their politics on an equal basis. By 1950, such a life was difficult if not impossible. Even in their progressive milieu, their political affiliations had to be hidden. Their relationship had taken on the contours of the conventional fifties marriage.

* * *

Theresa Boyle lived another kind of political life during the fifties. As a young wife and mother, she was part of the movement of progressive Catholics whose goals were an active laity, independent of church hierarchy, and working for social justice. Theresa, who weathered a bitter divorce in 1978, now lives in St. Louis where she teaches English in an adult education program. Outside her cool, dim kitchen, St. Louis shimmers in one hundred degree heat. Theresa pours me a glass of iced tea and sits down across the kitchen table, shy, but eager to tell her story.

Theresa grew up in a series of Iowa towns and cities, the daughter of a Catholic mother and a non-Catholic father. When she was a sophomore in high school, Theresa's family moved to Cedar Falls, where she went to a high school on the campus of Iowa State Teachers College.

"I always felt like an outsider in that high school, partly because of our family problems—my father's drinking—but also because the town's culture was based on its large Danish Lutheran population. I can still remember that I was accepted at one of the high school sororities, but they withdrew their invitation when they found I was Catholic. This was the first time I realized that being Catholic could be a problem.

"We lived in a house called the Newman Club, a Catholic club right across the street from the college campus which my parents ran. We had the run of the house, but the large living room, dining room, and solarium were open to Catholic students for meetings. This was a kind of financial rescue for our family. My mother was really carrying the ball at this point. She was a devout Catholic and I think I've stayed a Catholic because she was such a strong person, and she had something to offer, where my father offered me nothing in the way of goals or ideals."

After high school, Theresa waitressed and worked at the telephone company for a year to earn money for college. The following year, she went to Iowa State Teachers college, where she quickly gravitated to journalism.

"I became editor of the college paper in my freshman year." She laughs. "Well, that was 1946 and most of the boys hadn't come back from the war yet. I think this idea about journalism came from teachers in my high school who recognized that I could write and encouraged me. It also seemed to be a career that might pay. But I didn't know any women in journalism. I just mapped this out all by myself."

The following year, Theresa transferred to the University of Iowa, which had a well-known journalism school. Shortly before graduation, Theresa was informed that, due to an administrative error, she was three credit hours short. Out of money and eager to leave, she was allowed to graduate with a blank diploma.

"The day of graduation, another girl and I drove out to Denver where we wanted to work. I put this down to a sense of adventure and wanting to take care of myself, but I was also very eager to get away from home. I went right over to the *National Catholic Register* to get a job. When I went in, they said, we don't take applications this way. You have to write us a letter and send a resume. So I went back out to the nearest five-and-dime and bought some stationery. Then I went to the library and wrote the letter, took it back to the *Register* and got the job. So I was pretty proud of myself. I did proofreading— they did not allow women to write for the *Register,* at that time. We could work in the proof room, but we could not be reporters. The men started out in the proof room, but then they were moved up to the editorial room. I knew this was unfair, but it didn't occur to me to challenge it. It was just the way it was."

Theresa met her husband-to-be, Hugh Boyle, in the proof room on the night shift. Hugh was from Green Bay, Wisconsin, an orphan who had spent his whole life in Catholic boarding

schools and had joined a religious order. On the eve of his ordi-
nation, Hugh decided against a religious life and the next day
he was inducted into the army. When he and Theresa met in
1948, he had just been discharged.

"I think what drew us together was the stimulation of the
shared Catholic background and the shared ideals. Hugh was—
is—brilliant. He had ideas of a paper written by Catholic lay
people, something both of us were intrigued with. Hugh
wanted to put out a paper that was not parochial, somewhat
along the lines of the *Christan Science Monitor*. He thought
what was needed was some really good journalism that didn't
say things like, 'Plane crashes in Texas: Three Catholics killed,'
when fifty other people had also been killed. I was so drawn to
his idealism. I saw in this man someone totally different from
my father, someone who, because of his Catholic background,
wanted to live a Christian life, who wanted a family because he
was an orphan. All these things were very appealing to me. My
own agenda was that I wanted children, a family—it was a hidden agenda, but it was there."

Theresa and Hugh were married in 1949 and had their first
child, Tommy, ten months later.

"At that time we were in love with 'holy poverty' instead of
what we perceived as the hypocrisy we saw around us—everybody nesting and accumulating things. We were also interested
in the 'green revolution' that was going on then—people were
gardening, living off the land. What went along with all this was
a kind of progressive politics—for example, we started the first
Catholic Interracial Council in Denver and we had some run-ins
with the archbishop because of it. He was going to bring in a
black priest to serve the black community and we protested,
saying it should be interracial. We were really on a blacklist in
Denver with the archdiocese.

"We were also involved in the Christian Family Movement,

which had started in Chicago. This was little cell groups of Catholics, most of them married with children—young people who met and talked about how to be better Christians in the family."

Hugh's radical views were increasingly putting him at odds with the *National Register*'s conservative editor and in 1950 he and Theresa moved to Chicago to start their newspaper.

"We had sent out a precursor letter—I don't know where we got a mailing list—saying this paper was coming, would you be willing to donate some money to help us get started. We raised nearly fifty thousand dollars just from that letter. Apparently people were hungry for this.

"While we were in Chicago I became pregnant with our second child. We were living in an absolute slum on the west side of Chicago. For a little Iowa girl, this was quite a shock. I saw no trees, no grass, the kids played in the street. The first day I was there a rat went right through my kitchen. I was so scared I kept Tommy, who was a toddler, on the kitchen table until Hugh came home. It was summer, very hot. We finally found another place, a nice clean apartment, in the Czech district. That was much better, but it still felt like a very foreign place to me. I'd go out each morning with my basket, like all the good Czech women around me, and do my shopping at the fruit market and the meat market. It was quite domestic. We were living in back of the offices this group of young people was using. I'd prepare lunch every day and we'd all eat together. I wasn't part of the meetings, and the writing and sending off of the letter. But I started a filing system, so I was part of it in that way.

"It was an uncomfortable time, but I don't remember longing for something else. This was a deep commitment. We were willing to put up with anything for this ideal. Though I was with Hugh on all of this, he was really the leader, he had the vision and the intelligence for it. I think, in fact, I was the back-bone in some ways, but he knew much more about the church. I backed him a hundred percent."

Denied permission to start a lay paper by Chicago's Cardinal Stritch, the group began to cast about for a diocese that would accept their venture. Eventually they found a home for the paper in Kansas City.

"We found this old house in the southeast area—a huge, stone, three-story mansion with eleven rooms. The whole third floor was a ballroom! Completely torn up, weeds all around—we just thought it was great! Everyone was very excited about the paper and people kept coming out to see us and help get the place together. The Loretta nuns sent their high school girls out to help clean up the place.

"I had six children in twelve years in that house. My father had died just before I got married, so my mother came to live with us. Even with her help, it was a rough motherhood. We had no clothes dryer for years so everything got hung out on the line. At first we had no central heating—only two wood-burning stoves. Later we hooked them up to gas. There were rooms we'd just close off and never use in the winter. I walked to the grocery store which was seven blocks away, usually with a stroller and this throng of kids around me.

"Of course, we used no birth control. There was no pill yet and I'm not sure I would have used it anyway. Rhythm was barely talked about. And besides, Hugh and I both bought into the idea that you take the children as they come. After each birth I went through the ritual of cleansing, a Catholic ritual called 'churching.' It was not a public ceremony—it involved being ritually cleansed and blessed—I remember the words 'be cleansed.'

"After a while I think there began to be a conflict in my mind: I can't handle any more, but it's wrong not to accept them. I think Hugh was also feeling the burden of all these children, and realized that it was a burden on me. Frankly, I think one way we handled it was just not to have as much sex. We didn't talk about it. We had a kind of tacit agreement. Communication was not good on things like this. Besides, Hugh was working late into the night and I was often asleep when he got in. So there got to be a little more space between babies each time." Hugh's paper lasted only ten months. For a time he worked at whatever he could—driving a taxi, selling Wearever pots and pans door-to-door. In time he was asked by then-Bishop Coney to become editor of a new diocesan paper. Coney gave Hugh a free hand with the new paper, and it absorbed most of his time and attention.

"For most of the fifties I was left alone in the house to raise those children. But I was barely aware of resentment. My feeling was: he is doing a wonderful thing and that's his job, and I'm doing my part being a wonderful wife and mother. If I did have flickering doubts about the way we were dividing our labors I wouldn't have spoken of them to Hugh. Always I was afraid that if I demanded anything of him, his mission might be compromised, and what he was doing was so much more important."

Toward the end of the fifties, at her mother's urging, Theresa enrolled in a correspondence course to earn the remaining three credits for her degree.

"I'd go up to the attic and work and she'd watch the kids. I didn't really think it was necessary at first—after all, wasn't I going to be married forever? I mean, seventeenth-century English literature? It turned out I really loved it—I guess I needed the stimulation. It felt so good to go up into that attic and close the door and use my brain."

Like Ruth Friedman, Theresa Boyle now sees herself as both at odds with and caught up in the mainstream culture of the fifties.

"On one level we were very isolated because of our involve-

ment with the newspaper and because of our physical isolation—we were hardly living in a ranch-style house in the suburbs! At the same time, without realizing it, I was buying into a
lot of the same things other women in the fifties did. We were
also part of the mainstream *Catholic* culture of the time: we sent
our kids to parochial school, and whatever the sisters said, we
bought. In some ways we beat at the structure, but we
remained inside the gates."

Traditional party politics, always a male enclave, became even
more exclusive during the fifties. Women who had been active
during the New Deal era were aging, and had failed to bring
other women along to replace themselves. Newspaper and magazine articles rebuked women for not being more active in political parties, but had no suggestions about how to reconcile the
conflicting demands of domestic and political life. Nevertheless, a
few women with energy to spare and the economic resources to
free up their time for volunteer work, did make forays into local
politics. Adele Schreiber recently retired from a long career in
local Democratic politics. We talk on the patio of her sprawling
Spanish-style house overlooking the Berkeley hills.

"As soon as we came out here I went to the local Democratic club and volunteered to work. I had always been very
interested in politics, and I was damned if I was going to be out
watering the lawn at 8 A.M. like everyone else. At ten in the
morning all the wives would get together and have coffee and
talk about their sex lives, and how awful their husbands were
and what they were cooking. This was not for me. I was immediately sent out to canvass door-to-door. Within a year I was
president of the club. I'd cook and clean and take care of all my
other stuff, but then I'd go do this. The other women thought
I was peculiar. When they wanted me to bring something to a
PTA bake sale, I'd always bring something store-bought
because I didn't have time to bake. They thought that was odd,
and would say, 'Oh, you and your politics!'

"At that time, the club movement *was* the Democratic party. We hadn't had a Democrat in the entire state legislature at that time. Herb got involved too, but he was sort of seen as 'Adele's husband.' We campaigned hard for Stevenson, whom we adored. I'd get the kids off to school, prepare dinner, and then go off to headquarters. Back at six in time for the kids, then I'd often go back to headquarters after dinner. And I loved it, I just loved it. Then I ran a campaign for a local congressman. That's when I started to *really* work! He won and it was a huge upset. He was entitled to make one political appointment and he asked me to be his deputy. Well, I almost fainted. I didn't even know where City Hall was. I said yes. This was an important job, a *paying* job.

"So I went home and told Herb, I'm going to work. He was very upset. He said, 'Did it ever occur to you to ask me?' I remember this so well. And I said, 'No.' I hired a full-time housekeeper. This was in 1956: my daughter was five, my son was three. I must admit that I was not concerned about whether or not this was going to be good for the children. I just never had the feeling that they were going to suffer. I went to work and I was never happier in my life. I loved my job, loved my boss, we worked so well together. But it didn't last long because I was the first woman who'd ever been proposed for that position and I had to be approved by the city council and they opposed me—because I was a woman and, worse than that, a Jewish woman.

"Well, he stuck to his guns, but there was a whole brouhaha, with the Chief of Police involved. He said he had a file on me because I was a Communist. I gave my boss my word I was never a Communist, but I told him he shouldn't appoint me, that it would be a blot on his political career. But he insisted, he went back to the city council and insisted on seeing my file. They had gone back to people I'd gone to high school with, but there was nothing there, really. Finally they approved me. I was there for two years before any of them would talk to me.

"It never occurred to me to run for office myself. At one point, when my boss was elected to higher office, he wanted me to be his interim appointment. But they wouldn't have it.

"In those City Hall days, we were trying to get a park for our district. My boss couldn't go to the hearing and he asked me to go in his place. Well, I was very nervous, but I prepared my case well, and I really knew my stuff. So I made my presentation, and my opponent, a man, presented his case. After we were through, the Commissioner said, 'Well, how could we say no to such a charming young lady?' So I got my park. That was the attitude I always got. But I went ahead and did what I had to do and I got what I wanted."

As a dedicated Communist, Jean Williams has spent a lifetime challenging the system that Adele Schreiber was trying to break into. Jean, now seventy-four, comes from a long tradition of activists. Her mother's family, descendants of escaped slaves, worked with the underground railroad in Ohio. Her Communist affiliation brought her into a direct confrontation with McCarthyism in the 1950s. Sitting in her modest, comfortable apartment in Brooklyn, surrounded by African figures and photos of Paul Robeson and W. E. B. Du Bois, the ordeal she describes seems unreal, like a distant nightmare.

Jean joined the Party and plunged into political work while she was in graduate school at Fisk University in Nashville, Tennessee.

"I lived in a settlement house in the middle of the black ghetto in Nashville. That was the first time I had spent time in a southern, urban slum. I saw some of the most horrible things I had ever seen in my life. It seemed to me that something drastic needed to be done, and I came to believe that only a revolutionary change in the kind of society we had would help these people."

In Nashville, Jean met her husband, Ernest, a fellow Party member, while they were both working for the Southern Negro Youth Conference, a forerunner of the Student Non-Violent Coordinating Committee (SNCC). They married in 1941 and moved to Birmingham, Alabama, where Jean stayed for seven years, working for SNCC, while Ernest was in the army.

When Jean and Ernest and their two daughters came to New York in 1950, the McCarthy era was in full swing.

"We had been living in Michigan for two years—I was working on the Wallace campaign and Ernest was organizing auto workers—and we wanted to go back down South, but at that time it was too dangerous to be in the South if you were on the Left. So we came to New York and in a matter of months my husband was indicted under the Smith Act. (The Smith Act, passed by Congress in 1940, banned, among other things, the advocacy of the forcible or violent overthrow of the government.) There had been one Smith Act trial already where people had been convicted and gone to jail for five years or more. Hundreds of people had been arrested all across the country. You either stayed and went on trial or you went underground.

"It was decided that a certain number of people should go out, go underground—not because they were running away, but so that they could continue to work. We knew they were looking for Ernest because every day more and more people were around the building, talking to the neighbors, around our daughters' school. There was no question that Ernest was going to be arrested, so it was decided that he should be one of the ones to go. Frankly, I didn't have a lot of input into the decision, but we did discuss it, and I think if I had put up some big opposition he might have had second thoughts. But, you see, it wasn't as if he was choosing between going underground and staying home with me and the children. He was certain to be arrested at any moment.

"Our daughters, Charlotte and Mary, were eight and three

and a half. They already knew about and identified with the Rosenberg children, and children whose parents had been lynched in the South, so this wasn't so strange for them. They were a little frightened, yes. He took nothing with him when he left. He couldn't do anything that would draw attention to himself. Just walked out the door. Three days after he left, they knocked on my door with a subpoena.

"He was gone for five years and we didn't see him once during that time. It was hard, but don't forget, we'd already had years of separation—in World War II, and when we were in the South, when Ernest was working on some case, he would often disappear and wouldn't be able to get in touch with anyone. So it wasn't as if I'd been in some cocoon. But I didn't know that it would be five years."

As profoundly as it challenged American society, the Communist Party did not concern itself with questioning prevailing gender arrangements. Jean's job was the job of the wife of every traveling man in the 1950s: to hold the home front together while her husband did the "important work." Few women went underground because, as Jean points out, "there weren't that many women in the leadership, so the people most in danger of being indicted were men. Besides, someone needed to stay and take care of the children."

Jean heard from Ernest only occasionally and in clandestine ways. "I'd be sitting in a meeting or a concert and somebody would come by and hand me a note and disappear into the crowd. One day somebody handed me an envelope with nothing in it but my husband's wedding band. Oh, my heart went into my throat when I saw that. But I learned he was all right. He'd just gotten concerned that the ring might identify him.

"I used to have to fabricate these long messages from him for Ernest's parents in Virginia, so that they wouldn't be too frightened. So I had my children on one side and my in-laws on the other that I was trying to reassure. The way I handled it with my children was, I got them involved in the defense of the Rosenberg children. So my girls could see that at least they were not facing their father's execution and they felt lucky. I gave them a sense that people were fighting back.

"There were people who supported us even though they couldn't come out publicly. Progressive camps would give the girls a camp for the summer, free. It was sort of a schizophrenic existence for the girls, I think. On the one hand, they were living this enriched, middle-class, life, with summer camp and piano and music lessons—all donated, of course—and at the same time they were deprived of their father and they were being followed by the FBI everywhere they went. When my older daughter went to the park with her school class, FBI men would jump out from behind trees. They thought she was going to meet her father there! If I took them to see Santa at Macy's, I'd look over and see these very obvious FBI guys, always tall, always blond, with hats, they stood out like sore thumbs.

"The black community in Brooklyn where I lived was a great source of support for us. We lived in a brownstone, and during the first two months, two carloads of FBI agents were stationed down on the street in front of the house. We made a flyer explaining who they were and what they were doing and why and we put them under the doors of everyone in the building. We didn't run away from it. Some people lived in communities where their neighbors turned on them and isolated them and they were forced to move. We tried to organize our whole neighborhood about what was happening, and what my husband was, and what he believed in. Our only problem was that a woman on the first floor of our building was running a numbers operation and she was sure this was interfering with her business.

"I worked part-time as an assistant to a doctor who had been a Spanish Civil War vet. The FBI used to sit outside his office, too, and even visited some of his patients. The idea was to put pressure on him to get him to fire me, but they sure had him figured wrong. He used to drive me home sometimes and he'd say, 'Let's have some fun, let's lose 'em.' And he'd go tearing through alleys and up and down side streets a mile a minute until we lost them. Of course, I knew they'd be waiting for me outside my house because they knew I wasn't going to leave my children, but this doctor used to say, 'Let's make 'em think you're going to see your husband.'"

The FBI never caught up with Jean's husband. In 1955 when the climate started to improve, Ernest Williams surfaced and turned himself in to a friend, a black lawyer in New York.

"It was on the TV news and a friend saw it and called to tell me, Ernest just turned himself in down at West Street. So I made a beeline down there. Then I came roaring back up and got our daughters and brought them to see their father. We had to raise twenty thousand dollars bail and my mother and I raised ten thousand dollars of it ourselves. I went down to Virginia and we got into a cab and went 'round to all her friends, all our old friends, black and white down there and raised ten thousand dollars in about two days. Other people raised the rest of the money.

"After he turned himself in, he went on trial for eleven months and by then there was a Supreme Court decision [*Yates* v. *United States,* 1957, reversed the Smith Act convictions of fourteen leaders of the Communist Party in California], so he never had to go to jail.

"I was frightened for the country. So many terrible things were happening—people dying of heart attacks, committing suicide, having to leave the country, people going to jail. There was a lot of terror in the land. Some people actually thought fascism was coming to the country. Now, of course, when we look back, our fears were perhaps exaggerated. But the things that were happening made us fear that the situation could only get worse."

Feminism as an organized political movement itself fell victim to the anti-Communist hysteria. The women's rights movement was a natural target for Communist witch-hunters, many of whom viewed the ERA as a Communist-inspired idea. Many feminist leaders scrambled to establish themselves and their organizations as anti-Communist, and attacked each other as "Left-leaning." Already weakened by internal conflict and confusion over goals, the women's movement became virtually paralyzed by distrust and suspicion.

Nevertheless, a handful of women journalists and critics— Marya Mannes, Diana Trilling, Mary McCarthy, and Lillian Hellman among them—spoke out against the McCarthyism with courage and passion at a time when many of their male colleagues were either tentative or silent.

Epilogue

Decades don't usually begin and end sharply in their first and last years. The fifties, for example, really began in 1946, the year after the war ended. But in many ways the year 1960 really does mark the official end of the 1950s. In that year the birth control pill was introduced, John F. Kennedy was elected president, the first sit-in took place in Greensboro, North Carolina, and 24,000 women responded when *Redbook* magazine asked its readers, "Why Young Mothers Feel Trapped." The following year 50,000 American women took part in a Women's Strike for Peace—something that could not have taken place a mere five years earlier. Looking back, we can see 1960 as a demographic watershed as well. It was the year the trend in early marriages began to reverse itself, and indeed, the year the marriage rate itself began a thirty-year decline. Although material changes in women's lives were still years away, the events of 1960 were harbingers of a revolution to come.

In 1963, when Betty Friedan published *The Feminine Mystique*, she was deluged with letters from women responding to her diagnosis of "the problem that has no name." These letters, most of them pervaded with fury and regret, told the same story over and over—of talents and education wasted, of careers and interests abandoned, of years devoted to mindless house-work and child care. Women were also beginning to understand and deplore their retreat into the "cozy cocoons" of family life. The National Organization of Women was founded in 1966, and as the messages of feminism began to be heard again, women emerged from their doldrums and, in various large and small ways, began to change their lives. They returned to school, went back to work, and divorced their husbands in large numbers. They organized against the war in Vietnam and eventually began to organize on their own behalf.

In the fifties the central issues of feminism were starkly exposed. Everyone understood very well that women's independence threatened the very heart of American society, the family. It still does. For women to be able to truly control their reproductive lives, and to have real economic equality with men would irrevocably alter the power relationships within all our institutions, from the family to the U.S. Congress. The very nakedness of fifties attempts to control women attested to a profound fear that their sexual and economic independence would mean a radical change in the way we all lived.

And indeed, in many ways that fear has been justified. Most Americans recognize that the realities of family life have changed dramatically. The benign paternalism of a Jim Anderson in "Father Knows Best" simply won't wash if Margaret Anderson is working herself and making an indispensable contribution to the family income. The very face of the American family has had to change to reflect the growing numbers of women raising children alone or with other women.

Inevitably, the fear that invariably accompanies such change has also resurfaced. The renewed ferocity of the attacks on abortion rights reveals that fear in its most elemental form. But it can also be seen in the government's attempts to roll back affirmative action legislation, and in the Far Right's clamor for a return to "family values."

Feminism is reemerging as the all-purpose scapegoat, as Susan Faludi documents in *Backlash*; the old 1950s language about "pathology," "dehumanization," and "gender uncertainty" is creeping back into some popular discourse about working mothers. A recent full-page *Good Housekeeping* ad in the *New York Times* introduces "The New Traditionalist," a woman who "finds fulfillment in traditional values that were considered 'old-fashioned' just a few years ago."

Does all this mean we've wheeled around and are steaming back into the Dark Decade? I don't believe it. Women have progressed far beyond the point of no return. They're in medical schools and law schools, and they're inching into the upper echelons of the corporate world. They've entered the political arena and are even beginning to make inroads into that ultimate male enclave, the U.S. Congress. They've had a taste of equality, even a taste of power. They've experienced the shift in the balance of power in a marriage that occurs when a wife is earning as much money as her husband. They've experienced the autonomy that comes from being in control of their own reproductive lives. They will almost certainly have to fight for these things again and again, losing ground, gaining ground, running in place. But they will never go back.

Bibliography

For lack of space, I'm unable to list all the books I read for an understanding of the 1950s. What follows is a selective bibliography of recent books on which I relied heavily as sources:

Bailey, Beth, *From Front Porch to Back Seat: Courtship in Twentieth Century America* (Baltimore: Johns Hopkins University Press, 1988).

Bérubé, Allan, *Coming Out Under Fire* (New York: The Free Press/ Macmillan, 1990).

Chafe, William, *The Paradox of Change* (London: Oxford University Press, 1991).

D'Emilio, John, *Sexual Politics, Sexual Communities: The Making of a Homosexual Minority in the United States, 1940–1970* (Chicago: University of Chicago Press, 1983).

D'Emilio, John, and Estelle Freedman, *Intimate Matters: A History of Sexuality in America* (New York: Harper & Row, 1988).

Eisler, Benita, *Private Lives: Men and Women of the Fifties* (New York: Franklin Watts, 1986).

Giddings, Paula, *When and Where I Enter: The Impact of Black Women on Race and Sex in America* (New York: William Morrow & Co., 1984).

Hartmann, Susan M., *The Home Front and Beyond: American Women in the 1940s* (Boston: Twayne Publishers, 1982).

Jezer, Marty, *The Dark Ages: Life in the United States, 1945–1960* (Boston: South End Press, 1982).

Johnson, Joyce, *Minor Characters* (New York: Houghton Mifflin, 1983).

Kaledin, Eugenia, *Mothers and More: American Women in the 1950s* (Boston: Twayne Publishers, 1984).

Komarovsky, Mirra, *Women in College: Shaping New Feminine Identities* (New York: Basic Books, 1985).

Luker, Kristen, *Abortion and the Politics of Motherhood* (Berkeley: University of California Press, 1984).

Messer, Ellen, and Kathryn May, *Back Rooms: Voices from the Illegal Abortion Era* (New York: St. Martin's Press, 1988).

Morello, Karen Berger, *The Invisible Bar: The Woman Lawyer in America, 1638 to Present* (New York: Random House, 1986).

Rich, Adrienne, *Of Woman Born* (New York: Norton, 1976).

Rupp, Leila, and Verta Taylor, *Survival in the Doldrums: The American Women's Rights Movement, 1945 to the 1960s* (New York: Oxford University Press, 1987).

Walsh, Mary Roth, *Doctors Wanted: No Women Need Apply: Sexual Barriers in the Medical Profession, 1835–1975* (New Haven: Yale University Press, 1977).